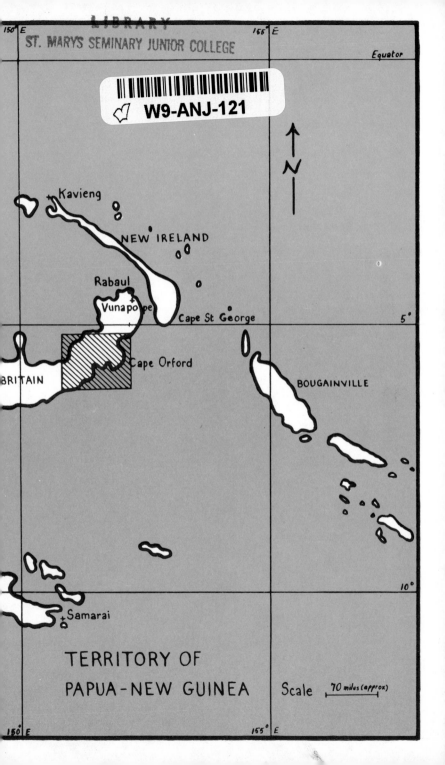

150 E

155 E

Equator

↑
N

+ Kavieng

NEW IRELAND

Rabaul

Vunapope

Cape St George

5°

Cape Orford

BOUGAINVILLE

BRITAIN

10°

+ Samarai

TERRITORY OF
PAPUA-NEW GUINEA

Scale 70 miles (approx)

150° E

155° E

AND WE, THE PEOPLE

© *Rhodes Tremeer, F.I*

Tim O'Neill, M.S.C.

AND WE,
THE PEOPLE

Ten years with the primitive tribes
of New Guinea

by

TIM O'NEILL

P. J. KENEDY & SONS - NEW YORK

Imprimatur : Georgius L. Craven Vic. Gen. Epus Sebastopolis

Westmonasterii, 13a Augustis 1960

Imprimatur : M. G. O'Leary, M.S.C. Prov.Sup.

Cork, 13a Augustis 1960

MADE AND PRINTED IN GREAT BRITAIN

Contents

v

Illustrations

Preface

This book is written by a man of wide experience and deep understanding of the native people of New Guinea.

The scenes depicted of the natural beauty and fertility of the country are in vivid contrast to those of the life of the poor frustrated native who was on the point of extinction when he received the benefits of Christianity and civilization.

The book, unintentionally, also reveals an explorer of the wild jungle and its people, a missionary not looking for fame but for souls to save. Living alone among the people has given him a rare insight into their ways, their outlook and their deep-rooted beliefs in pagan idols, sorcery and magic. He draws sound comparisons between their native laws and those of the white man.

Here is not only an excellent manual for missionaries and anthropologists but especially a book that will be enjoyed by all who have an interest in those of their fellow men who have only now begun to emerge from a most primitive way and standard of living.

Written with humour and pathos and with an underlying faith by an active, zealous and learned missionary it is an invitation and a challenge to the youth of to-day to carry on the work that has been begun.

As his Bishop who knew and esteemed the author very highly I wish 'And We, The People' wide publicity and every success.

Most Rev. Leo Soharmach, D.D.
Bishop of Rabaul.

Foreword

If you have opened this book in the hope of finding it laden with thrilling adventures, you may be disappointed. It is simply a casual glance at a few day-to-day events of no importance to the world at large, little events that unroll themselves with severe monotony and a touch of boredom in the lives of a few primitive and self-effacing people in an island of the South-west Pacific.

I have no 'experiences' or 'adventures' to tell you about, unless perhaps in your magnanimity you consider it thrilling that through my own fault I was nearly drowned a few times, a thing which could happen to any man anywhere, and that once I was bitten by a woman.

I have never seen poisoned arrows flashing in the sun, nor heard the blood-curdling battle-song of the tribe going to war, nor seen the steamy alchemy of the sorcerer at the new moon. I have never had to shoot my way in or out of anywhere because I have never carried a gun into danger.

Here among the people of the jungle, despite superficial indications to the contrary, viewing them from the common level of human nature, you will find the plainest and most down-to-earth person, the perfect average man, the man in the street, the man in the jungle.

We all know the average man. We know several and they are all average and all different, and it is these little differences that make life interesting. Although life here is just the ordinary life of simple people, yet it is ordinary in a different way. It is about these little differences that I write.

You may gather some impressions from this book which are contrary to what learned people believe. I do not claim that my impressions are correct and should you corner me to defend them I shall flee to Elalona in the jungle where you cannot follow me, and that for two reasons : with a greater knowledge I might very well have received other impressions and, also, the subject is so irregular and elusive that often when I thought I fully understood what made the other fellow tick and was sure that I could forecast his reactions, that indefinable thing called Personality or Free Will stepped in and he tacked off at a tangent, leaving me with an armful of useless theorisings.

Leaving individuals as such and observing only the tribe or the race, one will notice that the main body is usually guided by an accepted set of ideas which differ from those of another tribe or race. Technically-minded people might say that the two races have different fundamental first principles motivating and guiding their observable reactions to certain external stimuli; whereas ordinary folk would say that the two races take different things for granted. The average civilised man seldom questions the truth of those things, the average uncivilised man never.

Native places and persons are mentioned here and there in this book, and where the mention might have been embarrassing I have garbled those names. Lima, of some of the stories, is a type, not a person. As a person he appears elsewhere under his own name. Some events may appear to be specific cases, but they are not purely so. I mentioned them not for their individuality but because they represent a type; several similar cases have occurred every year and will, no doubt, continue to occur. As isolated events they would not be worthy of mention.

I have walked a thousand miles of jungle, probably more, through the habitations of God's most primitive people, over their rough tracks, rocks and mountain-ridges, over their rickety wobbly bridges and along those seemingly endless and dungeon-like trails that forever wind in, out and around like a dying snake, covered all the while with a dense jungle canopy of leaves which turn the noonday sun to twilight, and yet I am surprised at my ignorance of the people and their country.

There is scant mention of Europeans here because this book is about the Natives. There were a few Europeans in the parish and I am indebted to them all. Some came and went in a few months but the ones I knew best and who had been longest about the place were the Coulstons of Palmalmal, the Bodes of Unung, the Auchettls of Matale, the John Young-Whitfords of Pomio, the Burkes and later the Broomfields of Cutarp, the Wests and later the Morrises of Bergberg and the Hummerstones of Manguna. They were all kindly good-hearted folk who though mainly of other religions always made me welcome in their homes with a good meal, a shower and a bed for the night, and never let me go empty away: it may have been just some fresh food or eggs or vegetables but these things were more valuable than gold when one was on the track. They also complimented me by accepting my hospitality when occasion brought them my way. I have thanked them already; I thank them here again.

Tim O'Neill

Part One

THE PEOPLE

War and the Aftermath

I MET him only once. It was on a hot summer's day in 1939 when I was studying for the priesthood. He was tall, lithe and middle-aged, and his complexion was bronzed by the equatorial sun of New Guinea. Father William Culhane was on holidays, his first in twelve years.

I was one of a group of Irish students who had joined the missionary Order of the Sacred Heart, in Cork, and were then in a house of studies in Gerdingen-Bree in Belgium. We had completed our year's Noviceship and were ploughing steadily through our last year of Philosophy: Metaphysics ... in French with a marked Cork accent.

Father Culhane had come across from Germany where he had been visiting some priests who had worked with him in New Guinea. The mission out there has been run by the German Province of our missionary society since 1880, when most of New Guinea was a German colony.

At this time the world war was only six weeks off. Everybody seemed convinced that it was coming and the only disputed point was the date. He was glad to be getting away from it all. 'I don't want to be around here for the next few years,' he said. 'New Guinea is the only place safe from war just now. I'll bet there isn't one person in a thousand who could point it out on a map' . . . but he had not thought of the Emperor of Japan.

He told us many stories about New Guinea, in which there lived then, and live now, some of the most primitive people in the world: how in 1932 he opened the first mission to the Mengens* on the South Coast of New Britain, and in tracking down the rest of the tribe, found himself one day on the other side of the island, some fifty miles away; and how his Bishop, when he heard of it, frowned an episcopal frown, because he believed that one missionary in the hand was worth any number in the pot.

Father Culhane had a very noticeable characteristic which caused us considerable amusement. When walking, he always pitched his eyes a few feet in front and never turned his head, even to speak. This, he said, was the result of habit, for in years of plodding through the trackless primeval jungle he had learned to keep a careful eye where he was walking, because it was so easy to trip up or step on a snake or a rotten log which turned out to be a crocodile.

For the few days he was with us, his stories were the principal attraction, but with time they faded and were forgotten and the picture of the man himself emerged: a serious-minded dedicated man who felt he had the finest job in the world; a man who was probably never once afraid in his life, either because he was peculiarly blind to danger or because he had drilled himself to ignore it when it stood before him.

In later years there were many questions I wished I had asked him, for I did not know then that one day I would have the spiritual care of his Mengens, and cover the trails he had blazed and others that were then beyond his reach, though not beyond his desire. Nor did I foresee that twelve years later, accompanied by Father Tony Gendusa of Chicago, I would dig the black sands of the Uvol shore in the hope of finding his decapitated body, to give it the Christian burial which it had never received. I was not aware of it then, but his short visit must have shaped my years to come.

* Pronounced : Meng-en.

The four years after this visit were spent in our House of Theology in Moyne Park, Co. Galway, and I was ordained priest in Fermoy on Trinity Sunday, 1943, by the Bishop of Cloyne. At this time I had made up my mind that if the opportunity offered, I would ask for appointment to New Guinea. The opportunity came three years later. The war was over and we learned for the first time of the serious losses which the mission-staff had suffered during the Japanese occupation of New Guinea. The mission was anxious to rebuild its staff and six of us, young priests from Cork, applied to our Superior and were accepted.

Our group consisted of Fathers Pat Walsh from Sligo, Eamon MacSweeney, Kevin Fleming and Steve White from Kerry, and Michael Kelleher and myself from Cork. The usual rounds of farewell parties followed Christmas 1946 and spilled over into January and February of '47; the goodbyes to parents, brothers, sisters, relatives and friends; and at night-fall on February 16th we had bid farewell to them all, even to the gulls that had followed us out from Cobh that morning, and which now glided up into the air and wheeled for home. We watched them from the deck of the S.S. *America* and some-one remarked: 'The gulls are going home,' and another replied 'So are we,' and that seemed to sum up the position. From now on, New Guinea was to be our home.

We were all in high spirits, evidenced by the fact that nobody took anybody seriously. Kevin Fleming asked Michael Kelleher 'Tell me, to what do you attribute your wonderful missionary vocation?'

'To the Irish weather,' said Mike.

'One can put up with the weather,' said Pat Walsh. 'It would take more than that to shift me. But I'll tell you why I'm here now. When we buried Father Gerard some years ago, I thought I had never before seen such a doleful undertaker, and I made up my mind then and there that he'd never bury me. When they plant me let them do it by a blue sea on a sunny day, under green swaying palm trees and red flowers, and let them do it with a song, preferably "The Irish Rover" . . . and

New Guinea is the only place where that is ever likely to happen.'

Pat had an extraordinarily captivating tenor voice and only a little persuasion was necessary to get him to launch into:

> Magee, MacEntee and the big Portuguee,
> And Johnny O'Brien from Dover,
> And the man, Mick MacCann from beyond Turkestan
> Was the Skipper of the Irish Rover.

A crowd was gathering, so we thought it proper to go to our cabins.

Though shipping was unpredictable from San Francisco to Sydney, we were not unduly worried, because America is a wonderful country and we spent ten weeks there, before sailing on May 9th on a converted troop-carrier from San Francisco, Sydney-bound, via Pango-Pango, Suva and New Zealand.

We ploughed on through the tropics where, the ship's billboard told us, the surface temperature of the sea was eighty degrees; on to Pango-Pango in American Samoa, which rose from the ocean one morning with the dawn: black mountains with grey clouds, changing to deep green with white clouds when the sun rose up. The ship slowed to a few knots as she manoeuvred the narrow channels between the reefs, and without the cooling breeze of her speed we felt for the first time the heavy humid heat of the tropics, and we rather liked it.

The Pacific Islands will always be different from the rest of the world. In a way, they seem not to belong here at all. Even the Europeans who live in them have changed. They have lost the nervous bustle of home; they lounge more easily and work more casually; they go to rest at midday and re-appear only when the day has cooled. The sun sets regularly around six o'clock the whole year round, and after a twenty-minute fast-fading glow, the night is in, dark and warm and with a sky full of fiery stars. Let it be Samoa, or Samarai, there is no difference: just the same snug soporific warmth intoxicating you into a dreamy carefree frame of mind, drawing you out, melting you, deceiving you; gently and imperceptibly lulling you into a state of semi-comatose, satisfied laziness.

Auckland in New Zealand, when we got there, was more bracing. Late May was nearly winter there, but many trees were still green, though some displayed the glorious russets, golds and browns of late European autumn. Regrettably, we had only a few hours here before we moved on to Sydney.

If, as you round the Sydney Heads and swing into the Harbour, you hear a heavy pounding, you know that it is not from the ship's engine-rooms, but from the breast of every Aussie on board, as his heart thumps with pride at the sight of the most beautiful harbour in the world. 'Wait till you see the Harbour Bridge,' he'll tell you. 'Isn't that magnificent? Can you beat it, mate? They can have the Golden Gate and the rest with it.' And most people will agree with him.

A sprawling, bustling growing giant of nearly two million people, Sydney expanded faster than the architects could draw it. Out from the narrow-alleyed centre it grew, gobbling up one suburb after the other, stretching out its fingers along the beach through Randwick, Coogee, Bondi, Parramatta and out to Botany Bay. But the Sydneysiders appreciate their leisure too, and nowhere else will you find the cricket-grounds, tennis courts, golf courses and beaches with so many people at ten o'clock in the morning. And the realisation will come to you that Europe is the most crowded continent of all. Nowhere else are the people so ready to take your place because, there, the struggle for life is keenest. The Aussie does not understand that yet and often gazes in amazement at the frantic industry of the emigrant from Europe. If he could only know what the European left behind, he would be better able to appreciate his own continent.

Our short stay in Australia was spent at the Mission house in Coogee and as guests of our Australian confreres at their monastery in Kensington. We regretted that the M.V. *Malaita* was leaving for Rabaul so soon, because Australia gave excellent promise of providing us with another interesting holiday.

It was not, of course, our intention to discover New Guinea. Its existence was first reported in 1512 by a Portuguese sailor, and the first Catholic was baptised there in 1514; after that great burst of activity it slumbered on for 350 years, apart from some sporadic raids by seamen and pirates: Dampier, Carteret and Bougainville, to mention just a few. In 1828 the Dutch occupied the Western portion of it but nobody seemed to mind. British explorers twice claimed the rest for England, on both occasions she repudiated it. Finally, in the 1880's Germany forced the issue by establishing a Protectorate over the islands of New Ireland, New Britain, Manus and the North-west portion of the mainland. England then claimed the remainder.

Since 1919 it has been administered by Australia, first on a mandate from the League of Nations, and later on one from U.N.O.

After eighteen weeks voyaging from Ireland we disembarked from the *Malaita* at Rabaul, on July 7th, 1947. Bishop Leo Scharmach was there to meet us, and his predecessor, Bishop Vesters, who was then in retirement, together with some priests from the Central Mission Station at Vunapope*, which lay about fourteen miles across the harbour. We set out for it in the Bishop's own boat.

In the Common Species of Bishop, missionary Bishops are an Established Variety. Except for the ring on his finger, our new Bishop was dressed no differently from any of his priests: white drill pants and white short-sleeved shirt with a Cross pinned on the lapel. He had a home-made cigar in the corner of his mouth, tucked well into his cheek, and he wore a straw hat at an angle which was not handed down from the Apostles. Out in the harbour he said: 'Let's go below and see the boat.' We followed him down companionways, through the cabins, the galley, down another deck and into an engine room where the temperature was 120°. 'Twin-engines and twin-screws,' he

* Pronounced: Vúna-pópay.

shouted over the infernal noise. 'We run only one engine at a time, but the screws are inter-coupled. One engine gives her eleven knots and the two together only twelve.' He scanned the panel: revs. per minute, temperature, oil. . . . 'She's revving more steadily today,' he shouted, 'since we changed the lubricant. More body in this one. We've been having trouble with the fuel too, THE FUEL. . . . Yes. A lot of water in it recently.'

Back on deck Mike Kelleher cracked: 'In this outfit, My Lord, it seems a Bishop must know as much about Diesel oil as about Holy Oil.' The Bishop eyed him from tip to toe with amusement and then added a piece of fatherly advice for us all: 'In an outstation, Fathers, even with a pint of Holy Oil you can't anoint a sick man unless you know enough about Diesel oil to get to him in time.'

'Have you heard how Vunapope got its name?' he asked. We had not.

'In the early days here,' he continued, 'there was another Mission down the road. Each was trying to expand and consolidate as quickly as possible, and indeed there was no love lost between them then. The Natives from the other Mission used to tease our fellows by calling them Popeys. Bishop Couppé was here then and he had a sly sense of humour. Vuna is the local Native word for settlement. In German we say Stadt; you say town in English. So he named the place Vunapope, or Catholictown . . . and then the jibe lost its point.'

We were now nearing Vunapope. The bombed-out hull of a thousand-ton cargo-vessel lay in a few fathoms of water, forming an excellent breakwater for the jetty. We nosed gently around it, tied up, and with a clanging of telegraph bells from the wheel-house, the engines stopped. We had arrived.

'Let's go straightway to the Church,' said the Bishop. 'There I will welcome you officially before the people; then we will have Benediction of the Blessed Sacrament, and after that, count yourself one of the—what did Father Kelleher call it—the outfit? Yes, one of the outfit.'

In 1947 Vunapope resembled a swarm of bees without a hive. For sixty years prior to the war, from the very first day when the Mission cleared that spread of jungle, the missionaries had slowly but very thoroughly built up a do-it-yourself Mission. This was necessary in such a backward place where supplies from the outside world were often scarce and always dear. The lay-brothers of the Society did the work. They were men qualified in the various trades: builders, carpenters, mechanics, shipwrights, electricians and so on. Since all the houses are of wood, a sawmill was a prime necessity. They established one at Ulamona and ran miles of narrow-gauge railway into the jungle to haul the logs to the mill where they were cut to all sizes. From the labour of this sawmill came the timber to build every Church, presbytery, convent and school in the Mission's forty-five stations. This timber was converted into pre-fabricated buildings at the workshops at Vunapope and sent out to the stations, complete with furniture. The mission was 'made in Vunapope'.

Many of these mission-stations were hundreds of miles distant and the only communication-route was by sea, so the Mission built its own boats to maintain a life-line to the outstations and bring them all their needs, for none could live off the land. Since many of those outstations covered a hundred miles of coastline and many islands out to sea, each one was supplied with a small motor-boat, and the boat-shed at Vunapope was seldom without one or two of these cockles on the slips for repairs: a propeller chewed to ribbons on a niggerhead, a few sheets of copper shorn off here, a bent shaft, a leak below the water-line, a damaged keel or an engine that would not fire. The lay-brothers of the Mission took these invalids and painstakingly made them seaworthy again and sent them back to duty in all corners of the islands.

Before the Japanese arrived Vunapope had a twin-towered Cathedral, Bishop's house, a house for priests and brothers, two convents, a hospital for Europeans and Natives, boarding-schools, day-schools, technical schools, a dispensary, a mission-doctor's house, store-houses from which the missionaries were fed and supplied, workshops, a butchery, bakery, laundry: everything that was useful or necessary to carry on the work of evangelisation. It was, in fact, a fully grown Vuna or town.

Then, in February 1942, the Japanese lined up a few warships a mile out to sea and in half an hour had shelled the place to pieces.

The Japanese Army then took over and sent all the Mission staff off to Ramali Valley behind barbed wire, where there was no shelter apart from the trees, and the only asset was a running creek. For houses the internees dug mansize rabbit-burrows into the hill-sides and there they remained till the end of the war.

Meanwhile the Japanese occupied the old site; but the change of ownership did not long escape the eye of the American reconnaissance planes from Port Moresby and Australia. The inevitable result was only a matter of time and tactics. Long before the war ended, Vunapope had been wiped out and had reverted to a tangled mass of tropical undergrowth. Sixty years of toil and not a rafter left!

The outstations of the Mission fared no better. Forty-one were totally burned out and the remaining four were heavily damaged. At the end of the war, then, the outlook was dismal: forty-five of the staff were dead, the remainder were hungry and in poor health; over two hundred major buildings had been bombed and burned out, and there was neither a hammer nor a nail left to commence rebuilding. But the Mother of God was smiling through the paw-paws.

Early in the war, Australia felt uneasy about the Japanese and expected some form of trouble. Hence the Government compelled all property owners to contribute to a War Damage Fund. This regulation extended also to New Guinea. When the war was over the Government decided to allocate the entire fund to the rehabilitation of damaged properties in New Guinea, irrespective of whether they were owned by Europeans or Natives. The Mission got its compensation on the pre-war rates, but on account of the soaring post-war prices the amount was very inadequate. And again, a new compensating factor appeared.

In Manus Island, the Americans had built a war-base for nearly a million men. It contained, as the phrase goes, everything that opens or shuts. When the war was ended, the Americans were selling out their base at bargain prices. They had pre-fabricated Quonset huts of corrugated iron which could be dismantled and rolled up by undoing a few bolts, and re-assembled by reversing the process. They had all kinds of furniture, vehicles, mobile workshops and churches . . . they had more than everything the Mission needed.

The Mission's General Manager, Father O'Connell, set off for Manus and it was not long before the much-needed goods began to arrive: food, clothing, medical supplies, hospital equipment, buildings, furniture, whole up-to-date workshops, electrical machinery and what not. The lay-brothers got back on the job again and with this new American equipment they built their workshops and turned out the needs of the Mission as before.

Less than five years after total annihilation the Mission, it was officially announced, was built anew. This extravagant claim was more a joyous expression of exuberant hope than a strict statement of fact. The real situation was that by this time it was over the hump and felt that it could manage the road ahead.

Newcomers are kept at the Central Station for quite a while to give them a chance to become acclimatised, to learn the rudiments of a new language and to do an elementary course in tropical medicine. Unmentioned, but definitely present, is the intention of giving the authorities an opportunity to judge what sort of a character has blown in, and on which mission-station he is most likely to do the least amount of damage for his first few years.

Due to the general shortage of priests, we were not detained too long. Father Peekel found time to teach us Tokboi (see

Appendix) and Dr. Schuy and the Sisters at the hospital put us through our course in medicine to qualify for a Government certificate.

The object of this medical course is to train a person to diagnose and treat the commoner disabling and killing diseases found among the Natives. Its scope is well-defined, which is just as well, because in that way it offsets any fancy notions a person might have about his own special ability to go a little further.

The diseases most common to the Natives are malaria, pneumonia, meningitis, dysentery, yaws, hookworm and tropical ulcers. In the more remote areas where medical facilities are rare, a priest can save quite a number of lives, even in a short time, by a judicious use of his limited medical knowledge.

All the while, the Mission was sorting fact from rumour on the fate of its missing staff-members, who had died in an area of some 20,000 square miles. The later account of the death of Father Culhane which I heard at Uvol did not differ much from the one I heard at this time at Vunapope.

It happened in an unusual manner, unusual even in New Guinea. He had returned there in 1940 and left his first foundation, Malmal, in the hands of Father Harris while he went sixty miles west along the coast and opened a new mission-station at Uvol.

In 1942 the Japanese invaded New Guinea and occupied Rabaul, in New Britain, its second largest town. The whole island of New Britain, including Rabaul, had scarcely a thousand Europeans. The invading Japanese force was over a hundred thousand strong. Soon they had companies of soldiers stationed all over the eight hundred miles of the island's coast-line. One such company was in Father Culhane's district at Uvol, which was about one hundred and ninety miles from Rabaul, on the south coast of the island.

This is the local Natives' version of the story. Tavalo, a neighbouring village, had two important men who were newly converted Catholics, but who held that on account of their village-importance they should be allowed to have an extra wife. In that they fell foul of Father Culhane. They threatened violence if he would not acquiesce, and there was some proof that they actually assaulted him. Later, they openly boasted that they had gone to Confession to him and threatened that if he refused to give them absolution or to permit them to keep their extra wives they would find a way of getting the Japanese to kill him.

Early one night, about February 1943, four Japanese soldiers arrived at his mission-station and led him away. They forbade anybody to watch or to follow. There were, however, a few Natives on the beach who hid in the undergrowth nearby when they saw the soldiers coming along with Father Culhane. About a hundred yards to the west along the beach the soldier in the rear of the party drew his revolver and shot him in the back of the head. As he was falling another severed his head with a Japanese sword. The body crumpled to the sand and made the Sign of the Cross.

The Japanese left it there and called at Uvol village to warn all the people that anyone who touched the body would be shot. In due course it disappeared: whether it was swept out to sea, buried in the sand by the tide, or whether a crocodile took it, has never come to light.

The Genesis of Appointments

THERE WAS an old saying at Vunapope that the only permanent appointments were the temporary ones, meaning that, if you were appointed to some station with full ceremony, something would always occur to change it but if, on the other hand, you were casually asked to help some Pastor for a week-end, most likely you would take over and continue there for ten years.

By September our group was scattered to outstations over the islands, with as much as six hundred miles between some. With luck, we might meet every two or three years but, in fact, we never did. Twelve months later Father Pat Walsh died after an abdominal operation. He was buried as he had wished: under green palm-trees by a blue sea; the children filled his grave with hibiscus flowers and chanted his last Requiem.

My 'permanent' appointment came in September. It was to Lemakot, in New Ireland. There was nothing left of the pre-war mission-station, so I was to stay at Lugagon with Father Hoffman till I could get Lemakot back on its feet again. I was to take three months' rations along; the mission-boat would come with further supplies at three-monthly intervals. I had no idea of what three months rations consisted, but the general mission supply-store at Vunapope stocked all the items.

The lay-brother in charge knew a man's needs for three months and he saw to it that they were packed, labelled and put on board the mission-boat. He worked from a standard list.

The boat would sail in three days, my rations were being packed ('cargo' they called it here), and I was in my tent scanning the list of goods when Father Rudolf strolled in. 'So you're leaving us in a few days,' he said. 'Got everything packed up?' and he eased himself on to a collapsible stool.

'Yes,' I said, 'This is the list,' and I offered it to him.

'You don't have to bother,' he said lazily. 'I knew it by heart fifteen years ago: 9 tins of butter, 3 tins of jam, 6 tins of tea, 24 tins of condensed milk, 24 tins of waxed matches, 6 bars of soap. . . . Smoke a decent cigar,' he continued. 'I got a present of five today from the Chinaman at Kokopo.'

We smoked for a while and then he said: 'There are no cigars on your list. See what I mean?'

I did not.

"Look," he said, "let me tell you something. Since Vunapope was founded in 1882, the best brains of the Mission have gone into the compiling of the three months' ration list. With devilish accuracy it contains the exact number of calories to sustain life in the average man for exactly $91\frac{1}{4}$ days. You'll never want, but you'll never grow fat either. And if for instance, you have a visitor for a week, you will spend the last week of your term without rations.'

'I could kill a chicken for the visitor,' I said.

'Have you got chickens at Lemakot?'

'No,' I said.

'Then how are you going to kill one? See what I mean about the cigars? If you want "extras", Vunapope expects you to find them for yourself. How much rice is on your list?'

'One bag,' I said.

'I thought so. It's in short supply just now but you'll need three at least for your boys, and if you go without it, you'll do without it. "We'll send it on later" means "Come again, sucker". Now we must see to that! Have you got four sheets of corrugated iron and a galvanised 44-gallon drum?'

'No,' I said. 'What for?'

'Water! Do you think there is going to be a tap at Lemakot before you? You'll put those four sheets on the thatch of your hut and let the rain run down into the drum. That's for drinking and cooking. How many pairs of trousers?'

'Four,' I said.

'Enough for modesty, but not quite enough for comfort in the tropics. You'll need eight. We'll see to that too.'

'How?'

'Oh! The Mission-store here has got them all. The problem is to collect them. You mustn't steal or thieve, of course,' and then he added in a faraway voice 'We do, however, collect. . . . And by the way, when you are on a collecting errand, you must never sidle up with a hangdog, ingratiating smile. Sure to be recognised right off! When you are short of, say, two bags of rice, as you are now, then you take *four* boys along. Walk into the store boldly with your team and make a reasonable amount of noise, enough to attract reasonable attention. Everything must be reasonably done. Go straight to where the rice is stacked and put one bag on each boy's shoulder and get out with reasonable assurance and in reasonable time. If anybody notices you at all he'll presume you've surely got the O.K. from higher authority . . . and also . . . please remember: never collect trifles; it's not done . . . only essentials and in a big way.'

A few days later I boarded the mission-boat *Waimana* for Lemakot. The Bishop came to see me on board and to give me his blessing . . . 'and if you're short of anything, Father,' he said, 'be sure to let us know and we'll send it on later.'

'A cigar for the road,' said Father Rudolf, casually drawing a Havana from his shirt-pocket and dropping his left eyelid.

❧

After twenty-seven hours, the *Waimana* dropped anchor in Kavieng Harbour at the northern tip of New Ireland, and put me and my cargo ashore in a dinghy. Lugagon was fifty miles down the coast and linked with Kavieng by a very pot-holed track through coconut plantations and jungle. I met a Chinese trader who had an army-truck and after we had agreed on a fee, we set off and completed the journey in just four hours.

But I was not long enough at Lugagon to have unpacked my cargo when I received word from Vunapope to leave everything there except my personal belongings and to return immediately.

My first 'permanent' appointment was over and the second one was waiting right at hand.

❋

This appointment was to be outside the Mission. The Bishop in Papua, about six hundred miles away, felt his mission-field was too large for him to give it the attention he desired. Would two Irish priests come along to see the place? Father O'Connell was appointed and I was to go with him as caddie. We arrived in Papua in March 1948.

The Papuan Mission with its central station at Yule Island had been founded about seventy years. It had been run by the French Province of our society. When they first arrived there they found the entire coastline occupied for evangelisation by non-Catholic denominations. The Government system in operation at that time was known as the Zoning System: whichever denomination first hung out its shingle, as it were, was to have the area to itself and no other denomination could muscle in. This, it seems, was done to prevent spiritual cannibalism amongst holy men. So the Catholic missionaries had no choice but to head for the mountains, which they did.

On account of the tremendous difficulties attached to the evangelisation of primitive people hidden away in inaccessible mountains, the mission's progress was slow. Yet it had now almost a dozen established mission-stations, some of them even fifty miles from the coast, as the cockatoo flies, and about twenty-four thousand Catholics. They had built bridle-paths right into the mountains and sent their supplies in by pack-horse.

The field we were to examine stretched about three hundred

miles, from the Fly River on the borders of Dutch New Guinea to the Purari in the Eastern Gulf. Our Papuan Mission knew nothing about this area. It was our job to learn about it. The Bishop put some population-maps at our disposal, impressive but not quite reliable, because the area had not yet been patrolled and the enthusiast who had drawn the map had never been nearer than four hundred miles to the area. Ironically, the map was coloured in rose.

We had misgivings about the reportedly dense population in the Upper Fly, because this 600-mile river oozes through three hundred miles of swampland. We eventually succeeded in going 550 miles up the river, and the results were disappointing. The population thinned out as we receded from the coast, and wherever there was a workable population at all, there was already a long-established mission of one or other Protestant variety. Further upstream we found very little indication of people, beyond some few who built their houses on trees, high above the water-level. The river was not a single stream but a network of channels that joined and separated through the swamp. Five hundred miles upstream, the elevation above sea-level was only seventy feet.

His Lordship was disappointed with our report but there was one consolation for him—he did not have to lose any more sleep thinking of the unevangelised Fly River.

We then turned our attention to Kutubu, a lake in the Southern Highlands. It was known that the adjoining population was four thousand and it could be reasonably presumed that the healthy hinterland held many more. To get there we would have to charter a Catalina flying-boat. Our intention was to go in there with six months' rations and have the Catalina collect us when we had done our patrols. But before we had completed our arrangements for this new trip the Bishop changed his mind. He said he felt the area should really be patrolled from the North Coast of New Guinea, and so the whole thing came to an end, and the Bishop of Rabaul invited us to resume duty with him.

When we left Papua in 1949 no one knew what was in the

hinterland of Lake Kutubu, but five years later I came across some information bearing on this same region that interested me, in the 'Handbook of Papua-New Guinea 1954':

Southern Highlands District: comprising an area of some 7,000 square miles. . . . This is Papua's newest district and it was formed only in 1950-51. The Natives whose numbers are officially estimated at 80,000. . . . Administration Headquarters are at Mendi . . . some 45 miles north-east of Lake Kutubu. There is no European population in this district outside Administration personnel and the staffs of the Methodist and Unevangelised Mission stations, of which there are a number at Mendi, Tari and Lake Kutubu.

It might have been. . . .

✵

In the Rabaul Mission there were nine vacant stations, Malmal, which had been founded by Father Culhane, among them. I would like to have been sent there but the Bishop had already asked me to take a desk position as Director of Catholic Education for the Mission. I had no love for the job and luckily he had gone overseas without confirming the appointment. At Vunapope I argued that I was unfit for the position as I had yet no first-hand knowledge of the people. Why not let me take an outstation 'temporarily' till the Bishop returned? The argument seemed to make sense and I was 'temporarily' appointed to Malmal, and in a week I was on my way. This temporary appointment lasted for nearly seven delightful years.

I had envisaged Malmal as a large parish, but in fact it was a district, and quite extensive at that. It was almost as extensive as the entire Papuan mountain Mission which I had just left, but lacked even the primitive Papuan amenities of bridle paths. It had no paths at all. The hinterland was primeval forest; it took me years to learn what primeval rain-forest was, and a dictionary could never tell me.

I first saw the parish from the bows of the Mission boat *Teresa*, as they rose and fell and lolled and plunged in a long low swell. We were about a hundred miles out from Vunapope and just past Cape Orford, of which Navigator Dampier wrote: 'When we were abreast of it, I called my Officers together, and named it Cape Orford, in honour of my noble Patron; drinking his Lordship's Health' (*Voyages*, 11-533). Cheers!

The western boundary was now appearing over the horizon some sixty miles away, a three thousand foot spur of the Nakanai Mountain Range. Between it and us were two long stretches of coastline and two large semi-circular bays, Jacquinot Bay and Waterfall Bay. Such was the foreshore of the parish. The hinterland rose abruptly from the sea and unfolded upwards in successive mountain stages, leaping in majestic sweeps to the clouds five thousand feet above.

Pulpul village was on our right, 'on the starboard beam' said the skipper, but only the trained eye could pick it out because it was as well camouflaged as a wild bees' nest in a meadow. Look along the coastline or up into the mountains, look to any point of the compass and you find only the same unbroken colour-pattern: the blue-green of the tree-clad mountains, spurs and peaks, fading to dark green in the gorges.

We passed twenty villages on the coast in the four hour run to Malmal but could see not one of them, for the jungle was all over them, all around them, in front of them in tiny islands, and in the mangrove trees that grew up through the sea. The little grass huts of Pulpul peeped through the trees from a ledge a hundred feet above the sea. Below was a mile-long reef over which the sea surged and curled and pounded as it leaped in green-white breakers kicking up colonnades of angry thrashing water.

This was the land of the Mengens; the land of We the People.

We took a steady course for Malmal some thirty miles distant. The land fell away on our right into the open maw of Waterfall Bay. The hinterland here held a few Timoip villages, a vanishing remnant. Further inland in the basin of the Bergberg River and of the Iso you would find the primitive tribe of Kol; deeper inland and over Nakanai Mountains you would contact the unknown Sui tribe. It was all part of the parish.

Fifteen miles west and Cape Jacquinot was on the starboard beam. This was a narrow, high promontory which divided Waterfall Bay from Jacquinot Bay. This latter was of larger expanse and the mountains rose more abruptly around it. It was the centre of the Mengen Tribal grounds. From Pomio, on the north shore, you could walk seven days northwards till you came to the other shore of the island, and you were still among the Mengens.

Malmal was deep in the bay on the southern shore. The tribal land extended a further thirty miles west to the Tolo River, a fast mountain torrent some eighty miles long which drained a goodly portion of the southern slopes of the Nakanai Mountain Range. On the eastern side of this river, and right up to its source, from one to five thousand feet up the mountains, lived a section of the Mamusi Tribe. The Mamusi and the Mengens are related tribes.

The whole parish, then, covered about 2,000 square miles with an average of four persons per square mile. Of those 8,000 people, about 1,500 were Catholic and the rest pagan, many of them, so far, with no white contact. At the time I was not aware of all that. But when I looked out over the taffrail of the *Teresa* to the pale blue mountains that merged in the distance with the sky, and knew that the ends of the parish were still further on, and that the only way to get there was on foot, then I had an indefinable feeling. Later on I would be able to define it very sharply in the Mengen phrase: My liver has turned to water.

There was a mission-station to the east, some sixty miles away and another to the west, about the same distance. In between were matted jungle and an open sea. It occurred to me that this could be an isolated and lonely life for a priest. I had 8,000 parishioners of whose various languages I did not know a word, and there were then only three white settlers in the whole area.

The Malmal mission was on a clearing a hundred yards square, the sea in front and the mountains right behind it. The sea was corroding the foreshore in a frontal attack and the jungle was always creeping up on the rear.

A pre-war Church, a legacy from Father Culhane, capable of holding three hundred people seated or nine hundred standing was still substantially intact. The Japanese had used it as a store-house and American planes had machine-gunned it. It had a corrugated iron roof and weather-board walls. The bullet holes in the western wall were still there, and the new cement patches on the floor and on the Altar-steps marked the path of the bullets. It was, however, one of the four churches of the Mission that were still serviceable.

The wartime Pastor had been Father Ted Harris of Sydney. After the fall of Rabaul many Australian soldiers trudged along the south coast of New Britain in rags and tatters, ridden with jungle sores and malaria, living off the inhospitable land and hoping to find their way south to Australia and safety. Father Harris helped them along with food and whatever medical supplies they could use from his store.

Sometime later, the Japanese came to Malmal in a warship and took him on board. Nobody knows the rest because he has never been heard of since. But when the war was over, the Army remembered. I erected at the mission station a slab sent by the grateful survivors of the 2nd/22nd Battalion A.I.F. to acknowledge their debt to him. The soldiers' story is told on the slab: 'I was sick and you visited me'.

Fifty yards from the Church and half hidden by palm trees, lau-lau and mango trees, was a low ironroofed shack hastily put together after the war, which now served as dwelling house for Father John Askew. A few more huts did duty as kitchen, bathroom and store-room. I had arrived too late to see the school, because a huge galip-tree had fallen on it a week previously. Twisted iron, broken beams and fragments of shattered school-equipment stuck out through the grass. The whole set-up was shabby and drab, but Vunapope had not yet begun to re-build the outstations, and at this time Malmal was easily the best equipped of all.

Father John Askew, M.S.C., an Australian, had been Pastor at Malmal since the end of the war. He was now being transferred to Japan and would leave for Australia in two weeks, from Palmalmal, on a Catalina flying-boat.

'On Sunday I'll induct you formally as Pastor,' he said, 'but in the meantime let us pack some rations and visit some of the outstations by launch.'

On the third evening, we anchored off Pulpul; the wind began to rise and the sea was heavy. The anchorage behind the reef was only a fair-weather one. The launch pitched and rolled, and strained stiffly at her cables. John Askew was an unhappy man.

'The last time here,' he said, 'I had two anchors out and lost both, and almost lost the launch too. We had to find our way by instinct out through the channel in a heavy sea and at night. What do you think of the weather?'

'Looks nasty,' I said.

He consulted his boat-boys, and they were not very hopeful either.

'Let's get out,' he said, 'while there is still light.'

I was glad he did because I was beginning to feel queer all over me. We got back to Malmal in four hours and by then I was well under with a dose of gastric malaria which made me half-delirious for ten days.

There was no induction ceremony, but I was able to get out of bed to wish him God-speed at the plane.

I was now long enough in New Guinea to know that few people were more subjected to scrutiny than the new pastor in a Native parish. He is watched day and night, seven days a week, by we the people. 'What does he eat?' they ask one another. 'Can he eat our taro if it is baked in the ashes? I wonder does he say a lot of prayers?' They must also know whether he can shoot wild pigs and crocodiles, or whether he 'just-fires-up-nothing' with his gun. A big question is: 'Does he swim in the morning or in the evening?' and also: 'are his swimming trunks of a different colour from the last pastor's? Anybody here seen the skin of his back? Is it still sickly-looking or is it brown? Is he lame, like the rest of his tribe, when he walks without shoes on the gravel?' They will also want to know whether he is a no-nonsense fellow or a man-of-pity. (To be a man-of-pity is to have a very lovable weakness.) But then: 'Can you pierce his nose (pull his leg) and has he a sense of humour? Is he soft-tempered or would he sizzle the skin off your back with his words? Just how far can he be pulled around? Do you think if you provoked him sufficiently that you'd get a clip on the chin?' And by the way: 'How does he compare with the last man for bandaging sores and for giving injections?'

More serious investigations follow: 'How is he in Confession? Do you think you could tell him everything . . . and he would not be vexed? As a preacher is he one of those fellows who talk "water-nothing" (slop)? Has he a big mouth that shoots a lot of wind or can he really pierce the liver of a man with the noise of his neck?'

The older men will want to know whether he can use a trout-spear and manage a canoe, but especially whether he was a man of substance or just a 'boy-nothing' in his own tribe.

These were the weighty problems that tormented the minds of the parishioners. After a few months they would have their own answers to them all, usually the correct ones, and they would know their pastor better than he could ever hope to know any of them.

I had not been long at Malmal when one day I went into the Church to see how two fellows were getting along with a job of painting.

'I am the Father now, and you're the boy,' one of them was saying, as he put his foot on a bench and adopted a posture I recognised as my own. 'You up there!' he continued. 'Get on with the job. Man! Do you think for a moment that I'm paying you just for looking ugly?' Both roared laughing at this. I slipped out before they could see me and watched the remainder from hiding. They already knew every word and gesture I used, and reminded me of a few I was not aware of. They even imitated my voice and included all my pet grammatical errors. I could only bite my lip and ponder.

Malmal

I N THE first few weeks I was trying to sort out who was who among the people. They were all alike in appearance: average five-foot-six, shiny copper skin, black fuzzy hair combed upwards, brown eyed and barefooted. The men wore a loin-cloth (laplap) and the women wore two little aprons of croton or coleus leaves (purpur) from a waist-band. After a while I was able to recognise familiar faces and with more acquaintance I wondered how ever I came to be confused in people whose features bore such marked personal characteristics.

Native people have similar difficulty in differentiating Europeans. A few months after my arrival I was one day walking to Pomio village ahead of my carriers, when I met a man from the village on the track.

'Good day, Sir,' he greeted me.

'Good day, Friend,' I answered in Tokboi, the lingua franca.

'How is it you walk unattended?' he asked.

'My boys are following on,' I said.

'Have you come a great distance, Sir?'

'From Rabaul. I left over a week ago.'

'Oh! That's a long way off. And what is your business, Sir?'

'Recruiting Native labour.'

'Not many available here,' he said.

'Is there a village nearby?' I asked.

'Yes. Pomio is just ahead. Are you staying there the night? It's a big place. We've got a Government Officer and a hospital too. And there's a Mission over across the bay.'

'So you have a Mission, have you?'

'Yes, Sir, we are all Catholics here.'

'Is that the meaning of the silly medal you've got round your neck?'

'Oh! Sir, you must not speak like that. The Father gave me that just a few days ago.'

'Tell me, what's the Father like?'

'Just like all white men to me, Sir. I wouldn't recognise him if he were to stand in front of me.'

✳

In getting to know the people I also came to understand something of the Tribe. Here amongst the Mengens there was no Chief in the accepted sense of the word, no Father-of-the-Tribe. Groups of villages had established a special bond, due mainly to their proximity to one another, and each group, and even each village, enjoyed autonomy in its own affairs, but this autonomy was guided by the general traditions of the Tribe. The arrangement was similar to that of the British Commonwealth. The different units of the tribe held together in virtue of a strong internal cohesion arising out of a common outlook, interests and language.

Two questions glared at me from the day I arrived in Malmal, because the answers affected my whole life and work: are all people capable of the same development? And why are some people backward or primitive while others are progressive? The Mengens were primitive, although they had advanced quite a lot in the last quarter century. The Kols and Mamusis were much more backward. Since the Mengens, then, had made an advance, they had partially answered my first question. With encouragement and teaching, all peoples seemed capable of progressing. But since the whole human race had an even start, why had one branch pushed ahead while another had not; what spurred the fathers of our civilisation to leave their primitive level and seek wider horizons in social and cultural life; and why have others been content to remain as they were?

Anthropologists have done extensive research into the social structure, customs and beliefs of primitive peoples. They have shown us that the apparent chaos of Native life is, in fact, a highly-ordered existence, governed by age-old laws, customs and beliefs which reach down to the last tribal relation between each and every member. No person or circumstance is unprovided for in the Native scheme of things.

But if you look more closely at their highly complicated social structure you may come to the conclusion, as I did, that there is no *a priori* organisation among primitive people; and that that is possibly why they always remain primitive and backward. There are codes and observances which have grown out of the daily burden of living: codes which result from the repeated experience of the past, but no codes formulated to change or improve life for the future; codes to restrict and confine life to what it has always been, but none to expand it to create a better future. Backward or primitive people live in the past and guide the present by the light of it, but they never try to mould their future. This attitude to the past has guaranteed their survival as a race; and their inability or unwillingness to come to grips with the future has kept them forever a primitive race, for it seems that the basic and only difference between a primitive man and a progressive one is mental: the primitive is wholly pre-occupied with the past and the present, the progressive with the present and the future. The one allows the past to mould the present, the other uses the present to mould the future. The backward man allows the world about him to mould and dominate him, while the other tries to mould and dominate the world about him. The hallmark of the primitive man in any society is his frozen backward glance.

Both types are to be found all the world over but where the majority of any race is of the primitive frame of mind and outlook it will stifle the exception; and where the majority has the progressive outlook, this will prevail. The Mengens and all other South-Sea Islanders have the primitive outlook, the frozen backward glance, and that is a far greater handicap than the fact that they are materially backward. In fact it is their only real drawback, at the root of all the others. Worldly improvements, therefore, are largely a waste of time until their mental attitude is changed, until they are convinced that by their own efforts they can improve their lot and shape their future; until they learn how to switch on their mental headlamps to light the road ahead, and not to depend for guidance on a mere tail-reflector; until they learn to use not only the receptive but also the creative half of their brains.

They are given the occasion to improve themselves by the three classical intruders into Native life: the Government, the Trader and the Missionary, each working from different motives and from different angles. The Government does not ask questions. It lays down the Law and has the power to enforce its wishes. Over the years the people can see that those laws have helped them to improve their lot. As long as those laws are helpful they afford the Native a prop by which to drag himself out of the age-old primitive pit from which, by his own efforts, he has never raised himself an inch, and so set his feet on the road to material progress. But whether he continues along that road or drops back again to his former slough will depend exclusively on his ability to change his outlook on life and the world about him. If he cannot change his outlook, he stands a poor chance of ever growing up. No Native people ever had a more helpful Government than the people of New Guinea have now in Australia. If they do not reach maturity in record time, the fault will lie with themselves.

The Trader's profession is well known. He offers new goods or money for work or for native goods. The Native envies this wealth but at the same time realises that he too could become as rich as the Trader. Few have attempted it in New Guinea, because the general answer is: 'Maski. It does not matter. I'll remain as I am.'

The Missionary, however, has neither the persuasive power of the Government nor the enticing power of the Trader. To the eye, he has nothing to offer for exchange, nor any show of power to display. So, if he wishes to have any helpful influence over the people, he must be, above all, a talker. He must be able to talk his way into and out of anywhere. When he has talked himself into the tribe he must be able to talk them round to his way of thinking. And if he can talk sense he will know that he is influencing them, because they will say: he has given us the answers to those things which we, the people, have never been able to discover for ourselves.

Although it may not be at once apparent, the Missionary is, of all three intruders, in reality in the most advantageous position. The other two bring something new, but he works with very old tools, common to all mankind: common sense and the Natural Law. By Natural Law I mean those things which every human being instinctively knows to be right, such as love of parents, or wrong, such as murder, stealing of wives or goods, defamation of character. These things are set down in code-form in the Fourth to the Eighth Command-ments, which state these Natural Laws and merely add Divine sanction to what every human heart, even the most primitive, would never dream of questioning. Natives break those laws as everybody else does but they would never think of arguing that to do so is to do the right thing. Here the Missionary is on common ground with the native; his ideas are not revolution-ary, and it matters little whether the native has the backward glance because, fundamentally, the ten commandments are en-shrined in his tribal laws. They are old stuff. They are the belief of the ancestors. Hence, a Native will take more easily to the religion of the white man than to any other thing he brings along. His backward glance is an obstacle to Admin-istration, Health, Commerce and Progress, but it is totally insignificant where Christianity is concerned.

The scope of the Missionary is limited however, though in

his enthusiasm he may be tempted to over-reach himself, for he must always remember that his kingdom is not of this world. His job is primarily with the individual and only in a secondary way with society. The material progress of his people is not, strictly speaking, his work, though he may contribute to it. The material progress of society is the burden of the head of society: the Government. No matter what form of society individuals adopt, it is the missionary's duty to work under that social form and to gain the individual for heaven. He has no mandate to change society, to decapitate kings, over-throw republics or to establish modern democracy, even though one or other of those things might help his own work. The Man who said: Render to Caesar ... fulfilled His own mission only by co-operating obediently with Pilate after He had given him the authority to condemn Him unjustly. He had full certitude that Pilate's act was an outrage against God, a certitude the modern missionary might often lack in regard to whatever he might consider his own special personal Pilate.

The point is important, for surely every missionary has had to face it one time or another. He enlightens people more than any other man, with the natural result that they come to him with their woes, all of them, and his enthusiasm or love for his people could easily draw him outside his own sphere. It happens amongst the most primitive Catholics, amongst those emerging to political maturity and even in established nations. People sometimes feel that the Church has let them down when it does not ally itself with them to satisfy their political ambitions or to vent their political spleen. A short medi-tation on Christ before Pilate should help.

It was necessary to say all this even in Malmal, because I felt that the people should know just what part of their lives the Church was primarily interested in, and in what part it would do its best to help, as a work of charity; how they as Catholics should worship God, and how as Catholic laymen they should make the best of every material help that came their way, so that they could worship God all the more fully.

From that you may conclude that the Mengens were

a highly enlightened body of men. They were not. I am sure it all went clean over them. Perhaps a little stuck. At any rate, I felt better for having said it.

❦

Amongst the Mengens I was the only grown male who had neither wife nor female relative, and I soon began to feel the loss because I had to be my own cook. Certainly, I had inherited a cook from John Askew but cooks were ever a tricky business. They develop a personal attachment to their employer and are rarely a success with a new one. Each man has to train his own.

I spent some hungry months before I solved the problem. I had no scarcity of applicants but I needed a boy who was clean, tidy, reliable and intelligent enough to adapt himself to the work; and, above all, one who would be prepared to accompany me through the jungle, for good food counted more there than anywhere else, and this last condition was always the great obstacle.

I preened myself in remembering that I shared a problem common to holy men. The Old Testament solemnly reminded me that 'Mathathias, a Levite, the first-born of Sellum the Corite, was overseer of such things as were fried in the frying-pan,' and the New Testament backed it up with: 'then the twelve, calling together the multitude of the disciples said: It is not right that we should leave the word of God and serve tables.' My Mathathias would have to do more than watch the frying-pan. He would have to take care of the house, the washing, the poultry, the pigs, the garden and me.

At last I found such a one in Joseph Kenpale from Malmal, and we parted only when I left on holidays. He had a helper, Gerard Kalorea, better known as Lonra, who was almost as good as Kenpale. Between them they ran me and the mission-station.

From a cookery-book I chose those recipes we could use and translated them for Kenpale. In a short time he had a reasonable selection to choose from. Baking bread was our greatest problem because the yeast often gave trouble. It was a home-made brew consisting of sugar, flour and the milk of a green coconut. As time went on, ready-made yeast became available from Australia, and this changed all the rules of bread-making. By experimenting we mastered the new technique, down to the precise moment at which we should add the pinch of salt.

An endearing quality of these two Mengens was their unfailing good humour and pleasantness of disposition, and perhaps more important, the willingness with which they accompanied me on many a long and arduous trek through the jungle where, under the worst possible conditions, they cooked my food, washed my clothes and pitched and broke camp a few hundred times. From an old bush-diary I see that Lonra accompanied me for 300 hours of actual walking-time, and Kenpale for over 350. Only rarely were both on the same trip. To say that I was grateful to them seems wholly inadequate.

Kinkale was another Mengen built on the same lines. He had messed about with Mission-boats since he was a youngster. During the war he had served with the Australians and on big occasions used to display his five war-medals with pride. He was now Luluai or Mayor of Malmal and also skipper of my twenty-six-foot motor-launch. In the six years he was with me we logged over 15,000 miles; he never touched a reef or failed to bring his launch home. But the most astonishing thing about him was that every good human quality that you and I would like to find in our friends, he had.

When coming to Malmal I had remembered Father Rudolf's advice about 'extras' and hence had brought along some ducks, fowls, pigs and goats: male and female I brought them, each according to its own species. They all served me well except the goats. The nanny caused no difficulty, but the billy was a real problem. He was friendly and tame and had no respect at all for boundaries. The doors of houses in New Guinea are seldom closed at the best of times, but my house had not even a door, and so only too often I found the billy in my bathroom or on my bed or table; and wherever he went, his aroma lingered for days.

The young boys from the village soon found that they had a new playmate. If they pitched a high football his way, he would rear up on his hind legs and butt it. This was considered even more marvellous than the fact that he 'stank-too-much'. Once, during my absence, he cleaned up every flower and shrub in the place. I tethered him but he refused to eat, and I had not the heart to kill him.

During Benediction of the Blessed Sacrament one Sunday the volume went out of the 'Tantum Ergo' and only a few giggles saw it through. 'Next Sunday,' I thought, 'I must say a few words on Deportment in the House of God.' Then someone tugged me. I pulled an ecclesiastical frown and looked solemnly around. The billy was there, chewing the hem of my Cope. The Catholic Church is pretty far-sighted but this was a situation that was not covered by any rubric. 'Whoosh-whoosh him into the sacristy,' I said to the server. The young lad tried but the billy stood on his hind legs as if he expected a football. The boy now did some fast thinking. He walked slowly backwards towards the door making motions towards the goat with the thurible. Billy followed on, snorting and rearing capriciously. He did not know that he was making a solemn exit with incense and thurible . . . an honour the Church does not grant even to a Cardinal.

I had now made up my mind to get rid of him unless he changed his ways; and then he committed a mortal sin in public. Two women from Malmal were walking along the track with loads of food on their heads. Billy, apparently on his lawful occasions, filed along behind. There was some newspaper on the track, and that is a prized commodity for rolling Native cigars. One of the women stooped gingerly under her load to pick it up. The goat moved into position behind her and with a few deft flicks gobbled up her entire dress. She dropped everything and fled to the cover of the jungle shouting : 'It's the devil himself, I tell you.'

Shortly afterwards, I gave billy and his mate to a neighbour.

We, The People

I T IS unavoidable that in writing on a topic so obscure and uncharted as primitive peoples, a person should have his own approach and carry away his own impressions and conclusions; it does not follow that all or any of those impressions or conclusions will be correct in whole or in part. They are, however, though poor and unreliable, the only instruments he has to guide him in his life's daily course, and he will cherish them and use them so long as they are borne out by facts, and discard them as soon as a wider experience provides him with others which appear more correct.

My own experience of primitives is quite modest. It has in fact covered something less than ten years, though it may have gained from the fact that it was daily and uninterrupted, since I was alone on my Mission station. In that time my impressions and opinions suffered variations, oscillations and even complete gyrations. The ones I thought granite were only wax. This I know, that time did not bring certitude; in fact in many cases it brought only doubt. I became less sure . . . or perhaps I should say less cock-sure. I should like to think, however, that my field of vision became broader and truer, though in consequence the detail may have become less sharp and isolated.

In the following pages I propose to sketch in broadest out-line some of the ideas and behaviour of these primitive parish-ioners and thereby to draw the background against which the daily life of the missionary is set. Some things may seem ridi-culous or funny and may even be so, but to the people they are serious facts, which is of paramount importance when one has the job of helping them solve their problems and of bringing their ideas up to date.

It is the common belief both of the European and of the Native that the European is superior to or better than the Native. This is so obvious that neither party ever questions it. Yet it is a superiority of accomplishment and not of nature, because the European has inherited a richer culture and is trained to a higher degree of manual and intellectual dex-terity. Fundamentally there is no difference and if a primitive baby were brought up in exclusively European surroundings there is no reason to believe that he would be in any way dif-ferent from a white baby. Similarly, if a European baby were transferred to a primitive tribe he would grow up as the other tribesmen. The European has at his disposal a rich and varied culture, a mass of knowledge in trades, professions and intel-lectual pursuits which are entirely unknown to the Native of New Guinea.

European civilisation is mainly directed (in peacetime) to-wards making life easier; New Guinea civilisation is at all times totally absorbed in making life possible. Since the people know no luxuries their demands are simple, and once possessed of the two primary necessities of life, food and shelter, they are substantially content.

With this simple form of life they are less dependent on each other than are we. A labour strike in America could easily cause inconvenience in New Zealand but it could never affect the dwellers in the huts on Nakanai. Every bushman who has sound hands and teeth can carry on at his own level indepen-dent of the outside world. He does not depend on machinery or on tools of trade. We depend on these things; my parishioners depend on themselves. They have less interference from their neighbours and also less help. We are suited to our form of civilisation and they are suited to theirs.

If a primitive New Guinea tribesman found himself locked alone in a European house which contained everything necessary for life it is quite probable that he would die of hunger and thirst, for he would not know how to get water from a tap or food from a closed container. It would not even occur to him that taps and tins held such things. Nor would he know how to open a door to let himself out. And if a European suddenly found himself in the jungle he would be in a similar predicament.

The jungle is home to the primitive. He knows which roots, leaves and berries are nourishing and which are poisonous, and he can also recognise those foods which are edible in one season or locality and poisonous in another. Using only his hands and teeth he can make traps for animals, birds and fish. He can make a fire by rubbing two sticks together and a water-container by putting a few twists in the leaf of a waterlily. He is not worried if he has to sleep in the open without blanket or clothes. As he must learn the ways of our civilisation from us, so must we learn the ways of the jungle from him, because in jungle-lore he is unquestionably our superior.

I have trekked possibly more than two thousand miles of jungle and mountain with him and I readily admit that he is hardier, a better walker, a tougher climber, less subject to fatigue and weariness than I am. He can thrive on little. He can sleep in the open without fear of chill. He needs no chair, bed, blankets, boots, clothes, pots, pans or any of the other paraphernalia with which I must encumber myself in order to survive. For untold generations he has, with bare hands, wrestled with the savage and unyielding jungle and forced a living from it. If all my tools and material equipment were taken from me how long would I survive?

The extremely difficult circumstances in which he has lived for generations have left their mark on him. Things are always scarce and times are always hard. Hence, in order to survive, the human product has to be healthy, wily, self-centred and independent. If a person can not look after himself there is nobody with the wealth or leisure to care for him. Only the heroes survive.

The battle against the forces of nature is continuous and the stakes are always high, for it is a fight not for holidays with pay but for survival in the nude.

To steal a man's mate or to steal his food is to attack his very life and the penalty, death. Their laws are simple, hard and final. Selfishness on our part may be a vice, but for him, in his circumstances, it is a primary necessity in order to preserve the individual in an exacting country which gives nothing for nothing and only a sparing return for the sweat of the brow.

Great and small are relative terms: that which is trivial to one may be tremendous to another. In Native life where good things are scarce nothing is small. Any favour or gift is important and demands reciprocation. That is why we notice the tenacious memory of the people for even the smallest service that they may have done one another. Kolapana reminds Varalona that he gave the roots of four sweet potatoes to his father and why has he heard nothing from him since?

It is an accepted axiom that there is no such thing as a charitable donation. I do not mean that they understand the idea and reject it but rather that, from lack of material, they have never even got as far as considering it. Each man knows that he must return what he received and receive back what he gives. In the eyes of the primitive, only a fool gives something for nothing and he is to be despised because he does not know the value of things. It is therefore a difficult undertaking to make a gift to a primitive. He will attribute to it the same value as you do; if you insist the thing is free and not to be returned he will conclude that the gift has no value and hence that it does not merit a return anyway, as you are doing him no favour; but if the gift is obviously something of value, such as an axe or a knife, he will probably show his bewilderment by shaking his head and saying: My eye is dark to the fashion of the white man.

A close student of our own customs will admit that we differ little from the primitive in this matter ... or in any other. Christmas presents, wedding gifts and the like all carry the tacit implication that they must be reciprocated on a suitable occasion, if not in justice, at least under the risk of social censure. Only when people are generous or wealthy or both do they remove that invisible tag from their presents.

It is an important thing in dealing with the primitive man not to be in his debt. The cost of keeping clear is usually only a trifle to us, though to him it may be a thing of great magnitude. Most of us who fail do so because we neglect to view the affair from his angle. He is ashamed to ask us to pay our debts, though he resents the non-payment. Little trifles with primitive people can often cast long shadows.

But things like this give only half the picture. The world in which the Mengens live is open for all to see, but no two people see things in the same light, interpret them in the same way or draw the same conclusions from them. The Mengens and I saw the same daily events but usually drew totally different conclusions because our beliefs were not the same; we took different things for granted and this naturally affected our conclusions. We saw common facts in a different light, the light of our upbringing and traditional beliefs. Hence, in order to understand why he sometimes acted in such an unusual manner, I found it necessary to try to learn and understand his superstitions and religious beliefs, which were the key to his behaviour. These beliefs are commonly known as taboos.

A taboo (pronounced by South Sea Islanders as 'tamboo' with the accent, as usual, on the first syllable) is something which is forbidden. It may be a place, a person, a thing, an action, a word, a gesture and so forth. The taboos then, are the Thou-shalt-nots or the laws of the tribe. They differ in strictness and in penalty according to the nature and importance of the thing they are designed to safeguard.

It is taboo to steal from a man's garden or to alienate the affections of his wife. Since this taboo was meant to safeguard the life of the individual and of the race, the penalty was death.

Betrothed persons may not be seen together even in public in a group, nor mention each other's name under any pretext whatever lest the people 'think-no-good' of them or suspect them of improper familiarity. The consequence of this would be 'loss of face' for the betrothed, which is the greatest possible loss and often leads to suicide.

A woman may not enter the Men's house lest, among other reasons, she hear men's conversation and become coarse. I might add that this taboo has failed to curb either the women's volubility or their vocabulary.

A young lad may not refer to a married man by his name as that would be cheeky and impolite. He must speak of him as Golurea's father or Tangulele's husband.

Men may not walk within a certain distance of the women's bathing place and vice versa.

People abroad near the village at night must notify their presence by carrying a lighted ember or by whistling or singing at sufficiently frequent intervals, lest they be suspected of trying to spy or steal or make evil sorceries.

People may not linger near certain trees or rocks, or near burial places, because the genii of the place could then take possession of them and cause sickness and even death.

A son-in-law is heavily burdened with taboos towards his mother-in-law. If he sees her on the track he must avoid her by making a timely detour. He may not sit, eat, smoke, chew betel-nut or speak in her presence. Pressed by grave necessity he may speak to her but then in the most formal manner addressing her as 'My Love. . . .'

Now, if a Mengen tribesman may not sit, eat, smoke, chew betel-nut or speak in the Presence, it is fairly sure that he will not seek out that Presence, or, should he find himself in It, he will, as the Australians have it, 'go off like a Bondi Bus'. I asked old Omokena why all these taboos on two people who are so obviously united in 'love and harmony', and he gave me a roguish smile and said: 'Ach, Father, a bachelor would never understand.' It has been suggested in other circles that this taboo might, with certain advantages, be circulated more widely.

There is a taboo which cost me a lot of money but which saved a few lives. Only brothers can nurse each other's children. By brothers I mean sisters, because among the Mengens sisters are called brothers. I hope that's not too complicated because brothers are brothers too. Jack and Mary are sisters. ... Jack is Mary's sister just as she is his. Jack and Jim are brothers, so are Kate and Mary. It is quite simple if one remembers that, in the children of a family, those of opposite sexes are each other's sisters and those of the same sex are brothers. However. ...

Kate had a child and then she died. The people have no artificial means of rearing a baby and the good book says that in such circumstances one must find a wet-nurse. Catharina was there, whose week-old baby had died and in her condition would have been glad to accept the orphan, but it could not be. It was taboo. Catharina was not Kate's brother, and so, had it been left to them, the baby would have starved to death. Local taboos, however, did not extend to the white man's bottle-and-teat and I found myself with a squawking pikinini. Over the years I acquired four others in much the same way. Incidentally, they were very healthy and easy to rear. Malmal village supplied the foster-parents. The bigger girls used to bring these babies to school with them, collecting the bottles from my kitchen on the way, and getting a refill as needed. Since the children here do not wear nappies till they are seven years old, each baby had a complete wardrobe when I had supplied him with towels and a blanket. Baby-food, towels, blankets and the other odds and ends which he needed for his first fifteen months never cost me more than £60, which was a cheap price to pay for a human life.

❊

Side by side with these and hundreds of other taboos dealing with secular matters, are the taboos relating to the supernatural, for the Mengen tribe and also the Mamusi have always believed in the other world. Their religion is an extensive and in some points a contradictory affair, so I shall record only the main and undisputed tenets of it, as I gathered it from the ancients.

Nutu is Master of all things. He always existed. No one made him. He made everything, especially our tribe. Nutu is good and can do no evil to anything or to anyone. He made all things before anything was. First there was nothing and he went around creating as he went. He came from the east with the sun and journeyed westward along the coast to the end of our tribal ground at the Tolo. Then he veered from the point where the sun goes down and followed his good (i.e. right) hand creating the land and the river as he went. He pushed the land to both sides thus making the mountains. Away up in Nakanai mountains, beyond Paka village he grew tired and sat on a newly made boulder in the river which was still soft and so he has left his imprint on it, and it bears that imprint even to this day; and close beside it another boulder bears the imprint of his little bag. Nutu, refreshed, continued his journey till he thought the river was long enough and then he pushed his finger into the mountain and said: Let that be the eye (source) of the Tolo, and so it was.

He then created our ancestors and gave them this land. He did not make them from nothing as he made the mountains and the rivers. No, he made them from two nuts of the betel-nut palm. But Nutu saw that he had made two males and he said: this will not work. So he changed one into a woman. And this is how he did it but the Father must tell no one for it is taboo for the women to know about it. This man and woman, then, understood many things and they said: Ke Minamina mana: That's how things are.

Nutu made man but he made him different from other things. He is not like 'pinolo' the wild pig or 'lausa' the bush-wallaby, nor is he like the cassowary nor the possum, for they all die and are dead; but Nutu, when he made man, placed a 'kanu' (soul) inside his lona (liver), and that kanu never dies. It leaves the liver at death and at the following sundown it is escorted to Nutu by a procession of 'soare' (departed souls). The kanu becomes a soare too, once it has been escorted from the liver of the dead man at sundown. The kanus of each totem have their own resting place and each resting place is by a river. They live for ever with Nutu by the river. As each person dies his feet must be pointed to the river where his kanu will later reside. Nutu lives by all the rivers at the same time but the departed souls are confined to their own place, for it is a well-known fact that a soare (ghost) cannot cross running water.

Nutu is good and his name is taboo. He is always willing to help and that help must be invoked by all; some however, invoke only the help of Saia, the Evil One.

When we the people clear the jungle to make a new village and find a boulder, that rock is consecrated to Nutu. If we find no rock, then the first post driven in the ground is dedicated to him. Everything we do, all our work, all our gardens must be placed under him, but some invoke only the help of Saia, the Evil One. and cast spells on things by his power.

Nutu is good. He gave us land and he gave us the taro to eat and the coconut too. It was he who commanded us to circumcise our boys and that is why we always do it. Some other tribes do not do it and that is why they have customs which are not as good as ours. Our customs and habits are good.

Our newborn babies are given to Nutu and the mother speaks saying: 'As Nutu is strong, Oh let my baby be strong; as Nutu is great, Oh, let my baby be great; as Nutu is good, Oh let my baby be good.' But some invoke only Saia, the Evil One.

Saia is a spirit and has been in existence from the beginning. He was always there. Nutu did not make him. Nutu had nothing to do with him. Nutu makes only good things. Neither is Nutu interested in Saia's goings-on. Nutu and Saia are neither friends nor enemies. They just ignore each other, each one following his own bent. If Nutu wishes to do good, that's his business, just as it is Saia's to perform all evil. Neither interferes with the other's work and Nutu has no power whatever over Saia. There is only one Nutu but there are 'plenty too much' Saias, some more powerful than others.

Saia is evil and the cause of all evil, accidents, sickness and death. Without him they could not happen. He is the source of all these things, urged on by his own devilment or enticed by the agency of man. To bring about an accident or to cause a sickness Saia enters into the thing or person. Thus sometimes he takes possession of an axe and diverts it from the tree to the foot of the man wielding it. Sometimes Saia acts like that just from his own perversity, sometimes a sorcerer puts him into the axe either for a fee or because he does not like the owner of the axe. If Saia were not in the axe, the accident could not possibly occur.

Saia sometimes enters a tree and cunningly weakens a branch and waits for an unsuspecting tribesman to climb on to it. There is no end to his mischief. He will even inhabit a loose stone on the track and attack a man's toe. Such a small dwelling place would not be any of his permanent ones, however. But he permanently resides in all deformed trees, large creepers, grotesque boulders and rocks, high mountain peaks and waterfalls and in everything that is unusual of its kind. Consequently, all these things must be carefully pointed out to the young and sedulously avoided by all. (In the 200 yards between my house and the village I know of eight abodes of Saia.)

Saia often takes possession of people and when he does so they become sick. If he leaves them they become well. Sickness means the in-dwelling of Saia and the only cure lies in his eviction. He can take possession either of his own accord . . . if someone passes near any of his abodes without having been fortified by the appropriate sorcery or charm . . . or he can be induced to do so by a sorcerer. It is useless to ask Nutu to get him out because that is none of Nutu's business and anyhow, Nutu has no power over him, but Saia can be commanded to leave by another Saia or in response to certain charms, spells and incantations by a sorcerer.

Sickness usually means that Saia has been put into the sick man by someone, although occasionally here too Saia works on

his own initiative and when he does so he causes either fatal
pneumonia (sometimes its result can point to the origin of the
sickness) or cerebral malaria.

By way of personal observation I may remark that those of
us who have experienced a severe dose of malaria, even of a
type less terrifying than cerebral, are quite sympathetic to
the Mengen's view of its origin.

The people's idea of right and wrong falls plumb within the
Natural Law and the Ten Commandments: Man must honour
Nutu; he must obey authority; he must not kill a person without good reason; he must not interfere with other people's
mates; he must not steal; neither may he tell lies or defame a
person, for if a person lose his good name the only honourable
course left to him is suicide . . . 'but he who steals my good
name. . . .' Moses and Shakespeare would have felt quite at
home in Salumpuna.

When we see how the people believe in this brooding presence of Saia, how they see the daily accidents, sicknesses and
deaths as all coming from his hand, we must admit that they
are in sore need of enlightenment and sympathy, for they are
the most permanently scared and terrified people in the world.

The Mengen's cosmos is, however, peopled with more beings
than God, Man and Devil. There is also the shady world in-
between, about which they are extremely shy to speak.

From different remarks which I had overheard during the
years, those very informative remarks which one is not meant
to hear, I had concluded that there was another race of
beings about the place. To give strength to my surmise I had
noted certain rites that were carried out in regard to babies.

There is a man in the village of Malmal whose name is not
Lima but I shall call him Lima from now on, because in the
circumstances it is taboo for me to mention his name. Lima has
quite a broad and intelligent outlook on life. I had marked him
as the best source to tap about these strange beings and had put
it off for years because I knew that discussion of such a topic

needed a very special atmosphere. I should need to have him alone with me for a considerable time and he should have a good excuse for being with me, because everybody's comings and goings were watched. His enemies in the village would say that he was carrying stories about them . . . as if I did not already know them all.

Lima and I had worked the whole day on the motor-launch. We had done all the repairs and the tidying-up that were within our scope, but one job had eluded us, a damaged shaft bearing.

'Let us run it over to Master Harry,' said Lima.

Master Harry was Mr. Harry Bode who had a coconut plantation in the vicinity. He had all the things necessary to do the job: the equipment, the skill and a generosity of soul which was at all times embarrassing. He might say to me: 'I heard your boat pass a few days ago and it didn't sound quite right. I think you should bring it over some time.' Goodenough was not good enough for Harry, even when it was only a question of my boat. It had to be one hundred percent, otherwise it was a sin against the fitness of things in the Bay. Harry was my friend-in-need, and also my friend when the need had passed.

Lima's suggestion would have to wait till the morrow. Now we called it a day and took time off to have a smoke and to straighten our backs. The conversation began by comparing motor-launches with his ancestors' mode of sea-faring and gradually came round to the Mengen's ideas and beliefs in general. Our job was done and our mood was relaxed and satisfied. There was no possibility of being heard because the launch was anchored off-shore. It swayed like a cradle as the gentle ripples licked its sides.

'You have mentioned Nutu,' I said, 'and Saia and all the spirits of the dead, but isn't there something else, something which is none of those things, and which nobody ever mentions in my presence?'

Lima wiped a spanner with a rag and put it carefully in the toolbox and closed it. He picked a scrap of copper wire off the deck, and leaning over the side let it drop into the sea. Both of us watched it sparkle and wriggle down through the clear water, chased and nibbled at by colourful little fish. We gazed till the little fish came back to the surface.

'Oloman!' said Lima, 'the Father hears everything.'

'That's what they say, Lima, but don't you believe them.'

'If I tell the Father, he'll make fun of me?'

'Have I ever made fun of you yet on account of your beliefs or customs?'

'True.' Lima looked around to make sure that no one was within earshot. 'Let the matches come,' he said, 'my smoke has died. Are these things too in the land the Father comes from?'

'I don't know, Lima, until I hear your story.'

'We the people say there is a Porekanu,' said Lima. 'He is like a man in every way only he is not as high as a dog. He lives mostly in holes in the huge trees. You know that old tree that's now dead, the one between the Father's house and the village, below the breadfruit tree at the left hand side? Well, a Porekanu always lived there till it withered recently. He hides by day and by night in the tree unless the moon is up. He lives on "nasi", the dew on the leaves. He may be seen at dawn dancing on the sea-shore, and when the sun is a little higher he likes to bask on the sand like a lizard or a crocodile. His hair is long. We the people like him because he is frolicsome and happy and never does an injury to anyone. We call those fellows the Good People.'

This Porekanu, which Lima pronounced very similar to Porrkawn, intrigued me because he resembled, not only in habit but also in name, that little Irish elf the Leprechaun. Drop the 'Le' and you've got him. I asked Lima to pronounce it again, because frankly I was suspicious of this all too obvious similarity. Perhaps some European had told him about leprechauns and he was now coming out with his own garbled version.

'Porekanu,' said Lima, 'Po-re-ka-nu. You know that place there around the point where Master Harry used to anchor the *Susan*? We call it Pore. That's the name of a tree and there were

a lot of them growing there . . . just the same with Gugulena
. . . gugul-ena . . . a lot of gugal trees, because they used to be
plentiful there at one time.'

It was now clear to me that there was nothing common in
name between the Porekanu and the Leprechaun. The Mengen
rival was simply Pore-kanu or the Sprite of the Pore Tree. Kanu
is the Mengen word for spirit, sprite, or soul. It is used in the
Catechism and prayers. Kanu e Tupu is the Holy Ghost.

'Now there is another one,' said Lima, 'and we name him
Sanauga. He is very like the Porekanu only that instead of
long hair he wears a long hat. He lives on the tree-tops and
comes down only occasionally, and if he sees or is seen by a
man he will run up the tree. Women do not frighten
him. In fact the women are afraid of him; later I shall tell
the Father why. Sanauga is most active at the full moon.
We have often tried to capture one and nearly succeeded
on one occasion. Does the Father know my relative, I may not
mention his name, the husband of Kiulona?'

'You mean Lolotuparea?'

'Yes, that's the man. Has the Father seen the white patch
on his poll?'

'Yes. It was pointed out to me one day by Gulu, and when
I asked him how it happened he only made fun of Lolotuparea
and would not tell me.'

'That's it! Now, my relative is very sensitive about it and
people seldom see it because he always has his hair well dyed
to cover it. This is how he got that white spot.

'One day, my relative (the Father knows I may not mention
his name) and Momokulu got between a Sanauga and his tree.
The little man weaved and jumped and jigged and finally got
to his tree in spite of them . . . out between Momokulu's legs he
went . . . but as he was scampering up the tree Momokulu
grabbed him and held him fast. Just between the ribs and the
hips he held him as you'd hold a little pig. The little fellow
was so small that Momokulu's fingers met around his waist.
The Sanauga was really "mad-no-good" now and he screeched
like a cockatoo and tried to bite Momokulu's hand. My relative

saw what was happening so he took hold on the Sanauga's hat. Aiii-i-i-i! That was a pity! Ten men could not hold the little fellow then! He broke clean away from both of them ... the moment my relative touched his hat they felt his strength increase ... and he ran up the tree squealing and muttering. When he was out of reach he turned around and wet. He hadn't much, just like a kitten, but a few drops fell on my relative and that's what caused his white patch.

'It was only later that we the people remembered what the ancients had always said: All the Sanauga's strength is in his hat.

'I think if my relative had not touched his hat we might now have the Sanauga in the village ... but no ... we wouldn't.

'O sorrow, Father, let the matches come again, my smoke is dead.'

'Have one of these, Lima,' I said, 'it lights better. . . . But tell me, why are the women afraid of the Sanauga?'

'You see, Father, the Porekanu is good and he harms nobody. Sanauga we call the Little People. They are mischievous. Now when a woman has a young baby she must be very careful to hide it from the Sanauga. He may be around the houses at night and if he sees a new fat baby he will want to take it off and leave a sickly one in its place. He cannot enter a house, but if the mother brings the baby out in the open too soon and if the Sanauga is nearby he can swap babies so fast that the mother won't even be aware of it. The last time a baby was changed was at Laikatokea village above Motong in 1942. The changeling is still there ... a sickly idiot of a boy.

'The mothers protect their babies against the Sanauga by making a mixture from the resin of a tree ... we the people call it "kuoina" ... and they burn that kuoina in the house and the scent of it clings to the skin of the baby and when the Sanauga finds that scent he runs away because he doesn't like it.'

'May I break the speech of Lima?' I asked.

' 'Tis good,' he said.

'I notice, Lima, that when a woman brings her baby to the Church for baptism, he is painted and smeared with all sorts of powders and lotions and ointments, and also has charms hanging all over him.'

'The Father has mentioned it,' said Lima, 'I too may now speak of it.

'When Father Culhane first came here, I was only that high then, he made a ruling that the children should be baptised a few days after being born. He said it was not right to delay Baptism because many babies died young. Our women did not want to bring their babies out in the open so soon, but the Father was insistent. The women now made plenty-too-much talk and some wanted to run away and leave the village. Father Culhane did not know about this.

'There was a woman in the village; she is now dead. Samosi was her name. Pirakurumea was her mother and she had no father. She happened in the jungle. Samosi was a lively girl, always laughing and talking and it was said that some of the men from the village used to steal her. Now, when all the talking and discussions were going on about baptising the young babies, Samosi's own time was coming near, and her baby would have no father either because she would not speak.

'One night a group of women were talking and gossiping in Keloa's second house and Samosi was there and she would not tell them who the man was. The other women were curious to find out and mentioned lots of names but Samosi only laughed. Then they said: "Ah! Go on! Tell us. We're dying to know. We won't tell anyone. Truly!" But Samosi only laughed. Then they scolded her saying: "You can't hide it forever, anyhow! We'll all know when we see the baby's face." And some of the women, trying to force her further, spoke saying: "Ha-Ha! If you don't tell us who the man was, we'll fix you! When your baby is born you must take him right away to be baptised." But Samosi quite unexpectedly only laughed and said: "That won't be very difficult."

'The other women knew now that Samosi, contrary as ever, would do just that, and they were afraid of their foolish talk because they knew that if she took him out so soon, the baby would die, or the Sanauga would change him, and they would be blamed. Some, maliciously, spoke thus: "Samosi is ashamed of the way she got her baby and she wants it to die but we cannot let that happen." They realised now that Samosi would reveal their foolish words and shame them (draw their bluff).

'A little later they decided how to get out of the trap. Vole-vole, Gerard's grandmother, had made a new charm and so they agreed that when Samosi's baby would be born they would try out this new charm on it and then send it off to be baptised. And then if the baby happened to die later or to be changed by the Sanauga, no one could say that they did it with their tongues.

'All right. Very good. One morning Samosi gave birth to a baby boy and the village-women performed the new sorcery on him just after they had washed him. Before midday, that same day, Samosi took her baby over to Father Culhane to have him baptised.

' "Laga-laga manangana ikia," said Father Culhane speaking. "This is a freshly-born baby."

' "So it so," said Samosi, "just now I bore him. I obeyed the Father's ruling that it should be baptised immediately and so I brought it along."

'And Father Culhane was so pleased that she had done what he had asked that he could not scold her for the way she got him.

'And we, the people, laughed.'

'And the baby, Lima, did he die?'

'Not at all. The Father knows him . . . the fellow who went on the *Teresa* last trip. He's working at Rakanda now.'

'Is that the man!' I said. 'And tell me: is it because they saw that no evil came to him that they now bring along their babies without fuss?'

'No, Father, that's not true. They still resent it but they know that the babies are safe from the Sanauga as long as they use Volevole's charm.'

'From the Sanauga? Not from the Saia, the Evil One?'

'That's it. It is used only against the Sanauga to prevent him from swapping the baby.'

❧

Why is it that we can look at a thing a thousand times or more and retain only the haziest picture of it, and then suddenly and for no apparent reason some hidden camera snaps in the brain and the picture is made fresh and definite and indelible and so dominating that it excludes all others?

A shutter clicked when Lima had finished his story and I can still recall the picture with the clarity of sight. The sun was westward over Serunguna in the Mamusi and the soft tips of white cloud were edging upwards over the mountains on the horizon. The trees were already casting long shadows and the smoke that curled up through the roofs of Gugulena on the hill was a transparent blue with a tinge of white. It rose lazily and hung like a halo in the air. Over to the North across the Bay, Malekur village looked black and lonely, for the high mountains behind it had already cast their shadows out over the sea. Galue still caught the sun and its white strand sparkled and glittered. Further east, Pomio, though eight miles away, seemed right at hand and the blue smoke filtered through its roofs, for now every woman in the tribe was baking the evening meal. Further on towards Bovalpuna and Motong the sea changed from blue to dazzling white and melted into the white hazy sky, at what point no one could tell.

A canoe rode easy on the glossy sea with its dripping, glittering paddles frozen forever in mid-air. Parakeets on their panting wings of red-blue, black and gold scurried homewards into the sun, swerving now this way, now that. A lone, fat, disgruntled parrot, purple and red with anger, lumbered lazily home against a background of jungle green, turning his head from side to side in curiosity and screeching raucous curses on everybody. A vulgar fellow.

A few dozen school-boys were playing football near

the Church. In half an hour the conch shell would announce the Angelus and the close of day.

Lima had been watching me from the corner of his eye. Our eyes met and he asked: 'Has the Father heard those stories already? Are those things too in the land of his ancestors?'

'If I tell Lima,' I said, 'he will make fun of me.'

'Have I ever made fun of the Father yet on account of any of his queer habits?' said Lima repeating what I had said to him previously.

'True,' said I.

'Did some man tell these stories to the Father?'

'Yes.'

'Who is the man?'

'I'm sorry, Lima. He is a close relative, a close taboo, so I may not mention his name.'

'You mean a tribesman of yours?'

'A tribesman. The same clan and totem.'

'Kwukwu! And we thought we were the only people that believed such things.'

'He told me the stories, Lima, but I don't know if I believe them. But isn't there anything else besides the Porekanu and the Sanauga? Isn't there any sort of a "kanu" that does the work in your garden while you are asleep ... that sort of thing?'

'No,' said Lima, 'but we have a Boré and Malovangana too.' (Presumably derived from *Malo*, a loin-cloth; *vangana*, unoccupied, untenanted, empty, vacant or uninhabited. *Malovangana*: The vacant loin-cloth, or as we might put it: The vacant chair.)

'They are new to me.' I said.

'The Boré,' said Lima, 'is like this. Sometimes when a person is going to die a man is heard around the village for a few nights previously. He wails and cries. Sometimes he is on the ground and sometimes we think he is walking along the treetops. I have heard him but I have never seen him. His cry is different from anything we have ever heard. Father, if you heard him his wail would twist your liver in sorrow and fear.

When we hear him, our bellies turn to water and we have no strength for anything. We fasten our doors and hide in the darkest corner of the house.

'Omokena got angry one night when we heard the Boré and he went out with a spear. Omokena's account of it is that he saw the Boré and threw the spear at him and the spear went clean through him and impaled itself in a palm. We the people saw it there in the morning. Omokena got a terrible fright and ever after he was more scared than anyone else.'

'And what does Omokena say the Boré looked like?'

'He doesn't know. He says he saw only an appearance.' (*Lelea*: form, outline.)

'And does the Boré come round often?'

'No, but at the moment they say he is at the Native Hospital at Matale, and all the doctor-boys are frightened.' (By a rare coincidence a few days later I met the Medical Officer in charge of the hospital and in the course of conversation he mentioned that for four nights running he could not find one doctor-boy on night-duty. He could not understand why, and I offered no opinion.)

'Why do you think he is hanging so much around the hospital?'

'There must be someone there that's going to die, someone special; you see, the Boré wails for only certain families. The Father has never heard of that?'

'Yes, Lima, I have. My tribesmen call him the Banshee, and that, too, follows only certain families.'

'The Father is fooling me.'

'I'm not. Ask Master Harry what a banshee is. But what about the Malovangana?'

'One man can see another,' said Lima with a rare economy of detail.

'Not much strange in that, is there?'

'Yes, because the other man is not there. You see, it is like this. If one of our people goes to a distant place and if something evil befalls him or if he dies, there is always someone in the village that sees it happening, and sometimes he even talks to him. We often know these things as soon as they happen. Later on, somebody sends the news.'

'Is there any special place or time for these happenings, Lima?'

'No. Some people see them at night, some by day on the track or in the garden. The day Piragona's brother died in Lae, Piragona was talking to him just out there in his canoe and he came back to the village and told us all about it.'

Telepathy? Second sight? Clairvoyance?

'Well, Lima,' I said, 'some of my tribesmen too speak the words you have spoken.'

'I did not wish to speak of those things,' he said, 'because I thought they belonged only to us the people, and I thought the Father would make fun of me, and now the Father himself believes them.'

'I don't know if I believe them, Lima, and I can't say that I don't. You know how hard it is to go against the crowd, even when you think you are right. They have knowledge and they have prejudices and most of them mistake one for the other. And if you don't agree they'll say you are crazy and have got an evil spirit and when you pass along, the mothers will grab their children out of your way and say to them: Beware of that Nanasa. But let me tell you this.

'My ancestors too had their Porekanu and they called him Leprechaun. They also had their Sanauga and their Boré. These Porekanu dwelt in the tribal grounds of my ancestors and everyone was fond of them. And the people said: Let us build a place for the Porekanu and plant trees around it to shelter it from the cold rain. Let us call this place a Rath, the place of the Porekanu, and let it be taboo. And many of those Raths still remain and many places are called after them, as Rathmore and Rathbeg and Rathluirc and so on. And so it was in the olden days. But now things are changing. Many of my tribesmen now say: There is no Porekanu and some say there is no Nutu; we have never seen them. But you and I know that Nutu and Porekanu have their pride and their feeling and hide themselves from those who only mock them.

'It may be that the Porekanu does not exist, or it may be that he has deserted his Raths because my tribesmen have built roads through them, and noisy motor cars and rude and irreverent people pass there by day and night. He likes his sanctuary in the solitude of forgotten glens and remote places where he is safe from frivolous people and from busybodies. And he is now finding it more and more difficult. Here, of course, things are different. He has the endless depths of the twilight jungle with giant trees full of holes and draped with creepers of shapes grotesque and weird, and no man to interrupt or profane his solitude. If I were King of the Fairies and lived even at Bru na Boinne on the Boyne I'd leave it all for a hole in that ancient gnarled Pore-tree on the craggy rock that overlooks the pool at Lakalona.'

'Is it good to believe in these things then?'

'I don't know, Lima: anyhow it isn't bad, and it might be easier to believe it than to explain it. But I know that it is often easy for me to believe it in my own ground and it is always easy here, just as I find it easy to be good in the Church and not so easy when I am away from it. But I may not say that to my own tribe because they would laugh at me and say I was wrong because they thought differently, and then I'd be ashamed and . . .'

'. . . and the Father would have to commit suicide?'

'Not quite, but the result would be the same . . . but when I'm dead I want to be among the dead, and not among the living.'

'But did Nutu create the Porekanu, Father?'

'Lima, you're an evil spirit for questions. Look! It's like this: we are told of things He created but it is not said that they were the only things He created, and it's not said anywhere that He didn't create the Porekanu, and might it not be nice to think that He did?'

'Maski,' said Lima, 'we the people are fond of this little man.'

He pulled on the stern-line and drew the launch up to the jetty. The conch-shells were booming for night-prayer.

'One last word before you go! Lima. Your Boré is a man:

our Boré is a woman, the Banshee. So if ever you hear a high note in the wail of your Boré you must speak to your people saying thus: "Hear, O People, the noise of my neck. That is not our Boré. That is the Banshee of the Father's totem wailing round the places he has lived in. The Father's soul has left his liver. His toes are pointed to the River Dalua. May the Good God forgive him.'

'Aio-o-o-o,' said Lima, 'I'll do that.'

Sickness and Sorcery

Sickness and death are the two arch-enemies of the people, not because they are mysterious or inexplicable but for the very good reason that they finish the fun. In fact, nothing is more easily explained or more rationally satisfying when explained than the cause of sickness and death. For a Mengen, a Mamusi, a Kol or any other it is simply the indwelling of an evil spirit. The cure: get him out. Nothing mysterious so far. Since they accept that as a full and true explanation of the matter they no longer exercise their minds on it and there is no mystery whatever about it for them. Death is no more inexplicable to a Primitive than it is to anybody else. The fact that we know his explanation of sickness and death is wrong does not make that explanation mysterious to him. Why should it?

We believe that the sun sheds heat on the earth. But if someone proved beyond doubt that such is not the case, rather that the sun causes the earth to part with its own heat, no one could say after that discovery that previously the heat of the earth was a mystery to us. Our explanation satisfied us though it happened to be wrong.

In the same way, a Mengen's explanation of sickness and death satisfies him, too, although it happens to be wrong. And it is wrong because he has no knowledge of medical science.

Ultimately, and down at the grass-roots, the Catholic Church agrees with the Mengens, though not quite in the sense he means, for she holds that the Evil One introduced sin through Adam and, by sin, death.

For the Mengens, then, it is an unquestioned and an unquestionable dogma, a solid fact, a thing whose opposite would never even suggest itself to his mind, that sickness is caused by the Evil One. Since sickness is caused by influences of the other world, it follows, for him, that the cure must also be on the other world plane and the most important part of any healing is the appropriate sorcery. Spiritual evils need spiritual remedies. The man's logic is indisputable but his difficulty lies in this, that he started off on a false assumption and the farther he follows that assumption logically, the more he must go astray.

It might be interesting to pursue further and find out just why he so blindly accepted the false assumption that sickness is the indwelling of the evil spirit, but such a pursuit belongs to a very unsure field and is largely a matter of guess-work. Is it because his dream-world is sometimes more vivid and real to him than the one he walks on; or is it because he has not got an inquiring bent of mind; or is it just a bright idea that someone hit on and everyone accepted, just a fanciful prejudice? It may be all or one or none. Civilisation is only the accumulated answers to the question Why, and even the civilised man seldom asks the Why of his beliefs and prejudices.

Amongst the Mengens there is a comparatively high proportion of sickness and death, and it is due mainly to two causes; insufficient food and the presence of the malaria-carrying mosquito. As a consequence, therefore, the Evil One, Saia, is regarded as being always present and always actively injuring the people.

Except for the very old, who are a negligible minority, nobody is presumed to die from natural causes. If a tree falls on a person and kills him, we attribute his death to the injury caused by the falling tree and there the matter ends. A Mengen, too, will agree with us so far but now the most important question arises for him: who cast the evil spell on the tree that it should have fallen on our friend? Or who cast a spell on our friend that he should have been in the wrong place when the tree fell? A man's canoe breaks up in a rough sea ... who cast a spell on the sea to make it break the canoe? A woman has difficulty in giving birth to a baby ... who has put an evil spirit into her or into the baby? A person cuts his toe with an axe, he falls off a tree, catches cold, pneumonia, or dysentery ... it does not matter what ill-fortune befalls him or what malady grips him, the explanation is always the same: the Saia has been at work.

He usually distinguishes between the direct and the indirect agency of the evil spirit in sickness. Pneumonia, meningitis and cerebral malaria are attributed to him directly without any intervention of a human agent or sorcerer. It is probably because those three diseases are nearly always fatal, that the people attribute them directly to Saia. Other diseases are attributed to a human agent working in conjunction with the evil spirits.

With our modern drugs, pneumonia is no longer a menace and most cases of meningitis respond very well to Sulpha drugs, so much so that when I met with such cases I used to say to myself with relief: it is only pneumonia, or, with less relief: it is meningitis. But once a cerebral malaria case came along the grave-digger was not far behind, for this is a most terrifying and relentless form of malaria. I have seen only seven cases of it and of those seven, four died. It strikes with the speed of lightning; a few four-year-olds are playing in the village and one suddenly collapses with no previous warning. Fifteen minutes have elapsed before he is brought to me and by that time he is usually dead.

A mother wakes in the morning and finds the baby dead beside her. 'But I nursed him only a short while ago,' she says. 'An evil spirit took him.' No, it didn't, he just got cerebral malaria and died instantly. A ten to twelve year old boy may last a few days without treatment but he is in a coma with rolling eyes and dripping perspiration, pitching and tossing in a frenzy, with his head thrown back as if his neck were broken. Grown-ups make a longer battle and may last a week or two, they may even recover, but usually with severe damage to the brain.

One of the few cerebral malaria cases I saved was a girl from a local village. When she was brought along she looked as good as dead. I had seen her in school less than an hour previously. She was now in a deep coma. Yet she responded magnificently to treatment, though she remained unconscious for thirty-six hours and, luckily, she showed no after-affects.

I remember her especially for a particular reason that could happen only in a place like this. Normally when he hears of a sick person the priest thinks automatically of the Last Sacraments. He does so in New Guinea too, for a few years, but this instinct is inclined to become dulled, because of the hundreds of sick people he treats perhaps only one is in danger of death; and so, after a time, when a sick person is announced, he thinks more of medical treatment than of the Holy Oils. That is what happened to me on this occasion and it was only when the girl was out of immediate danger of death that I remembered my duty as a priest. Possibly the suddenness of the case put me off; at any rate it gave me something to ponder.

In normal village life when the symptoms of a disease have established themselves, the relatives of the sick person decide it is time to call on the sorcerer's help. In those cases where the sickness is considered the result of the direct intervention of an evil spirit, the duty of the sorcerer is to induce the evil spirit by means of charms and spells to leave the person. Each sorcerer has his own tools of trade and formulas but the usual contents are ginger, lime, chili, betel-nut, urine and all or any other substance which is hot or bitter. He may also use a type of incense which is made from the resin of a tree.

Sometimes he applies the concoction externally to the spot where the pain manifests itself, sometimes he does not apply it at all but holds it while he makes several trips around the sick person indistinctly muttering some formula in which the evil spirit is addressed. I have never been able to ascertain for sure what any of these formulas is like, because sorcerers, like professional men and inventors, keep their own secrets.

His duties are slightly different when he deals with persons who have been bewitched by a human agent. Here he must find out firstly who casts the spell, and in those cases where the person dies he must also find the actual charmed object which caused the death.

The one point I could never make clear to my own satisfaction was how far the people really believed in their sorceries. I sometimes had the feeling (it was only a feeling) that the individual might harbour a doubt though he never wavered in the slightest manner in public. My ultimate object was to nourish that little doubt if it was there, to create it if it was not, and to make it acceptable to express that doubt in public.

Hence I approached all cases of alleged sorcery with the greatest possible sympathy and tolerance and encouraged the people to speak openly to me about them. The results were slow at first and I did not try to hurry them because the people were wary. Later, they sometimes came faster than I could deal with them.

Death was always attributed to one of two causes: an evil spell had been cast on the person or he had been given food which had been bewitched.

I assumed in each case that one of these causes might have been the real one. I tried to establish from the evidence presented whether the cause of death as held by the people could be accepted beyond reasonable doubt. I never expressed a personal opinion or passed a personal judgement, but if I found a weakness in the argument I exposed it as best I could and then left it to the people themselves to make up their minds on the findings.

In all the cases which were at one time or another brought fully to my notice I have never found even a small fraction of the evidence which would be necessary to convince me that there was either foul play or evil spells involved. I am of the opinion that their spells and sorceries are ineffectual.

Kena came along to me one day with his wife, Lua. She suffered terrible pains in the lower abdomen. She had grown thin and could not retain food, and showed other signs which convinced me that it was beyond my very circumscribed medical knowledge either to know what was wrong or to cure it if I did. It so happened that a Mission-boat called a few days later and I suggested to Kena that he take his wife along by boat to the Mission hospital at Vunapope where a competent doctor could examine and treat her. This he agreed to do.

Some time later the doctor's report reached me. Lua was in the last stages of an inoperable cancer and could not be expected to live for more than a few weeks. In order that she might have the prized consolation of dying among her own people the doctor very kindly sent her back on the next boat.

I explained the situation as sympathetically as I could to Kena and exhorted him and his family to pray constantly for Lua that God might reduce her suffering and grant her a happy and a holy death. This they all did in a most exemplary fashion.

Lua sank more and more. I administered Extreme Unction and brought her Holy Communion each morning. She was not quite two weeks in the village when she died.

After the funeral Kena asked Tugulu, a sorcerer of sorts, to his house to find out who had caused his wife's death, and how he had caused it. Kena gave him a hint as to whom he thought it was, or at least wished it might have been, in this case Lima.

Tugulu was a young man of about twenty-five years and a very handsome looking fellow. He had not one of the characteristics usually associated with sorcerers. In fact I have never seen anybody who resembled the sorcerer of public imagination. To counterbalance Tugulu's good looks God had given him no brains. Possibly he was a novice at the game but he had recently come somewhat into the limelight by the death of his father. This good man enjoyed quite a reputation and was believed to have acquired a few new tricks in sorcery from the Sulka tribe further east. His most dreaded achievement was the one by which he claimed that he had only to lay his hand on a man's neck to bedevil him in the worst possible manner. Since he was now dead it was generally believed and assumed that he had passed on his powers to his son Tugulu. Public opinion and a little flattery had turned Tugulu's head and he let it be known that in the course of the past twelve months he had cast fatal spells on two men who had died.

I was already aware of all this, and was also aware that both of them had died of T.B.

Tugulu now set to work to establish the cause of Lua's death, and to identify the culprit. He chose four men, friends of Kena, and took them along to his house. To each he gave a small betel-nut, some lime and a ginger-leaf. Each now inserted these ingredients in his mouth and chewed the lot. Tugulu did likewise. When they were thoroughly chewed Tugulu got a portion of a banana leaf. Each of the four men now emptied the contents of his mouth on to the leaf and finally Tugulu himself did likewise. He wrapped the lot in the leaf and mixed it as best he could so that none of them could point to the portion that came from his own mouth. He accompanied all this with an indistinct formula part of which was '. . . as the termite bores through the timber so does the soul of man bore through his liver'. When he had finished his incantations and remarks he laid the leaf on the floor and all gathered round for the opening.

The point is this. Everybody saw what each one put in his mouth, everybody saw the mixture going on to the leaf so the matter on the leaf should not be more than the originals. The incantations were made to bring the object which caused death on to the leaf now with the rest. The sorcery 'has worked' if the leaf showed an extra item.

Tugulu opened the leaf and searched the pot-pourri for this item. He soon found it. It was a half-inch cube of taro, the staple diet. Obviously the sorcery was a complete success and this small piece of taro was the actual one which caused the death of Lua.

Tugulu now had to find out who in fact had administered that piece of taro to Lua. He daubed his face with different paints and dressed up in a fancy garb of amulets and bangles. He begged leave of his aides to be alone because he must now go into a trance and wait for the culprit to be revealed.

Tugulu closed the door and lay flat on his bed of rough bamboo poles. How long he remained there is not known. To add a dramatic touch he stayed confined to his house till midnight and then he burst open the door and blew long and loud on a tin whistle. In a short time half the village was around him and to this audience he solemnly announced: 'It was Lima. I saw him. He will come again' . . . and then he retired for the night.

Lima's name now went from lip to lip and everybody said: 'I always knew it. Wasn't I the first to say so?'

To guard the people against Lima the young men of the village armed with spears stood sentry at night, with orders to attack any suspicious sounds.

The first night brought results. Mologi was on duty at the eastern entrance to the village armed with a spear and an axe. In the darkness he heard the approaching footsteps. He waited tensely, straining his eyes to peer into the black night. The footsteps approached cautiously. There was no burning ember to be seen, no light, no song, no whistle; none of the approved methods of announcing an honest man. Mologi, prompted by the jitters plus a desire for glory, hurled his spear at the spot he estimated the man to be. His aim was accurate and his thrust was strong and Ruru's pig keeled over.

Anger mounted in the village. There was no blame placed on Mologi, in fact he was a popular hero. Lima's stocks slumped lower. Was there any end to his mischief? He had killed Lua and now he had cast a spell on Ruru's pig to cause him to wander in the path of the spear.

Everybody enjoyed the pork next day while new procedures were discussed. All except Ruru wanted the sentry business discontinued. (Presumably Ruru would like to have tasted the other fellow's pork.) It was clear to all that the devilish Lima would cause them to kill all their pigs, for he certainly had cast a spell on every pig in the village.

Democracy sprouted a tiny bud when the villagers decided by a majority vote to have finished with the vigils.

Since the actual thing which had caused Lua's death had been found and also the agent who had administered it revealed, the case was drawing to a close. All that remained was to inform Lima publicly that he had been detected in his mischief. Usually there was no question of restitution or of making amends in any way. Loss of face seems to cover all. Lima would be told that he is a sorcerer and an enemy of the people and would be expected then, since he has lost his good name, to do one of three things: commit suicide; pack up and leave the village (and, since his evil repute has gone before him, where could he go?); or brazen it out with small hope of ever re-establishing his name or that of his children. In fact, he was now a scapegoat (till the next one comes) for all and every drought, flood, failure of crop, or sow's miscarriage that may occur in any village he had visited.

I kept quietly in contact with the above developments and when I met Kena one day I asked how things were developing. On being informed, I asked him when Lima's mischief would be made known to him and to all, and he said it would be on the following Monday. I told him I should like to hear how they detected Lima and asked him would he mind showing me how the system worked. He would be only too pleased, and the following Saturday was appointed as the day of public demonstration.

The usual Saturday evening crowd was there for Confessions but there were also about a hundred strange faces, for word had got round that the show was on. Some passed the time playing football or fishing off the jetty and the women were busy brooming the Church or just sitting comparing babies. Kena appeared from the jungle and shuffled along the track followed by Tugulu and his four side-kick-charlies. The football bounced away to the hedge and nobody bothered to retrieve it; the women moved a little closer to where I was sitting, yet kept a discreet distance lest the men-folk should say they were curious old gossipers.

Lima was there, less than ten yards away, looking calm, stubborn and composed. By the end of the war, Lima had collected five war-medals with the Australian army in New Guinea. But normally he was a shy and quiet sort of fellow.

In order to avoid what might seem tedious circumlocutions I shall give a summary of Kena's explanation of how sorcery works.

The sorcerer by a power and a means known to himself is able to recover any charmed object which, by the power of Saia, the Evil One, has been used to cause injury to any person. When he retrieves that object he can induce a trance in the course of which he sees, as clearly as in daylight, the person who used the object to harm his neighbour.

Tugulu in this case, by his powers of sorcery, had brought back the actual piece of taro which caused Lua's death … 'there were four witnesses,' said Kena … and then in his trance he had seen Lima. The sorcerer's word, like Caesar's wife, is above suspicion. Hence there is no appeal against it. To be accused is to be condemned. The sorcerer cannot deceive or be deceived in any matter relating to his craft (axiom).

I asked Kena a few questions on this occasion which must have appeared highly heretical:

'Did Tugulu really go into a trance?'

'Of course he did. He says he did.'

'But did anyone see him in the trance?'

'No. But Tugulu says he was in a trance. Why should anyone want to see him? That's none of their business.'

'Even if he were in a trance, Kena, how do we know that he saw anyone? And more especially that he saw Lima?'

'But Tugulu says he saw Lima. What more is there to it?'

'Only this, Kena. Suppose some one else went into a trance too and saw a person other than Lima, what then?' (Kena smiles patronisingly.)

'But he couldn't Father, he could only see the man that did it, as Tugulu saw him; only Lima.'

'Let's put it like this, Kena. Tugulu performs a sorcery and he finds Lima did it. Kalap performs one and finds Moloi did it. Which sorcerer do you believe and why?'

'Tugulu, because 'twas Lima did it.'

'So, Tugulu said it because Lima did it, and Lima did it because Tugulu said so?'

'That's right,' said Kena.

The Mengens have no word for 'begging the question' but a few of them recognised it when they heard Kena's line of thought and little discussions broke out.

'Just one more question, Kena,' I said. 'Tugulu said he found, on the banana leaf, the piece of taro that killed your wife. How do we know that he had not put it into his mouth before he began the sorcery?'

'He couldn't,' said Kena, 'because it came up only after the sorcery was made.'

So many people laughed now that it was useless to carry on. I told Kena that they had better consider their evidence again. Eventually they dropped the whole thing.

From a few more questions later on, some interesting side-lights appeared: Yes ... Tugulu had been told by Kena to name Lima. He got thirty-five shillings for doing so and a small pig. Yes ... he did put the taro in his mouth beforehand. No, he didn't go into a trance but he could if he wanted to. No, he didn't see Lima in his trance. No, he knew nothing about sorcery but had tried this because Kena tempted him.

It also transpired that there was a running feud between Kena and Lima, and the root of it was Karena, the best looking girl in the locality. When she was young she was 'marked' for Qiaukaina, Kena's eldest son, but when she reached the age of indiscretion she married Lima. And was Qiaukaina leppin' mad! Half the things he said would roast a pig.

When it was obvious that Lima's wife would have a baby ... and these things are always obvious around here ... she seemed to run into a spell of hard luck. One day a coconut from a high palm crashed beside her. Qiaukaina was up the palm. What's wrong with that? It was his own palm, was it or wasn't it? He didn't see Lima's wife at all,

how could he when the palm fronds hid his view of the
ground? He was just getting a few coconuts for his poor sick
mother . . . the woman that Lima killed. The way people talk!
You'd think they never went to Church in their lives!

A few weeks later Lima's wife was walking along the track
from her garden in the jungle when someone in hiding pelted
her with large stones. Who can say it was Qiaukaina did it?
The eye of which man saw the hand of Qiaukaina lift the
stone? Malicious gossipers, that's what some people are!
Doesn't everybody know that Qiaukaina was out all that day
fishing with his father Kena? Ask Kena if you are not afraid
to hear the truth! O ye of unknown parentage.

On the track to Lima's garden was a dried creek-bed some
ten feet by fifteen. A single log spanned it. For the sake of his
wife who had to go there every day Lima replaced the log by
two stout ones and lashed them together with jungle-rope.
A few days later Karena, Lima's wife, told him that the wild
pigs had damaged the garden fence, and so next day he set off
with her to repair it. He walked ahead, according to custom.
When he was half way across his two-log bridge it collapsed.
He fell into the rocky creek-bed and escaped serious hurt only
because the logs came with him. He discovered that the
logs had been almost sawn through from underneath. 'I think
this was meant for you,' he said to Karena. He went back to
the village and without a word belted the tar out of Qiaukaina.

Yes . . . I remember the day Qiaukaina came to me to be
bandaged up. 'But I thought you told me, Qiaukaina, that you
got your injury from a falling coconut frond? Oh! So you
lied to the Father. Well don't take it so seriously, after all it's
the national pastime.'

More Sickness and
More Sorcery

MID-JUNE TO September is not a pleasant period on the South Coast of New Britain and even less pleasant at Malmal in Jacquinot Bay which, incidentally, is reported as the second wettest place on the island, averaging two hundred to two hundred and fifty inches of rain a year. Most of the rain falls between June and September, for that is the wet monsoon. It must have been during the wet that the American G.I. is reported to have said that if he were given a choice of Jacquinot Bay or Hell, he'd rent out Jacquinot Bay and go to live in Hell . . . but it is not quite that bad.

For most of the year the winds follow a steady pattern, sea-breeze by day and bush-breeze by night. But at the approach of the wet season they become jittery; they kick and veer all over the place. They put one in mind of a field of two-year-olds under starter's orders nervously trying to line up and, when everyone expects them to come, one tacks off at a tangent and the delicate process has to be begun all over again. The winds in June play in the same nervous way. The South-east has broken, we say. But no, it was a false start although we know it won't be long now. The winds are just collecting their forces and when ready they will come. They always do.

71

Then one morning we are treated to the great show. The barrier has been lifted and here they come! Thunder rolling and crackling all over the inky sky with lightning streaking from all points at once. This will go on all day and all night and all the next day and maybe for a week or two weeks before the first pause. The calm deep-blue bay with its green reef-waters and its white-ruffed beaches has been transformed, for the wind has come screaming in over it and whipped it into a grey-black heaving ocean pounding and groaning on the beaches. The coconut palms which for months have stood so languid and lazy are now bent over like a huntsman's bow, their backs arched to the gale and their twenty-foot fingered fronds flailing wildly like monstrous arms in agony. The little thatched gables of the village-huts are curling and every living creature is seeking shelter.

The rain has come, now blown along parallel with the ground, large fat drops hitting the sea with a hiss or rebounding off the ground in a grey spray. You hear it on the tin roof and say: I've never heard the like before, because it has drowned out the thunder. And then it gets heavier and you say: that must be the final burst, it can't get heavier, it must ease off now. But it does not! It only gets heavier still as it lets loose maybe ten maybe twenty inches of rain that day. You look out to see how the world is taking this lashing but you cannot see far because the sky is lying on the ground a few hundred yards away and there it will remain till the first round is over.

During the wet season I was often marooned, hemmed in on land by new mountain-torrents running bankers in old dried creek-beds, and barred by a sea too rough for boats. I would do the rounds of the mission-station, fastening all windows on the weatherside of Church, house, and school, and lashing down anything in danger of being blown away.

Back in my house, I would pull out last year's Christmas mail and prepare mine for next Christmas, for when the rains were over and the sun out again I knew I would be on the track and there would be neither time nor inclination for overseas correspondence.

I played old records and sang at the top of my voice, a privilege which is justifiably denied me in civilization. My tastes are proletarian and peasant : simple old Irish and Scotch ballads that I have known a long time. Now was their season. I've played them so regularly and exclusively at this time for the past four years that *Shannon River* now no longer calls to mind the Bridge of Athlone or the Siege of Limerick but a dozen newly born jungle-creeks riotously flooding the half-acre between the mission-station and the sea and flowing into Loch Lomond which has become Jacquinot Bay with the steep steep sides of Ben Lomond looming through the clouds, and the rain high up beyond the huts of Gomami.

It was also the time to renew friendship with Joe Gargery and with Pip, that little snob; with Barnaby Rudge and his raven and with Mr. John Willet of the Maypole, Sir. Thackeray and Carlisle were there too, but to me they are as heavy and as dreary as the weather and demanded of me an unprecedented expenditure of mental energy to garner the remuneration awarded to the pursuit of their circumlocutory verbosity. Lemuel Gulliver, R.N., had been smirking down at me for a twelve-month from the shelf, and if we can believe the Dean . . . and who could doubt so honest a cleric? . . . it was precisely in these latitudes that Lemuel commenced his strange wanderings. And so I imagined that if I could only trek far enough across the untravelled and unknown mountain-ranges here, I might one day reach Lilliput (Liliputput?) or the dens of the Yahoos.

The daily paper I had not seen for years, neither did I miss it. I rarely listened to the News. Nothing sounds more absurd here than the fanfare preceding 'Here Is the News' coming from the far-off land of the white man. That one Prime Minister said this or that another sent a stiff note interests me infinitely less than the news that the log over the creek at Vaungasupupuna has been swept away, that a python has swallowed the speckled hen that was hatching at the butt of the galip tree or that one of the young ducklings is lame. The news from the white man's world when it arrives here is dull, dead and distant, like the volcanoes on the moon. I remember my anxiety at first in procuring a good radio to keep me in touch with civilization. It is still here in showroom condition and you may have it for three Hail Marys.

In each village there was usually somebody who claimed to be able to influence the weather, bringing rain in time of drought and fair weather in the wet. If a rainmaker had a grievance against somebody he would claim a fee not to influence the weather to his disadvantage. None of the rainmakers seemed to know much about the monsoon and so it usually caught them unawares.

After a few days of the monsoon the people of each village were convinced that some one was paying off a grudge against them. The village savants and sorcerers got to work to identify the culprit and invariably came up with the name of someone in the next village whom they did not particularly like. Since the rain came mostly from the east, each village blamed its nearest eastern neighbour. Hence, village A sent word east to village B to stop the rain or else . . . and at the same time village B was sending word east to village C to do the same thing. It was an interesting period for all.

For a few weeks beforehand I usually advised the people of the approaching wet season, asking them to report any pneumonia and especially not to sleep at night in the shacks in their gardens but rather to return to their village houses.

One wet day Kesanarulu walked in. Would I go to see his sister Rotoparea who was very ill? She was a straight case of double lobal pneumonia. When I had treated her I returned to my house. Kesanarulu followed on. Obviously he had something on his mind. At my house and alone, he said:

'I would like to speak to the Father.'

'Go ahead. What's the matter?' I encouraged him.

'What's wrong with Rotoparea?'

'Pneumonia. She'll be up in a week or less.'

'She says she's going to die. She says she can't live.'

'Most people say that when they are very sick. She'll change her mind in a day or two.'

'I don't think so,' he said. 'This is different. There is something I'd like to say.'

'Fill my ear with the noise of your neck,' I said.

'Does the Father know Darulpita from Sunrau village?'

With Kesanarulu helping my memory I was able to recall him. Sunrau village is about three hours away.

'Well,' continued Kesanarulu, 'last Wednesday night Rotoparea slept in the shack in the garden with two other women. The wild pigs had been coming there at night. The other two women came back to the village on Thursday morning and two more went to relieve them. In the meantime Rotoparea went to sleep by the fire. When she woke she saw Darulpita just walking away from where she lay and she felt a sticky substance on her lips. She says Darulpita has cast a spell on her and that she will die. Next day she fell ill.'

'Did anybody else see Darulpita?'

'No. Rotoparea was alone. But four years ago three women from our village saw him here one day. He spoke to no one. Two children died shortly after that and we the people say that it was a result of a spell he cast on them. Does the Father know that Darulpita is a Nanasa?'

'What is a Nanasa?'

'In the eyes of us the people,' said Kesanarulu, 'Darulpita is not a man at all. He is an evil spirit who has taken on the form and shape of a man, but he is not a true man. And why? Because he has broken the strictest taboo, he is living as husband to his own sister.' (Actually a remote cousin, but cousins are sisters to most South Sea Islanders.) 'We Mengens believe that there is no recovery from a spell cast by a Nanasa. What does the Father think?'

I thought plenty, but now my immediate concern was to have Rotoparea persuaded that I had broken the spell of the Nanasa, for it is a common and observable fact that these

people are highly susceptible to suggestion and often can live
or die according as they are persuaded. The psychological angle
is a big factor in all cures.

'Leave this Nanasa business to me,' I said to Kesanarulu. 'I'll
take care of that. You just go along to your sister and by the
time you get to the house I assure you that she will be free
from the spell of the Nanasa. Your job is to convince her that
you have told me about the spell and that I have taken care of
it. Tell her that I said she'll be back to health in five days . . .
and compel her to believe you. And when you have done that,
fetch any two married men from the village. Let the three of
you come along here because the four of us are going on a little
journey.'

Kesanarulu was back in half an hour with his companions
and we set off. It was almost eleven o'clock. Three hours going,
an hour for the job, three hours to return and we should beat
the night.

The heavens had opened that morning and it still rained
an inch an hour. We set off at a good pace and got to Sunrau
village on time, and went to the rest house.

'What do we do now?' asked Kesanarulu for up to the
present I had made no mention of the object of our journeying.

'When the Luluai comes along, you will see for yourself,'
I said, 'only listen carefully, every one of you.'

In a few moments the Luluai came and did not seem at
all pleased to have left the fireside. A stick of tobacco compensated him and he was quite pleased to have earned it by
walking across the village square.

After a polite interval of commonplaces I asked him if he
could remember last Thursday. Most certainly. 'Was it not
the day of the dance and feast at Ivogona village?' 'Yes it
was.' I now asked him if he could recall every man he saw in
the village that morning, before they left for the dance at
mid-day. He screwed up his face and ticked them off laboriously
on his fingers. Darulpita the Nanasa was among them.
Then we called each man individually and asked him to name
everyone he saw. All had seen Darulpita in Sunrau

village at the time Rotoparea said she saw him in her garden.

On the return journey I asked Kesanarulu if he now knew what the hike was for. 'Yes,' he said, 'twenty-five people saw Darulpita at Sunrau at the time Rotoparea says she saw him in her garden. Rotoparea is wrong. It must have been someone else she saw.'

'What is your opinion, Kesanarulu? Did she see someone or did she concoct the whole story?'

'I think she's telling lies. She saw no one. Just like all women! There was no one in the hut. She made up the story. I don't believe her.'

'And yet, isn't her story as good as all the other stories that sick men and women tell and you all believe them?'

'I'm afraid the Father can never understand. That's the way with us. That's the fashion of us the people. When someone falls ill he must say who it is has bewitched him or give some reason for suspecting someone. You white people are different, but we the people are like that. We all believe that sort of thing.'

'Do you still believe it, Kesana?'

'I think they sometimes tell lies.'

... Only that I had not sufficient command of his language I would have said 'a most remarkable piece of understatement, old boy'.

After half a mile he asked: 'How did you know that Rotoparea was not bewitched by Darulpita?'

'I didn't. I only learned by enquiring. I find it is twenty-five to one.'

'Oh!'

'Ah!'

After another half-mile: 'Is it possible for one man to bewitch another or is this talk all nonsense?'

'When I see it I'll believe it, but I'll need more than the word of a sick old woman or of a sick man either.'

'I think we the people are ignorant. We still follow the tradition of the jungle.'

'Were you ever seriously ill, Kesana?'

'Yes, about four years ago.'

'And you named someone as having bewitched you?'

'Yes. 'Twas Kikomana did it.'

'What's that?'

'I don't know. I thought he did it. 'Tis possible I was foolish. I don't know. Maybe I only imagined it. I don't know. I thought 'twas he did it. The people said so too.'

'And where is Kikomana now?'

'He is still working in Madang. Paulus met him. He says he is coming back here no more.'

'Because you accused him of a sorcery he did not do, and he lost face?'

'Not at all. He's just a foolish fellow.'

We were making good time in the slush. The Mission was only half an hour away and it was not yet half past five.

'When we get back,' said Kesana, 'the people will want to know where we went.'

'Tell them of course.'

'And will I say what happened?'

'Naturally.'

'But the people won't believe us. They know that Darulpita cast the spell.'

'They what?'

'They think he cast the spell. They won't believe us. If we say otherwise, if we say Darulpita was at Sunrau village at the time Rotoparea says she saw him in the garden the people will say Darulpita has paid us to twist the evidence, or else that we have done it because he has told us to do so and that we too are afraid of him. They'll believe her, not us. That's the way with us the people. How about it? Could the Father come along with us?'

'And then they'd say you were only saying what I told you to say because you were afraid of me, and that I was present to see that you said it. And old Kena would shout around the villages again that this was another instance where I was helping murderers and sorcerers.'

'True, very true, O sorrow! What do we do now?'

'Just tell them what happened. Don't try to make them believe you. Let them pull the story out of you as if it were a secret you did not want to tell, and then let them make what they like out of it.'

'That sounds all right. We'll do it that way.'

'And will you tell them again from me not to sleep in their garden shacks in the wet season?'

❀

About the same period I was called out very early on a sick call one morning. I went in double capacity of priest and doctor. I arrived at the village at six o'clock and found the poor man Rekau down with pleurisy. I attended to his soul and body. As I was walking down the village I saw a knot of people at Loglog's house. Such a gathering at such an early hour excited my curiosity and I drifted towards the house.

'Loglog!' said a bystander, motioning his head towards the house, as if that explained everything. I went to the door.

'How did this happen?' I asked.

Lelurea volunteered: 'Rekau, the man you have just anointed. He fell sick and named Loglog as having bewitched him. Loglog denied it and the people did not believe him because that is the name he has got. So, he hanged himself.'

Loglog was a pagan too.

'Now,' continued Lelurea, 'the people are saying that it wasn't Loglog at all but Mokia.'

'And when he has hanged himself the people will say it was someone else?'

Loglog was not a Christian but in his death he reminded me of Christ, especially by the fact that He, too, was killed by the vox populi.

I went along to Mokia.

'Oh, don't mind Rekau,' he said, 'he's sick and he's crazy. He'll forget it when he has recovered.'

It was refreshing to meet one man with his senses about him.

❀

Samo is luluai of Bairaman. He is also a slippery rogue, a most agreeable liar and a great friend of mine. He has helped me in many ways, one of the chief ones being that he always has a canoe ready at the mouth of the Ba River to ferry me across. On one occasion, on my way home on foot from the western end of the parish I arrived at the river about midday and there was no canoe.

A loud whistle, some fancy shouting and indiscriminate yelling by everybody brought Tandeserea scurrying along in his canoe. Samo's absence was so unusual that I asked Tandeserea if he were ill. 'No . . . Samo's not sick at all but just now his youngest son, less than a year old, has died' . . . to die includes fits, faints, comas, in fact everything but what it says.

We paddled across the Ba and hurried to Samo's house. Samo was very worried and scarcely able to restrain his tears. Between stifled sobs he told me his child had been perfect up to five minutes ago . . . 'just when you appeared on the high ground over the river . . . but then he suddenly collapsed, and look, his neck is broken.' The neck was not broken but reacted as if it were, and the baby's head seemed to hang down his back. This symptom coupled with the suddenness of the attack indicated cerebral malaria. In any case, I had only seconds to make up my mind. I was at the end of my bush trip and all my medicine had been used up, all except one dose for malaria. I hoped it was cerebral malaria because I had no medicine to treat anything else.

I injected him with sterile quinine. He felt the needle sufficiently to make a tiny whimper. No music could have been sweeter for it meant there was still hope, no matter how small.

The usual treatment for such a case extends over several days. Yet no two patients react in an identical manner to the same treatment. The baby would have to be taken to the Government hospital at Matale for further treatment because I was not going home immediately, and as that was nine hours of open sea by canoe, I hoped that he was not only an exception to the rule but an exceptional exception. To strengthen the hope, Samo and the others joined with me in prayers for the baby's recovery. The injection I had given him might keep him alive till he got to hospital and then there was every hope.

I put the situation to Samo but he found a hundred excuses for not going. Finally I gave him no choice but told him to get off.

He made ready his canoe. He couldn't find the paddles. He found them but could get no one to go with him. He found those too, but then the sky was not promising ... and the women had no food ready for the journey ... and he was worried about leaving his garden because the wild pigs were in the locality ... and it was said that the Kiap (Government Patrol Officer) would be along soon and he'd have to have his village in order for the visit ... and it appeared as if the baby was improving ... and if he went he'd miss Mass next morning. ... Poor pious old Samo.

As he was bundling the baby on to the canoe he said: 'I think he's getting better. What medicine did the Father give him?'

'Glad you mentioned it, Samo. As a matter of fact it was a very rare drug and very expensive. Now you wouldn't have three shillings on you?'

Medical treatment is free but I liked to tease Samo.

'Three shillings!' said Samo. 'I don't know when I last saw even one. I haven't even got the price of a smoke. I am just like a bit of village garbage. Each day I have to scrounge around my garden to get a leaf or two of bush-tobacco. Even the few shillings I get for my copra. Futtt! 'Tis gone like that. But if I do get a shilling I won't forget the Father.'

I had occasion to recall that in the next twenty-four hours.

Samo pushed off down the river heading for the open sea. Rounding a sandbank he shouted to a man nearby: 'Tell the Father that if the sea gets up rough we will pull into some village but will continue the journey later.'

The statement was made in a loud voice and meant to be overheard by me; in fact Samo was really addressing me but in the common roundabout way of speaking to one person through another. And these remarks always fascinate me.

What he really wanted to make known to me was that he was thoroughly annoyed with me and had no intention whatever of going beyond the first village no matter what happened.

I paid particular attention to the sea that evening and it was dead flat.

Next morning I packed up about ten o'clock and moved out of Bairaman. After an hour's walk I saw a man coming towards me with a canoe-paddle on his shoulder very ostentatiously. As he drew near I recognised him as one of the men that paddled off with Samo yesterday. I knew the rest. Samo would be at Kaiton before me. He had sent this man along to meet me on the road and break the news. As I knew he was anxious to be observed I passed him hurriedly. Unfortunately, my cook-boy was with me and the Bairaman fellow now told him the whole story very loudly: how the sea got up and the great difficulty they all had in avoiding being swamped and how lucky they were to have been able to get in behind the reef at Kaiton, that the baby was cured and that Samo was waiting for me at Kaiton.

And so he was. I found him sitting on a log in the open shade, bouncing the baby on his knee. I sat on the log too, and we got chatting. Samo was somewhat excited and said: 'Maripa! I thought the little fellow was finished! But no, he's all right again.'

'That's good isn't it, Samo? And who cured him?' I was expecting the beggar would acknowledge my help.

'Anis,' said Samo, 'the doctor-boy of Kaiton.'

I realised now that if I could only keep casual I might get quite an interesting story. Samo led the way:

'Does the white man understand this sickness too?'

'Not quite, Samo, not quite. See, we're just fumbling along learning as we go, and of course, always anxious to hear more about it.'

' 'Tis all my wife's fault,' said Samo. 'Now, anyone can see that that baby is not sufficiently grown to be taken to the garden. All right. Very well. Good. A few weeks ago my

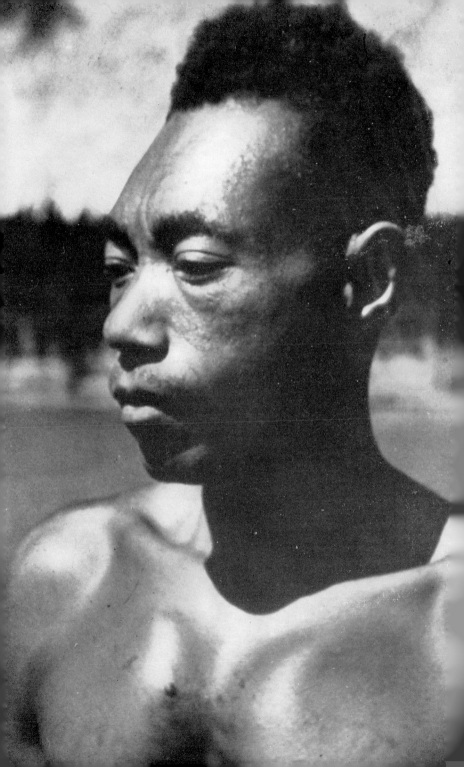

wife took him with her along to the garden, and she didn't put any lime on her ears or do a thing. She just took him like that. All right. Good. She was sitting under a tree and there was an owl on the tree. Does the Father know the owl?'

'Sure, I know him, Samo. But do you mean to say that your wife sat under a tree with an owl on it?'

'I'm telling you the truth. I'm not fooling. She really did. Now, you know of course that the owl is an evil bird. He does not fly like every other bird. No. He swoops down first. All right. My wife was sitting, sitting, sitting. All right. The owl swooped down over her and she had no lime on her ears. She had no lime on her ears, all right. Then the smell of the owl went into her ears and into her whole body.' (Here Samo shook his two hands as if he had burned the tips of his fingers.) 'The smell of the owl went into her whole body and then when she nursed the baby of course he became sick.'

'Well, well!' I said. 'Just like a woman, eh?'

'Oh! Father, they are stupid and do stupid things.'

'Have a smoke, Samo,' I said, offering him the makings.

'And Anis?' I asked. 'The doctor-boy?'

'Anis,' said Samo, 'is one of the few people that knows the spell to undo that sickness.'

'Any idea how it is done?'

'Only what I saw. He got the bark of a Masa tree and squeezed the juice out of it. He stirred and stirred and stirred the juice. And then he spoke to it.'

'And what did he say to it?'

'I don't know. I didn't catch it. Then he dipped a stick in it and tapped the baby three times on the neck. He said something. I don't know what it was. That's his affair. The baby became all right.'

'And how much had you to give him for all that, Samo?'

'Only fifteen shillings.'

The Wooing of
Tututoatoapaparea

Teresa Matetapu was head over heels in love with Tututoatoapaparea (Tutu for short) and their love was mutual, deep and cosy. Teresa came from the Malekur side over on the North beach of Jacquinot Bay, and Tutu was from the Banua direction, an inland village on the south side, putting about six miles between them. Teresa was the only daughter of her widowed mother Loto.

The relatives and friends on each side were agreeable to the marriage but a difficulty arose in connection with the place the young couple should live in after marriage. Tutu's side said 'Banua', Teresa's said 'Malekur' and Teresa herself said 'Banua' and that was the snag, because Teresa's relatives said: 'You silly thing, if you live at Banua who is going to look after your aged mother Loto? No! Both of you must live at Malekur until Loto dies and then you can go where you like.' 'That finishes it now,' said Teresa. 'Under no circum stances will I bring my boy Tutu over to live with my mother And if I have to live with her any longer, married or not, I' commit suicide. I never got anything from her but the rod o the ankles.'

'Oh sorrow! Sorrow!' said old Loto. 'Indeed it is my ow fault that you never got enough of it and if you did you woul

84

not now be the bad-word bad-word woman that you are. And as for that No-good you are marrying. . . .' (here Tutu covered his ears with his hands and turned his back to Loto). 'Oh! Father, I don't know how I reared that one! Or where did she come from? She's not taking after my side anyway. She has had a Saia in her from the day she pulled the first wind.'

A week passed and the deadlock remained.

I picked up an ancient Digest that gave me the facts and figures on suicide. Now I would be prepared. In a certain big country 2.46% more women than men committed suicide. Between the ages of 25 and 35 there were 1.0032% more suicides than between the ages of 35 and 45. That could be important. 9.303% more from 6 a.m. on Monday to 6 a.m. Thursday than from 6 a.m. Thursday till 6 a.m. Sunday, but if the percentage were taken from 6.08 a.m. it would be 9.307. A full 0.00012% more suicides among blondes than among brunettes . . . whatever you are, Teresa, my colleen, you're sure not a blonde. 3.02% more suicides in October than in May . . . and this is March. Of those who threaten it only 11.173% go through with it . . . Teresa may swing yet on the third decimal.

When it's all over, Teresa, we'll know where you fitted in. These figures are no guide to this race, they only tell us the winners of the last one.

It now became common knowledge that Teresa was going to hang herself. She definitely was. I was not so sure, but the possibility was there, because these people have a type of suicide which has escaped most statisticians: the fashionable suicide. Just as conkers or marbles become fashionable in some parts, so does suicide tend to become fashionable here. Two or three may occur in as many weeks and then we hear nothing about it for years. Three had occurred in the past six weeks and perhaps a new crop was ripe.

After Mass on Sunday Teresa disengaged herself from her relatives and came to my house:

'I would like to shake hands with the Father, I am going to hang myself this very day.'

I suppose nobody could blame me if I detained her by force,

in fact it might have even been a duty. The alternatives were: contact the Patrol officer, but he was already away in the jungle; contact the police: they were 140 miles away with neither phone nor road in between; contact a neighbour: he could do nothing more than I could.

Her relatives were now gathered around my house.

'Come inside, Teresa, come inside. It was nice of you to come to say good-bye to me, but I can't shake your hand from that distance.'

She came inside and I moved between her and the door.

'So you have decided to hang yourself, Teresa?'

'Yes, Father.'

'You'll do it in the jungle of course?'

'Yes. I'll go deep into the jungle.'

'And what are you going to use for the job?'

'A green double-laplap. My boy has it at home. It has a fancy yellow border.'

'And you'll tie the ends of it over a branch and make a sling out of it? And then put your head into the loop?'

'Yes. That's it.'

'And then you'll wheel round and round and the laplap will get tighter and tighter?'

'Yes. That's it! That's it!'

'And then?'

'Then I'll take hold on the branch and lift myself up and turn round hand over hand till I'm crazy and I can't hold the branch any longer. And then I'll drop and 'tis all over.'

'Oh! Wait now, wait! It isn't all over so soon! Don't you know that your head will first swell up and turn all blue?'

'It will not!'

'Indeed it will! And your eyes will pop out like the eyes of a crab.'

'They will not. You're fooling me. I never heard that!'

'Well, hear it now. And you'll be hanging three or four days before we find you. And the smell will attract the wild pig or maybe the crocodile and he'll grab one leg, that one

and go off with it with his head in the air and hitting it off the
trees leaving bits of it here and there as he drags it along.'

'I love my boy Tutu.'

'That's fine, but how is hanging going to help?'

'Tutu loves me too. And you're fooling me about the eyes
popping out. Loglog's eyes didn't pop out when he hanged
himself!'

'Indeed they did, Teresa. I saw them myself sticking out like
mangoes on a stick.'

'Ah go on! No one told me that.'

'Look here, Teresa. You don't have to believe me. Try it for
yourself. I'll put a rope over the rafter and there's a mirror
there and you can see the whole thing happening. Very well.
Come along. . . .'

But Teresa dug her teeth into my arm and vanished with a
rustle of leaves.

'Oh! you're the great one,' piped old Loto, 'you're the big
woman that was going to hang herself. Indeed my shame is
great today, I that brought you into the world and never gave
you anything but the best. Now I must stand here listening to
your foolish talk. Marila, Marila!'

❋

If there had been a newspaper in Malmal, the following
might have appeared in the Society Column:

'At the Church of St. Patrick with Nuptial Mass and Blessing, Teresa Matetapu married Francis Tututoatoapaparea (to
his friends Tutu). Our bride looked radiant in a pur-pur of
gaily coloured croton leaves, freshly plucked that morning
from the Father's hedge, and still moist with the heavenly dew.
It was kept in position by a string of beads and possum's teeth
around her waist (21¼). She wore no other jewellery.

'The bridegroom wore a green double-laplap with a fancy
yellow border. It was held as a good omen when, during the
ceremony, instead of putting the ring on the bride's finger, he
put it on his own, and the assisting clergyman had some diffi-

culty in persuading him to take it off. Afterwards the happy couple went away in Tutu's new canoe for Malekur, the bride's home, where a reception was held.

'Loto, our charming bride's resolute mother, followed along behind, paddling her own canoe.'

Gie . . . The Pig

YOU ARE leaning over the garden fence and Jones drives past in a ratty-looking little car and you turn to your neighbour and say: 'Didn't Jones drive a Bentley last year?' And if you and your neighbour are kindly folk you'll both feel sorry for Jones.

Or maybe you say to your wife: 'Wife, do you know whom I saw driving a new Cadillac today?' And she says: 'No.' And you say: 'MacGinty.' And she says: 'Never!' And you say: 'As sure as God made little apples.' And she says: 'Then it must be true that they bid ten grand for the house on Nob Hill . . .' and you both agree that MacGinty is an up-and-coming fellow.

Or you might say with studied carelessness: 'I saw Slattery driving the brat home from Jade College in Gentleman's Court today.' And there's no reply but the noise of a falling fork, or the little clacking sound your wife makes when her jaw drops.

Fashion of the white man! We the people have no cars to gauge the status of our neighbours, but we know it all the same. Lima says in a flat tone to his wife Karena: 'Rororea has a pig.' And there is no reply but the noise of a taro falling in the ashes or the little clacking sound Karena makes when her jaw drops.

89

In the local economy the pig holds the same place as the Gold Reserve and alcoholic drinks do in ours. He is too important to be bandied or bartered around for unimportant transactions. He takes his rightful place in large feasts, initiation ceremonies, marriage dowries and such like. Transferring pigs from one village to another has the local importance of the transfer of bullion.

Pork is a most valued commodity but only rarely is it used as food. Besides its actual value, its social importance is comparable with alcohol for us, for no Mengen would dare have a feast without an ample supply of pork. And these feasts occur only once or twice a year. To kill a pig because you need meat or because your family is hungry is just not done. There must be a reason of social importance.

If a person were to kill a pig without social reason he could be compared with the man who will not have a drink with his friends but drinks plenty when alone. Nor can a Mengen go around saying: 'I am fond of pork,' any more than you or I would say to everyone we met: 'I'm fond of rum.' But when pork is served on the proper occasion he is expected to compliment his host on the fine quality and tell him how much he enjoys it and how it far surpasses the pork he has had on other occasions, just as we compliment our host by enquiring of him the vintage of his wines or the ingredients of a new and pleasing cocktail.

In recent years domestic pigs of a breed better than the wild pig have become more plentiful and consequently the value has been deflated, so that while he still holds pride of place, he is of late often used in more everyday business. It is no longer unusual to find school-children with pigs of their own. The more old-fashioned and conservative tribal members view this change as you would view your school-boy son running his own racing stable.

The greatest misfortune that could befall a tribesman is to lose his 'name' and, conversely, the greatest gift is a big name. This is acquired mainly by the judicious use of wealth, pork. If he can give a party, even once in his life, where pork and food are in abundance he reaches the coveted position of being a big man.

To the casual observer, nothing would appear more simple than to breed up a great herd of pigs: they breed easily, there is an abundance of forage close-by in the jungle, they are healthy and apparently need little attention. And yet the picture is very different.

The pig has many natural and unnatural enemies: pythons eat up the young ones, cassowaries can fatally wound half-grown ones and the crocodiles carry off all sizes. The greatest menace, however, is the neighbour.

A typical case was Lalagona's. He had three sows, so I estimated that at the end of a year he might have over twenty pigs. I found instead, that at the end of two years he had only two, one less than he began with.

Lalagona expected his sows to mate with a jungle pig, but the war on these was so intense that he was out of luck. Why didn't Lalagona keep a boar? O foolish white man, don't you understand that in that case all the village sows would have young ones too and where would Lalagona's advantage lie?

After two and a half years' waiting, Lalagona was in luck. One of his sows had six young ones. Lalagona seemed to be on the road to prosperity. Nobody was more silently aware of this than his neighbours. In two weeks there were only four young pigs. A python? Perhaps. A dog? It could be. After four weeks there was only one piglet left. There was a row going on in the village. Lalagona was accusing Maito of killing his piglets. Did Maito do it? Only the dark jungle can answer that, and the jungle doesn't speak. Maito proved his innocence by asking: 'Now, why should I do a thing like that?' Why should he indeed?

Yet many suspected, but no one might say so, that Maito had been appointed to do it, just to keep Lalagona down to size. What would have happened if Lalagona had six pigs and no one else had any? That is too terrifying to contemplate.

If Lalagona can succeed, in spite of the kind attention of his

neighbours, in bringing some pigs to maturity, he will spread
a feast for them, not because he loves them much but because
he loves his own big-name more. At this feast, he or his family
may not eat of the pork. It is all distributed. Lalagona goes
hungry but he has secured a big name for himself, and a certain debt on the part of those who came to his feast. They will
repay that debt by another feast, or if they can't do that, then
they will work in his garden, whereby he will have a bigger
garden than most and lay on another feast, thus spreading his
influence. Whether they can or cannot do any of those things,
they must always keep an eye on Lalagona's pigs. Sometimes
they do and sometimes they don't. It may not be wise to let
Lalagona get too big a name and it might also be to their advantage to pretend they were looking after the pigs when in
fact they were stealing them. The jungle, like charity, covers
a multitude of sins.

There had not been a young pig in the village for two
years. Old Matemage asked me to procure a boar for him. This
I did. Then he realised he had to supply food for the boar,
otherwise he would go off into the jungle and come back no
more. He asked his neighbours to help out. They just laughed
and thought: what an old fool is Matemage. Matemage was
bitter. He pointed out that they stood to gain too and they
lied: 'Indeed we don't. There are plenty wild boars in the
jungle ...' at the same time cautiously attracting the boar's
attention towards their own pig-fence.

Matemage was no more foolish than the rest, less so perhaps,
because they had forgotten for the moment that they had left
the stone-age. Matemage came to me and said: 'Father, I
would like a razor-blade. An old one will do, but it must not
be rusty.'

The villagers came to me: 'Father, did you hear what Matemage did to his boar? Oh sorrow! All the neighbouring villages have plenty-too-much pigs and we have none. We are
rubbish in their eyes. We the people are at loggerheads about

a boar. Would the Father keep one and we will all pay one
piglet a year?'

I agreed, but knowing what they think in their hearts I
said: 'Very well. But if my pig breaks into some one's garden
he is not to spear him or put the dogs on him. Just let me know
the damage and I will compensate the owner, but the boar
must not be injured in any way. If anybody injures him I'll
... I'll ... I'll ...'

'That's it, that's it!' they all said. 'Excellent!'

A month later and I heard: Kena has speared the Father's
pig. The pig was said to have been in Kena's garden, but Kena
had nothing growing there yet. In fact, Kena had speared him
on the open track. 'I was so angry,' said Kena, 'when I saw
him in my garden that I forgot the good talk of the Father.'

Kena and myself had been neutral belligerents since a recent
sorcery case and it might have appeared that he was trying to
even the score. A little deeper enquiry, however, showed that
Kena knew that all his own sows had been catered for, and
well, why let those village rascals have pigs too?

Kena was very annoyed when I supplied a better boar.

When the time came for paying up, Kena said: 'O sorrow! I
forgot to "mark" one for the Father, and they are all marked
already, all twenty-five of them. Now, I'll keep two the next
time!'

I turned a very cold eye on Kena and said: 'I like this one,
Kena.'

'Oh! I can't give him. His face is the face of his father.'

'I shall be pleased to have him delivered this evening, Kena.'

That evening Kena sent me a scrub pig and said that he
could not catch the one I wanted.

'Take him back,' I said to the messenger, 'and tell Kena that
I have a rifle. Unfortunately I am a bad shot and so it might
happen that I would shoot the wrong pig first.'

The pig with the face of his father was delivered in fifteen
minutes.

In contrast to Kena, the other villagers offered me first
choice, and they could well afford to.

I was out one morning with my shot-gun looking for a few pigeons or hornbills. I was following the track from Valo's garden and came face to face with Valo himself. He had two spears and was accompanied by five snarling mongrels. His wife followed behind. She had a bush-knife and a few odds and ends in a basket on her head. A reluctant little wild pig trailed behind. He was in harness, roped and strapped like a toddler.

Valo's wife had him on a lead. Sometimes he ran ahead, sometimes he tried to break sideways for the jungle or he just sat piggishly on his haunches and had to be dragged along.

In a few weeks he would be quite tame and would need no harness. In fact, he'd trail along not looking left or right, the whole way to the garden. He'd busy himself there all day, and like a little dog, he'd trot home in the evening with Valo's wife. She'd have a load on her head and could not always see him so she'd say: 'Gie, Gie! Tst, Tst, Tst!' and he'd answer 'Ugh, Ugh!' and frisk along beside her. When they'd come to a log over a creek he'd wait and she'd bend down without taking the load off her head and lift him in her arm and shuffle along over the slippery log and deposit him on the other side. And no sooner would he find his feet on the ground again than he'd run off shouting 'Frout, Frout, Frout!' and suddenly halt and pretend he was digging for grubs.

But today, his ears were trimmed till they looked like a rat's, and his tail was snipped at the point where it begins to be called tail. 'We, the people, do it like that,' said Valo. 'Then when he grows up and moves about in the jungle nobody will spear him because they'll see his cropped ears and no tail and they'll say: "Behold, a village pig!" The Mengens are not much use at killing pigs,' Valo continued. 'I'm not a Mengen. I'm an Arowe ... from Gasmata. I only live here.' (He has 'only lived' here now for twenty-seven years.) 'I'm not afraid of even the biggest wild boar. Did I ever tell the Father how I killed a boar and I had no weapon? Well, it was like this. I had two dogs but they were only pups. I had a spear too. We put up a boar over at the back of Talie. The dogs cornered him

and I came up with my spear. I hurled it at him but it only
grazed him and the shaft broke. He charged the pups and
they ran. Then he came for me. I had no spear. All right! Very
well! I had no spear and he charged me. Very well! Just as he
was about to gore me I jumped like that! and I straddled his
back! Man, says I, what do I do now? I grabbed his ears like
that, and held on. Man, says I, I'll be here till sundown. No! I
whipped off my laplap like that! And I twisted it around his
long nose. Then I pulled his head up, up, up till I stifled him.
That's true. Ask anyone. Leka's father, he's dead now, he
saw me.

'These Mengens don't know a thing about pigs! Not like us
the Arowes!'

'Have a good day's hunting, Valo,' I said, 'and I'll give you
a stick of tobacco for the liver.'

It must have been a year or two later. Lima, my shoot-boy,
ran up to my house: 'The rifle, the rifle, quick! There's a wild
pig down off the track!' A few minutes later I heard the
rifle bark twice. Lima came back very disappointed. 'I only
wounded him,' he said. 'I followed the blood-trail but he
eluded me in the jungle because I had no dog.'

That same evening, Valo visited me, trembling with anger.
'I want thirty pounds,' he said. 'Your shoot-boy, Lima,
wounded my pig. Just now he came up near the village and
there's a fresh bullet wound on his leg. Only Lima did it! And
he meant it too. I know Lima's deceit. Says he thought it was
a wild pig. Wild pig! Even a fool Mengen can distinguish a
wild pig from a tame one.'

Lima had arrived too. 'Yes,' he said, 'I thought it was a wild
pig. Anyone could have made the same mistake in the circumstances. He was half hidden in the undergrowth and I could
not see whether he had a tail or whether his ears were clipped.
All I know is that the pig froze when he saw me and up-ended
his bristles. Only a wild pig does that.'

Valo's pig was a domesticated wild one and never lost its
jungle instinct.

'Isn't thirty pounds a lot, Valo?' I asked.

'He must pay for the suffering he caused my pig!'

'Only for the suffering? After paying you the thirty pounds who will own the pig?'

'I will, of course,' said Valo.

'Now, Valo, if I wished to buy that pig from you before anything happened to him how much would you have asked for him?'

'Two pounds ten,' said Valo.

'Very well, I'll give you two pounds ten now for the pig and he will be mine, wound and all?'

'That's all right,' said Valo. 'I'll take it.'

'And there is no further claim about suffering?'

'No. He's your affair now.'

'Then I'll send Lima to shoot him in the morning and bring him here to me?'

'That's fine,' said Valo.

As I was dressing some sores next morning a great hulla-balloo arose nearby. A couple of young lads came running along. Their story: Valo was on his way to his garden with spears and dogs as usual. The dogs cornered a pig and Valo came running up and hurled a spear at it, and killed it. Only then did he realise it was his own wounded pig that he had sold to me.

He was now approaching my house with the pig over his shoulder. 'Your pig, Father,' he said. 'I saw him on the track. I called him and he recognised me and came up to me, so I put a spear through him to put him out of pain. He's a male, but he'd have two litters before that fool of a shoot-boy you've got could shoot him.'

'True for you, Valo. Have a stick of tobacco. As you say, a fool Mengen can't distinguish a bush-pig from a tame one. Are you never afraid that living among them you might become like them?'

'Who? ... Oh? ... Do I have to give back this stick of tobacco now?' he grinned.

'No. No. Just give half of it to Lima, after all you'd never have speared him only for Lima having slowed him up.'

'The Father is laughing at me now!'
'Are not you able to laugh at yourself?'
He did.

❊

Does Valo know the difference between thirty pounds and
two pounds ten? Of course he does. If I am a penny short in
the fifty shillings he'll be right back to me.

Three factors combined to help Valo assess the damages:
Valo is much older than Lima, therefore the injury is much
greater than one among equals, as theologians say about sin:
you must consider the majesty of the Person offended. Also,
Valo knows that since Lima works for me he is sure to have
some money, and finally he knows that thirty pounds is well
beyond what Lima could afford to pay. In normal circumstances Lima would have to pay off in instalments and no
matter what he paid or when, Valo would still keep shouting
that he hadn't got five shillings yet not to mention thirty
pounds. There are no receipts and the big man is always right.
Valo is delighted because he has fastened himself like a para-
site to Lima's bloodstream and no matter what Lima does he
cannot shake him off.

Grieve not for the gallant Lima. He is doing just the same
thing to his juniors, because that is the fashion of us the
people.

Land . . . A Digression

THE MENGENS are matrilineal, that is to say they inherit and count their breeding from the mother's side; at least they used to, but a change is taking place.

They are not, however, matriarchal; they are not ruled by the women, at least in theory. No pur-pur government for us the people!

To put it briefly and broadly, the women own the tribal lands and the men administer them and the children trace their genealogy through the mother. That statement is not entirely true but it is true enough for practical purposes.

If we could go back, let us say, to the origins of Malmal village we would probably find that a few families which had for some reason broken off from another village decided to settle down here on the shore. They found the Kelamalagi River to the east and the Unung to the west. Between these two rivers they found an abundance of land for their needs. They would not go more than a mile inland. The hinterland is a no-mans-land and used only for hunting.

They would now divide the coastal strip between the two rivers and each woman would be allotted, say, a square mile of ground. This division would be more the result of usage than of planning. Her children and relatives would eventually appoint a man from their group to be in charge of that ground. Within the boundaries he would now portion out sections of it to each family or household for garden purposes.

There is no ownership involved. The patch cultivated now by one couple may be given to another couple within the same group later on. The people do not own the land in the sense understood by us. They recognise, as a village, their exclusive right to use a certain area and to eject any squatter by force, but they have never recognised or practised radical ownership as such. Their ownership never goes beyond usufruct.

That a person should own a piece of land in the same way as he owns a pig could never occur to a Mengen, any more than you or I could understand a person laying claim to the sun or the stars. Land, sunshine, water and air are there for everybody to use what he needs and to leave the rest. It is all, as it were, vested in Nutu; he is the only landlord and he collects no rent.

I have often thought that the Mengen, who lives so near to Nature, lives in many ways nearer to God than we do, and I like to believe that his idea of property is more in line with what God meant than are the ideas we live by. His attitude to the ownership and the use of land is unusual and interesting and perhaps worthy of a digression.

Four things abound in the tribal lands of the Mengen : land, water, sunshine and mountains. About two per cent of the Mengen land has been purchased by the European. For the rest, I estimate half an acre sufficient to support one Mengen at his present level for one year. The tribal land is available to him to the extent of about 3,000 acres per head of population.

When the European first came to buy land he presumed, on his own unquestioned prejudices, that the land was owned in lots by different people. The Mengen had no such conception. When the European asked who owned this or that area the Mengen in charge said he owned it (in the Mengen sense of being administrator). When the European said he wished to buy it (obtain absolute ownership) the Mengen was willing to sell (allow him to use it). Later on the Mengen discovered that the European was in and that he was out.

Quite a fuss is sometimes made about these old land transactions, usually by persons who know little about them. In their defence it may be said that no Native ever parted with any land that could be of the slightest use to him for gardens. What he sold was not rich and rolling pastures for a handful of beads but an area of unfrequented, unused and unusable tangled rain-forest. Had he not sold it, it would have remained till today as ninety-five per cent of his tribal land has remained: an impenetrable mass of fallen rotten trees and luxuriant primeval forest, the undisturbed haunt and sanctuary of the wild pig, the python and the cockatoo.

It has happened in countries other than New Guinea in the good old days, that the European went in and took the pick of the land without ceremony. When the Native bowed to the inevitable, a benign Government protected him by making it an offence for the European to shoot him without a licence.

In New Guinea, today, under the Australian Administration, the Australians themselves seem to think that matters have gone to the other extreme. Land can no longer be bought directly from a Native but must first go through the Government, which satisfies itself that the Native is protected from all possible exploitation. Yet here is what can happen: a European sets his eye on a suitable piece of farm land. He applies to the Government for permission to purchase. The Government assures itself that the land is not now or in the foreseeable future necessary for the Natives. Quite possibly it has never even been used or claimed by them. A Government officer now approaches the responsible tribal elders to ascertain ownership. They say it does not belong to anyone ... it is 'bus-nating'. 'But it belongs to your tribe?' 'No, it doesn't.' (We never administered it or used it for gardens.) 'Does it belong to village or tribe B?' 'No. It is a "ples-nating" ... ownerless.'

The Government now looks more closely at its map and says: We find it belongs to village A. Have the village suitably informed and enquire how much they will sell it for or if they are willing to sell it at all.

The tribal villagers geographically nearest the land are the owners. They must fix the selling price. As the Mission catechist may have taught them to count only as far as a thousand they presume this to be the limit in numbers and greedily ask for a thousand pounds, thereby assuring themselves that they will clean out the Commonwealth Bank of Australia and the Bank of England in one whip.

The Government now looks up its fat books on Ordinances, Regulations, Recommendations with their appropriate Additions, Mutations, Amendations, Qualifications and sub-sections and finds that: Whereas ... and Whereas ... the said land or lands consisting of so many hectares or thereabouts may not be purchased from Village A (hereinafter called the Owners) their heirs or successors ... for less than the statutory amount of five thousand pounds.

The village elders shake their fuzzy heads and speak thus: 'The eye of us the people is too dark to the fashion of the white man.'

The Aussie settler throws up his flamin' hands in holy horror and wishes his Government to a place where there is no ice. Oh Sorrow! But if you claim to be a Christian of any sort at all, which would you prefer to see: a primitive man underpaid or overpaid?

You're too smart, of course, and will say: 'Adequately paid', but I didn't ask you that.

The first necessity of every human being is food and the second is shelter. In prosperous countries most people have both and often forget that these are the cardinal needs of mankind.

In this part of God's world those two principal necessities are so far from being supplied that they constitute the main concern of the people, often to the exclusion of all or nearly all other legitimate desires.

Shelter is not as big a problem here as in colder climates, yet some form of housing is necessary, especially in the wet season. But such is the backwardness of the people and the poorness of the building equipment that the little houses they erect are seldom serviceable for more than two or three years. The shortness of the life-span is compensated, however, by the facility with which a new house can be built.

The food supply is the ever present problem and is nearly always insufficient.

How does the Mengen paterfamilias supply food for his family? Does he, as the glamour-writers say, just go out and collect delicious fruits that the uncultivated tropical soil produces in abundance? He does not.

Lima is about to make a new garden; let us accompany him and see, but first let us clear our minds of all previous notions we may have about any garden we have ever seen anywhere.

Lima has set his eye on an acre or two in his clan's area. He is going to plant the staple diet, taro. This is a very starchy tuber that varies in size from that of a small parsnip to a large turnip, and is much the same shape. It takes about ten months to mature. It is planted not from seed but from a sucker that grows together with a taro. Each sucker produces only one tuber. A man needs four average tubers a day or 1,500 a year, and that means he has to cultivate about half an acre of ground. Lima's household has six persons so he will need about three acres of garden.

Taro must be planted in virgin soil so when Lima says: 'We shall make the garden here!' do not expect to find fallow land or pasture cut off by a fence. Lima is pointing to a portion of forest no different from the rest of the jungle.

Some families work on their own but Lima follows the tradition of getting a few neighbours to give a hand. He has now organised his working group of men and women. The men carry axes and the women carry bush-knives. They have asked me to let the children off from school for the day. The girls bring the food for the workers and the boys go along with their fathers and are often more a nuisance than a help.

A temporary shack has been built near the new garden site, and the young girls under the direction of an elderly woman get down to house-work. A fire is lighted either by means of rubbing two sticks together, or from a live ember which has been brought along, or from matches or a cigarette lighter. Besides baked taro something special will be on the menu for the occasion, usually some vegetable such as cucumber or the young leaves of taro soaked in coconut oil and simmered. Lima, being a man of means may possibly have added some tinned meat and fish and also some tobacco.

It may be mentioned, too, that the new ground has already been subjected to many useful charms dedicated either to Nutu or to Saia or to both, and the eye that knows what to look for will see charmed sprigs discreetly stuck here and there on the approaches to the garden and within the area itself.

The women-folk set about clearing the undergrowth. The tropics abhor a vacuum and every square foot of ground has something growing on it which has to be removed. There are little scrub shrubs that grow almost as thickly as grass and no more than a foot high. There are shrubs that grow a few feet high, half a dozen to each square yard of ground. There are gangling sickly trees that couldn't reach the light, only six inches in diameter but maybe thirty or forty feet tall. There are ground creepers that have knitted together like lattice work, and climbing creepers as thick as one's arm that lie heavily on the branches. Next comes those trees equal to beech or chestnut in height and girth, commonly called secondary scrub ... they did not quite reach the open sky ... and over and above the lot are the giant trees of the rain-forest. The base of one of these could well fill an ordinary room. The bigger the tree, the fewer there are to a given area. Lima's three acres of prospective garden have to be cleared of perhaps ten or twenty giant trees, a hundred secondary scrub and an in-finite amount of creepers and rubbish.

At first you can only peer into the garden area for a couple

of yards, after that everything is confused and blurred. The
women now line up with their bush knives, grab the smaller
growth with one hand and lop it with the knife. The youngsters following along collect it in heaps.

After a few days' work you can walk unbent in the garden
area and see to the other end of it through the tall trees which
are still standing. In the meantime the men have been felling
the odd tree, but now they scrutinise the trees more closely.
There is a tremendous amount of felling to be done and they
will use their brains instead of their brawn where they can.
One giant tree is noticed leaning in a certain direction. It must
be felled that way and in falling must be made to bring down
as many trees as possible with it, hence all those smaller trees
in its line are first half-cut near their base to make sure that the
giant does not merely snap their heads off.

If two trees are connected by a hefty creeper only one needs
to be cut for in falling it will pull the other with it. The other
has to be half-cut or at least weakened otherwise a dangerous
situation could arise where the tree which has been cut
through may fail to drag down its companion and instead just
slip off its pedestal and dangle in mid-air from the creeper.

Every crashing tree is greeted with a resounding cheer and a
man really makes his name if he can so arrange matters that
in felling a giant tree at one end he causes it to cut a swath right
through to the other end of the garden. It is a feat that is
rarely achieved.

The time needed to clear the ground depends on the number
of trees and their nature and the number of woodcutters and
their nature.

Lima's trees are felled at last, three acres of logs and creepers
of all sorts, fallen over and tangled in each other in a most
hopeless mess. There are vicious red ants by the million there,
and centipedes, scorpions and often pythons, all in an angry
mood and ready to challenge any intruder. Lima does not
worry. He is bred to it and regards it as a rub of the green. He
is thankful that he has got a steel axe and a steel knife for the
job and not the blunt stone-axe of his ancestors.

The next few weeks are spent in lopping off the smaller branches and heaping them around the butts of the bigger trees. When dried, they are burnt in heaps as high as houses and the thick grey smoke curls up through the jungle and every neighbour within the horizon says: 'That's a lot of smoke from Lima's new garden. I wonder will he throw a feast this year. They say he has a lot of pigs.'

And perhaps, way out to sea, a white and blue luxury liner is passing with its cargo of tourists to Rabaul and he says: 'Look, darling, smoke!' And she says: 'Oh, those dreadful cannibals. How can they! But won't it be thrilling to tell Phyllis all about them when we get home!'

Not all the branches are burnt off. The long, straight ones are laid aside to make a palisade. This is a laborious work of lopping, chopping and digging. About a mile of jungle-creeper is first collected. A double row of stakes is driven into the ground all round the garden and heavy logs dropped between them. The stakes and logs are now lashed together with the jungle-vine making a solid palisade about six feet high. This is necessary to protect the garden from the wild pigs. Few of us are aware of the manual labour that goes into a palisade six feet high and five hundred yards long.

The accumulated ashes are spread over the entire garden but the soil is not dug, and the taro-shoots are planted by means of a sharp stick. That is the women's work. Growth is fast and so is decay. Swarms of weeds come up almost overnight so that the women have a full time job in keeping the garden clean. After a few months the logs of the palisade begin to soften and rot so that many of them must be renewed. Lima is well aware that the strength of his palisade is that of the weakest log. The wild boar always finds it. 'I'm sure he smells it out,' says Lima.

The wild pigs forage in droves. They cover thirty or forty miles a night . . . always trotting, tails not curled but erect, pausing for an instant to examine something more closely and then off again in the same fussy little trot, nervous, anxious, hungry and alert.

While Lima's garden is still young they pay it no more than an occasional reconnaissance trip but as it begins to mature they become more interested and insistent.

Lima now builds a shack and each night some two from his family keep watch over the garden. As the night wears on you can hear their chanting echoing through the jungle, surging and dying, rallying sporadically and trailing off in a lonely keen. For Lima, eternal vigilance is the price of food.

But ever since the days of Abel, people have been caught napping, and if it should happen in Lima's family it will mean six months back-breaking labour for nothing and six months hunger ahead. Lima knows that he is always fighting a losing battle, for he has no effective defence against the wild pig. He will never know what it is to eat the food of idleness.

St Paul said: 'He that will not work, neither let him eat.' Lima might truly say: 'O sorrow, Paulus e Tupu, we often work for six months and are still hungry.'

It is sad to think that Lima does not spend his day under a tree waiting for a delicious tropical fruit to fall into his open mouth, or that Karena does not spend hers with a hibiscus in her hair, throwing inviting eyes and kisses at the passers-by.

�֍

My own observations on the food supply led me to believe that the average parishioner had enough food for six months of the year, half enough for three months and was plain hungry for the other three. These periods of sufficiency and want were not sharply divided but intermingled.

This was not, however, as injurious to him as it would be to people accustomed to regular food, because he was bred to it and inured to it. Still, it was harmful, and although the result was not obvious among the stronger members it was all too noticeable among the weaker and older ones. Hunger, too, seemed to be the chief cause of most family squabbles and I soon learned that a good meal could shut mouths in more ways than one. A hungry man is always dangerous and hungry people may be pardoned if they do not give the Truths of the Gospel the attention they deserve.

❀

For anyone whose daily life is spent amongst these people it is essential to have as good a grasp as possible of their system of life and of the laws by which they govern themselves, not in order to be able to take a useful and intelligent part in their affairs but to know enough to avoid them like a plague. Anyone who relishes becoming involved in the people's private affairs is just asking for trouble and shall surely find plenty.

Once you know the traditions and procedures of a really primitive people you are in a position to forecast the way events will turn out, because the people will always follow tradition. But amongst those tribes who have had European contact and influence, the matter was not always so easy.

The Mengens, though they were mostly unaware of it, were no longer strict traditionalists. In the broad sense they still adhered to the old ways, but many European ideas and customs had crept in and split their allegiance. They sometimes tried to settle their tribal affairs according to European logic or laws, without being fully aware that they were not traditionally entitled to do so. The struggle lay between the advantage offered by the European custom and the age-old tendency to follow tradition.

It was often interesting to watch these two streams of thought flooding and confusing the Mengen's mind. A typical case was that of Kena and the Kaukau garden.

One bad harvest had followed another, yet the villagers decided that in spite of that they should all get together and have one large party: it was now five or six years since they had done so and they feared for their reputation. Two things are necessary for a successful feast: that an abundance of food be laid on and that great quantities remain over to rot. One of the most complimentary remarks that can be made about a feast is: 'You should have seen all the food that went to waste,'

implying that the generosity of the hosts far exceeded the
needs of the guests. Since the food cannot be preserved whatever is not eaten is lost.

The villagers merrily pulled out every taro they had, joy-
fully slit the throats of all their pigs and held an open house
for a week for all the neighbouring villages. The drums went
boom-boom-didi-boom night and day, the dancers bobbed and
wheeled and everybody was in the grip of frivolity and revelry.
There were competitions to see who could 'keep the floor'
the longest and who could eat a whole leg of pig at one sitting
and other competitions honourable and less honourable. The
usual good time was had by all and like all good things it came
to an end and the name of the village was now great among
the gentiles.

A week passed and hunger set in. A tiny taro overlooked in
the garden or considered unworthy of the guests was now a
cherished find. Another week had passed and even those scrub-
taros had disappeared, and ten months still remained before the
next steady food supply was due . . . but it was a good feast,
wasn't it?

The daily food which was becoming less daily every day was
coconut, fish and what could be scrounged from the jungle by
way of leaves, nuts and berries. Soon only the lucky ones
would have a meal every second day.

'Do you remember when Kukokale ate the whole leg of pig
and Murovona said he could do the same thing and they gave
him a small leg but 'twas stuffed with ginger! Ooo-a-ha-ha!
We'll never have as good a feast again.'

'Malekur are having their dance next Wednesday . . . are
you going?'

'I suppose I will.'

'We'll go in my canoe. Have you a big basket? A real big
one? No matter, we can make one. You should have seen the
size of the one they brought to our dance! I kept a close eye on
it. The whole side of a pig went into it and piles of food besides,
Ligaliga and Pulogana were just able to lift it'. . . and so on
. . . but a whole village cannot live for months on what

they collect at an occasional dance of their neighbours.

With caution, misgiving and a ha'porth of hope I rounded up the village elders and placed the seriousness of the situation before them. I proposed that they should get together and plant a few acres of Kaukau which, ripe in a few months, would tide them along to the next harvest.

Their enthusiasm was unbounded. That did not fool me however, because most things in the tropics flourish exotically for a day and then vanish forever.

The meeting dragged on, though the pangs of hunger knocked the gloss off the late feasting.

'Everyone is talking about our feast and dance. Our name is great in the tribe. We can hold our heads high,' said the proud and hungry Bolu.

'Hold it high in what manner?' asked Lima. 'Friend, I'm only fit for lying flat, my stomach is just water.'

'True,' said old Matemage, 'you can't eat your good name. It won't fill your belly.'

Everybody laughed because it was customary to laugh at everything old Matemage said anyway.

'I'm speaking truly,' continued the old man crossly, 'what is a reputation but wind on the lip of your neighbour? My young lad is hungry going to school in the morning. He asks for a taro but there is no taro. True! our name is great but does that give strength to his belly? We are just so many fools! Our pigs are gone, our food is gone. Now we seek food as the marmoset does, digging and scraping around the butts of the trees in the jungle. We are only rubbish!'

Bolu, who was still unmarried and who would go off to work for some European at the first opportunity, teasingly hummed a song from the feast-day. Old Matemage turned away trembling and spat viciously.

The net result was that it was agreed upon that the Kaukau should be planted immediately, and to make matters easier one huge plot would be prepared by all, where each should care for his own section later. After some discussion the men decided on a particular area and work was to be commenced next day to clear and prepare it. Axes and bush-knives were too few to go around so I supplied the necessary ones.

Great progress was made in the next week and every man did more than an honest day's work. Not quite every man. Four failed to show up at all due to a headache or a fever or a sore back. Trouble was around the corner but I could not imagine what shape it would take.

When the ground had been cleared, burned off and ready for planting the four who had remained aloof came along and announced (headed by old friend Kena) that on more mature consideration they were convinced that the prepared area was really theirs and any planting that was to be done would be attended to by them. Work stopped for a week and then two weeks. The Kenanites had no intention of planting anything, their intention was deeper: to lay a claim to the land, European fashion. The others would not, by tradition, plant in disputed ground. There was a deadlock which was not helped by a weed-covered garden and empty stomachs.

To solve this new tangle I had another round-up. Kena and his friends were there too. Not one of the village elders would admit Kena's claim but they agreed, for the sake of getting on with the work and without prejudice, to clear a new area to which Kena admitted he had no claim. This was done, and when the day came for planting, a notice was found posted at the entrance 'I Tambu', the Tokboi phrase for Trespassers will be Prosecuted. Kena admitted that he put it there because he said, on reconsidering the matter, he believed the ground to be his.

The older ones were inclined to let him have his way, but the younger men were of a different temper, arguing that if this were allowed to pass they might as well hand over their whole area to him. This view prevailed and the crop was planted. Let Kena now interfere at his own risk. He didn't.

❋

According to tribal custom Kena could claim no land at all, being a male heir, but he was substituting the European inheritance system for that of the tribe because he found it to be to his advantage. He had even sold some of his clan's land to a European and kept the money for himself. Kena was ridding himself of his backward glance. By disputing the Kaukau patch he knew he would stall off the older members because, by tradition, they would never plant on disputed ground; but he had not reckoned with his juniors. By the same tribal customs they should have had no voice in affairs but they too were breaking with the past. 'Why let one old man push us around,' they asked, 'when we know he is wrong?' Their fathers would never have entertained such heresy! Theirs not to reason why. . . . They would have obeyed their elders in all things.

In the next generation or two, it could well be that many other European customs will have become part and parcel of the Mengen's tradition.

In an earlier part of this book (fourth Chapter) I mentioned that I proposed to sketch in broadest outline some of the ideas and behaviour of the people, and thereby give some picture of the background against which my life as a missionary was set. In doing so, however, I have not followed the strict chronological order of events, but for the reader's convenience have grouped them together. These were all affairs of daily life with little reference to the missionary aspect, but they were important because they guided and controlled that same missionary aspect; an aspect which I have reserved for the pages that follow.

Part Two

THE PARISH

Clearing the undergrowth to prepare Lima's garden

Catechists . . . Done in the Green Wood

T HE MALMAL parish, like so many others consists of a number of villages scattered over a wide area of beach and bush. The population of the average village is about one hundred and fifty people, and it is found advisable to have at least one catechist in each village.

Though the title of a catechist may vary from one place to another, his duties usually consist in teaching the four R's: Reading, Riting, Rithmetic and Religion. He also collects the villagers for daily prayers, keeps track of those who are born and has them presented for Baptism, advises the priest on forthcoming marriages, sends for him in cases of illness, and in those villages whose distance would not allow time for the priest to be contacted, the catechist himself must assist the dying and, if necessary, perform the Burial Service.

Before the war, the Central Mission Station at Vunapope conducted a training school for catechists. Each missionary sent along some likely candidates to have them trained. The older and more advanced mission-stations had the better boys. In Malmal, which was founded only a few years before the war, Father Culhane could do no better than send a few pagan boys or recent converts in the hope that they would receive at least a good elementary training. They usually spent five years

Men sit while women stand to gather the last warmth from the setting sun at Bili. *Right* : Child descends a Mamusi stairway, a notched log.

115

in the school, a period which though inadequate was as much as the circumstances would allow. Of the original ten whom he sent, in 1933, only one was a failure, three have since died and the remaining six have given over twenty years' service.

The war disrupted everything and the chaos was greater in the outback mission-stations, because there they had fewer educated natives from whom to draw emergency catechists. They were entirely dependent on the more advanced stations, who, with their greater demands, were finding their own position quite difficult.

The first post-war work of the Mission was the re-organisation of its Catechist-school. The priests and nuns were still living in shanties or under canvas and going without many essentials while the Mission was building spacious and modern new schools and living quarters for the Natives. The system brought good results.

A lot of overtime work went into the building and the equipping of this school and it developed on lines far more extensive than those of the pre-war Catechist-school. In the meantime, the Government pressed forward with a new Native Education Ordinance. All schools had now to be registered and brought up to a certain standard. The day of the Mission-trained catechist was nearly over.

To meet these new standards the Mission converted its post-war Catechist-school into a Teachers' Training School and extended its capacity still further. It adopted the Government syllabus and put its students through the Public Examinations in order to qualify for Government Teachers' Certificates. As I am writing this, the Catholic Mission has, in its training centres, over seven hundred boarding trainees who are being educated by five priests, six Irish Christian Brothers (from Australia) and several Native teachers. Each year about one hundred students receive their Government Teacher's Certificate and move out to teach in the Mission schools.

The repercussions of all this were being felt even in Malmal. A few trained teachers came along and the schools improved wonderfully. The Mengens are quite brainy and make the best use of their advantage. Twenty youngsters have since gone to the Teachers' Training School and I feel sure a high percentage of them will finish the course.

It is now only a matter of time till all the old-time catechists will have disappeared. They have given excellent service and the Mission will have every reason to be glad if the new teachers handle their more difficult task with equal satisfaction. These new teachers are more efficient, are better trained and give a far higher standard of education.

Yet it is like changing from an old hat to a new one. You are very fond of the old one and hate to see it go. It slips on to your head like a cog in a mesh and you don't feel it there. You need no mirror to adjust it. The new one is stiff and you have to pull this piece down and push that piece up and pull out one part and squeeze in another before you have it to your liking ... and then your old suit shows up badly and you've got to get a new one to match the hat, and then of course, the only comfortable pair of shoes you've got must be replaced by pointed toes ... the changes never stop.

So too with the new teachers. There are Roll-books, Attendance Statistics, Reasons for absence, Progress Reports ... monthly and in triplicate; there is a diagram of the playground to be submitted, whether it is drained and/or fenced, materials used and cost and by whom erected; plan of school and materials used in construction, cubic footage per pupil, ventilation, lighting, and sanitation (my God, for us the people, and we are doing it all our lives).

Red tape is entering the jungle and hoping to tidy it up, but in doing so it will surely strangle the last haven of peace and simplicity left to us the people.

For better or worse the days of laissez-faire, the good old days are going. 'Ko Lolago! Ka momogo!' I say fondly. 'You go! I stay! Goodbye and God be with ye. It was good to know you.'

❊

The old-time catechists had not a very high standard of education but they were miles ahead of everyone else in the village. They were like the old village schoolmasters, especially in the place of honour they held in the village.

Kagogamana was one of these. He did a good job, never outstanding or original but it was a pleasure to visit his village. The tiny bush Church was spotless; the school children were well-mannered and happy and up to the mark in every way. The place exuded an air of efficiency and contentment.

But one day a dark cloud descended on the village and refused to be blown away. One of its solid citizens had become involved in a public scandal. It was not indeed a mighty affair, but small things are big in small places.

The villagers came to me during a visit to see if I could help straighten things out. The culprit was there too and quite proud of the fact that he was the centre of attraction. He did not try to excuse himself other than by saying: 'Well, well, if the catechist can do it why can't I?'

Later on the catechist came to me. He admitted that he was a great sinner. 'Ah, Judas was a decent fellow compared with me.' He said he gave very bad example, that he was weak, proud, selfish ... the whole list. And yet, I imagined that what he really wanted to say was: 'You like to hear that, don't you? But you know you can't do a thing about it.'

I had no choice. If I dismissed him nobody was going to conclude that morals were more important than manners. Dismissal would neither improve him nor help the villagers.

I consoled myself with the thought that I was dealing with people smarter than myself and that I was quite good if I could bring up the rear from a reasonable distance. I knew too, that they were not half as shocked as they pretended to be, and that most of the talk and gossip was due to the fact that they had so little else to worry them or occupy their minds. I recalled too, that Lupalupa village across the river had an excellent catechist and the villagers there caused me more worry than most.

Joseph Paluka was a catechist of another kind. As a sideline, he ran the local Meteorological Department, native-fashion.

His function was not to collect and correlate the data on the weather but simply to control it. In the village of Kulalona, no matter what he read in the Sunday's Gospel, during the week Joe did not believe that Our Heavenly Father made the sun to shine upon the just and the unjust. Joe Paluka did it and collected a fee for doing so.

When the villagers thought that sufficient rain had fallen Joe had to get out his bag of tricks and clear the sky. In times of drought he made rain. On grey days he taught school.

Then one day, the Angel of Death showed an abiding interest in Joe and he became worried and sent for me. When I had given him Holy Viaticum and anointed him, I spent some time with him.

As a catechist and a rainmaker Joe had always kept his eye on heaven and the future, and he followed that habit to the end.

I could see that he was now turning things over in his mind, because he was forming words inaudibly with his lips and occasionally nodding his head in approval or shaking it in disapproval. Finally he said: 'When I am dead, Father, how long will it take me to get to heaven?'

'Not very long Joe. You'll be there in no time at all.'

He pondered a while and then:

'Do you know what I'll do when I get to heaven?'

'You'll pray for us all, Joe, that the good God will keep and protect us.'

'Yes, yes,' said Joe testily, 'but do you know what I'll do? I'll ask God to take care of the weather. There is no one left here to do it now when I'm gone.'

Joe has gone to heaven but there is no change in the weather.

For a long time I was in a poor way with my catechists. I had only eighteen but estimated I could place a further forty without even pausing to think. I had been begging catechists all over the Mission and had collected a few.

One day when the Mission boat had called and left again, a

stranger approached me and introduced himself as Henry. He had sneaked on board ship as a stowaway. He told me he had been catechist for Father John for twenty-one years come December but now, alas, things had changed. New, young, smart teachers had gradually ousted the old ones in that parish and so he was without a job. He had heard that I was short-handed and had come along in hope.

Henry had not quite wasted his twenty-one years, for he had come without any letter of introduction from Father John and, very wisely, had let the boat move off before he appeared. He knew I could not turn him loose on the village and so he had three months to persuade me that he was worth his hire even without a recommendation.

I grilled him as best I could and he appeared quite satisfactory and I did not wish to probe the little secret which he kept so dark. I was in need of Catechists and was prepared to take a risk.

I sent him to an outback village where Catholics were few and where there had never been a school. His job was to start a school. A few weeks later I visited him.

'How are things getting along, Henry?'

'Fine, Father, heaps of children are rolling up to school each day.'

'And what are you teaching them?'

'A.B.C., Father.'

On my next visit I asked: 'And how is the school now, Henry?'

'Going fine, Father.'

'And what are you teaching them now?'

'A.B.C., Father.'

'But you were teaching them that the last day I was here!'

'Yes, but I'm teaching them more A.B.C. now, Father.'

Two years later he had his first class of catechumens for Baptism and he ran a fair school . . . after I got him to lift the needle in the A.B.C. groove.

At the last visit I paid his village he had a class of thirty adults under instruction. I read through the names and saw that Pompolona's was not there. She was a strapping hefty lass of twenty. Her two brothers were under instruction and so was her sister, or as they would say it: her two sisters and her brother.

'Pompolona seems to be an independent sort of girl, Henry, the only one of the family that will have nothing to do with us.'

Henry just gazed at the ground and made circles with his big toe.

'They tell me, Henry, that she's a good worker, and quite a good looking girl too!'

'O sorrow! The Father must not speak like that.'

'She should make a good wife for some lucky man.'

'The Father is teasing me now!'

'Let's go down to the beach, Henry, and we can sit on a driftwood log and no one will hear us.'

We sat on the log, on the steep gravelly beach and pitched white stones into the sea beneath us.

'Have a smoke, Henry, I'll bet you're short again.'

'If I say something to the Father will he be vexed?'

'Not at all, Henry. You never saw me vexed, did you now?"

Henry just smiled and glanced at me, smiled again and pitched a stone into the sea.

'I have a secret,' he said, 'that I have always kept hidden. You're a friend of mine?'

I smiled now and idly pitched a stone into the surf. 'Maybe I know your secret?' I said. 'May I guess? You're a married man? Am I right? Very well. You tell me the rest. I can't guess that far.'

'Twelve years ago,' he said, 'I put the ring on the finger of Catharina before the eye of Father John. Everything was fine for three years but she was a no-good woman and went off with other men. She did it, did it, did it, and then I kicked her out. She has been all over the place since then.

'Now, how could I teach in school and cook my food? I couldn't! How could I ask another man's wife to cook for me? I couldn't! Everybody would gossip about us. You know the custom of us the people: a man can take things only from his wife, his mother or his sister. Otherwise the people would whisper evil things. And I a catechist! So the Luluai of the village took pity on me and appointed his small daughter to cook my food. She was young and nobody minded; she was the Luluai's daughter and I was the catechist, a man of God. Very well. Then she grew up. O sorrow! But God blessed our union and she gave me a child, which Catharina never did though we were married in the Church and before the eye of Father John. Then everybody was gossiping about us and I asked to be sent to another village.

'When I was busily approaching that village I heard the women crying and I knew someone must be dead. 'Twas Catharina and no one else. I didn't look to the left. I didn't look to the right. No! I just kept going. That's how I got on the Mission boat *Teresa* and arrived here.'

'I see! And now, your love-affair with Pompolona?' I asked.

' 'Twas on the Eleventh Sunday after Pentecost,' said Henry, 'and I had finished the Church Service with the people and we all went outside and I said to Romorea thus: Romorea, brother, I feel sick and I am going to lie down. Very well. I was sleeping, sleeping, sleeping and this woman the Father mentioned came to my house with food and she spoke saying: "Pst! Catechist! Romorea told me of your sickness and I have prepared some food for you. If you eat it you will become well." She spoke thus.

'And I ate the food. Oh! 'Twas hot in my mouth and hotter in my stomach and I felt queer all over and I spoke to that woman thus: "What have you done to that food?"

'And she laughed and said: "I love only you!"

'And I said: "Hey! Have you put a malira (love-charm) in that food? Don't you know that that is sinful, and I am a catechist, a man of God?" But she only laughed and wiggled at me. And I was vexed and I scolded her: "You must not laugh and wiggle at me, your catechist and man of God. Someone may be watching." But she only laughed and went out and my eye followed her.

'Then I felt my skin become strong again and I got up and I washed. And that night I dreamt about her.

'And next day I told the Luluai about it and said the love-charm should be broken. And he said: "What love-charm, you idiot? No one cast a love-charm on you and how can we break it?" And I, now, am still in the grip of it, O sorrow!'

'That was a mean trick they played on you, Henry,' I said.

'Yes, Father. These Mengens are different from us.'

'And would you like to be free of that love-charm, Henry?'

'Father, I'd like nothing better. I'm through with women now. I've had enough of them. Finished! They're a bad lot.'

'Let me see if I can help you. You know that as a priest I have the power . . .'

'But, Father, don't you think we should be married first?'

Then there was Kaluapuna, a gentle, solid, shrewd and reliable fellow. When I first knew him he had already fifteen years service behind him as a catechist.

He accompanied me later on many a bush trip into the unknown and was a great standby in helping me to care for the sick whom we always found in abundance in the jungle. He gradually learned the routine and used to distinguish the different pills by the colour of the bottles they were in, which was quite useful so long as the next batch were not in different coloured bottles. Just from listening to the same question and answer between myself and the sick person, Kaluapuna would often anticipate correctly the different drugs I needed.

During the wet season, when pneumonia was common among the people, ten went down to it in the nearby village and there were others in the same plight in other villages. I was busy going from one to the other, when a letter arrived from Kaluapuna. I give here a transliteration because it is so typical:

Hallo, Father,

Now I wish to approach you in conversation about my insignificant affairs. Father, I am dying. I am really very sick with that sickness we found so often among the people of the mountains. My head aches, I am short of breath and when I breathe my two sides pain me. I do not know if I can recover. Father, I want you to bring me the Last Sacraments. Paulus is carrying this letter. He tells me the sea is very rough and heavy. If what he says is true you must not come, lest you get drowned, but send me some of the medicine we used for this sickness in the jungle and come as soon as you can afterwards. If I recover, that's good. If God wants me to die, I am ready. Father I am really very sick. Pray for me. Goodbye, God bless you. Good morning.

I, Kaluapuna wrote this.

Paulus, the dripping postman, arrived at dusk. 'Yes,' he said, 'the sea is very rough and the swells are heavy. Our canoe was swamped four times and we had to swim about while we were bailing it out. Once, we were almost capsized on a sharp high swell.'

'Kaluapuna told you that I will be going back with you?' I queried.

Paulus turned silently to his companions and they looked at their toes. Logpen said: 'The four of us were thinking of staying the night in the village here. We just managed in the daylight, now if we are pitched out in the night we might lose the canoe. And pitched out we will be! We can't even make it alone, and then if we have the Father we'll all be lost. True!'

I did not press them. They knew the sea and the performance of the canoe better than I did. I gave them all a meal and asked them to wait on and see if matters improved.

I could not go by launch, for one cannot steer a winding course in the dark just on a compass and clock. The predictable result would be that we would land on the first reef.

At midnight they woke me up and said the wind had dropped and so there was only the sea to cope with and they thought we might be able to make it. There was a heavy ground swell running but it was no longer being whipped up by the wind.

I had already packed my Mass-box. Inside it I had squeezed an inflated football tube. I wrapped the box in oilskins and fixed an electric torch on the outside over the place where the tube was. Routine procedure. When the Mass-box is washed overboard the oilskins keep it dry, the tube keeps it afloat and the torch tells you where to find it in the dark sea.

We pushed off, two men paddling forward, two in the stern and I amidship with the box on my lap. We had about six inches of free-board, which is a good average.

As we were passing by my motor launch, Paulus said: 'Are there life-belts in the boat? We might need them.'

'Yes,' I said, 'bring five of them.'

He climbed aboard the launch and disappeared under the canvases. When he re-appeared I teased him saying: 'The good old days are gone when the Mengens were men. The present generation won't go out in the rain without a life-belt. Just a bunch of old women.' He drawled out: 'Which of you fellows told the Father?'

'Nobody told me,' I said, 'but I catch on after a while. Thanks for thinking of me.'

Even before he boarded the canoe I knew he had only brought one life-belt.

We moved off, paddling as close inshore as was safe. In spite of extra hard pulling the current of the Unung River carried us some distance out to sea before we had crossed it. This was an advantage in one way because now we had a following sea for the remainder of the night.

I carried a pocket compass which I looked at from time to time as I could see no landmark whatever.

'How do you know your direction?' I asked Paulus.

'By the wind on my face and the sound of the sea,' he said. 'There on the left is the waterfall. There is no reef there; you can tell by the clean sound of the surf on the shingle. Further ahead is the first small reef that juts out. You can hear it noising oftener than the beach. And further still ahead is the long Baiena reef. It is from that we hear the continuous rumble because it is lying at an angle to the sea and the surf breaks first at one end and then runs crashing along the length of it. That occasional deep boom is from the submerged reef just in front of the channel we take. The boom-boom happens only when two heavy swells follow each other. When the first one passes over it it does not break but pulls the sea with it and exposes the reef and then the second swell breaks over the exposed reef. We have to be careful not to go too near that one. It is a long way off yet. We are listening for it.'

It is an eerie experience to sit in a little canoe riding the waves like a gull, with the night so dark that you cannot see the person beside you. We were not more than five hundred yards from the shore and yet there were probably two thousand feet of water beneath us. The waves were continually splashing into the canoe but most of the water went clean across, because the canoe was so narrow . . . maybe ten inches wide. A little water got in and there was always some inside the hull where the paddlers rested their feet; when they felt the water rising too high, the fore-paddler bailed it out. There was a steady sound of paddles against the sides of the canoe: bur-burrrp, bur-burrrp as they paddled a short stroke and a long one. 'Hau-si, Hai-si,' intoned a paddler to keep the team paddling in time, and I could hear the liquid swill of the water as it slipped below the keel. Then the swells were rolling shorewards. I felt the stern of the canoe rising higher and higher and then the whole canoe rushed madly forward, stern up in the air and the bows down on the water. I thought it would dig its bow into the sea and fill up, but it never did. Then the peak of the swell reached the stern of the canoe and passed along to the centre and out to the bows. The stern was down and the bows were pointing skywards. I thought the man in front of me would fall back on top of me for the canoe was now on the other, the receding side of the swell, and seemed to be sliding backwards down a mountain, lower and lower into the sea as the swell ran ahead like a huge black muscular jelly. Then we were as low in the trough of the wave as we could go, and the canoe evened out but only for an instant before the next swell was on us. If you are new to the business you'll look back and barely discern in the dark a flicker of light gleaming on the top of a high wall of water towering over you, teetering on top and ready to crash on you. And you'll scream because you are frightened and if you don't scream it only means you are too frightened.

But that water will not crash on you. The canoe will rise with it, stern up to the sky and the bows down and rush headlong as before.

What would you do if it did crash on you? I had long ago got the answer to that question, and it surprised me. You just sit tight and do nothing at all and everything works out right. The canoe will sink of course, but only a few feet. Then it will lean over at a slight angle as the balancing outrigger surfaces and there it will remain and all the water in the world can go over it and it will go neither up nor down. You just stand inside your canoe. Your head and shoulders are over the water. The canoe is safe in that position until it becomes waterlogged and that may take several weeks.

As long as the outrigger does not become separated from the hull, a canoe may swamp but it will never sink. But if the outrigger snaps off, as could easily happen in a rough sea, then you have just enough time to bless yourself.

The sky had now cleared a little and the first grey light of dawn was in the east. A faint cold outline of the mountains was in the sky. We were very near the reefs and the paddlers were watching and listening so as to reckon their position. We were still drifting when the sea broke over the submerged reef a few hundred yards ahead. Kunagome, in the stern, who also steered the canoe, now seemed to take charge. 'Let's go,' he said. They all had their bearings and needed no directions. They paddled along by the reef and then Kunagome headed the canoe in towards a narrow channel. It was full tide and the high seas sent rollers right in on to the beach behind the reefs. Getting safely through called for skilled manoeuvring, for even the smaller rollers could swing the canoe sideways and dump it.

Thirty or forty yards off-shore, the four men slipped into the water. The canoe bounded up and rode high. The four men took up positions along the side of the canoe to swim it ashore. From my exalted perch all I could see of them was four fuzzy heads above the water.

Kunagome was giving directions: 'Wait, wait. There's a big one coming. Not yet! Wait ... there's another!' Those two swells passed under the canoe and as it was settling back in the trough of the second one Kunagome shouted: 'A small one coming! Be ready! Let's go!'

Hands and feet shot out and we plunged ahead, slowly rising on the swell as it caught up with us. We'd have to ride it the whole way in, otherwise we'd be left in the shallows and the next breaker would make smithereens of everything. In half a minute I could see that they had won. The two men up front were now only waist deep in the spent surf and dragging the canoe along. Then it crunched on the gravel and we were there.

'How about that?' said Kunagome. 'Wasn't that well done?'

It certainly was, and the Mengens are so embarrassingly shy and go to such extremes to avoid anything that even savours of looking for praise that I knew the whole team must have been bubbling over with elation and a sense of achievement.

I did not spare the praise they deserved, and added an extra half pound of tobacco and a whole issue of a newspaper so that they could make plenty cigars.

I went first thing to the house of Kaluapuna, my catechist. The door was wide open and a log-fire blazed in the middle of the floor. Kaluapuna had company.

A villager who laid claims to the powers of sorcery was busy at work. He had already smeared Kaluapuna's face with a mixture of lime and betel-nut juice and what-not, and was now halfway through shaving off his fuzzy hair. He had discovered who had bewitched my catechist and this was the cure.

I bid them the top of the morning, as it was the most seasonable greeting just then. They gaped like two fish. It seemed that I was not expected. The quack gained his composure and tried to slink out. However, I excused myself first and told him if he could not replace the hair he had removed, the next best thing was to finish the job.

I returned to Kaluapuna in half an hour. He was crew-cut, washed and lone. He was not in a serious condition and would be well again in a week. 'If you had been here earlier,' he said, 'that would not have happened. You see, I thought I was going to die and I had to do something.'

It sounded common human practice to me. How many better educated people, when the doctors hold no hope for them, have recourse to charms, quacks and fortune-tellers? . . . 'And Satan answered and said: Skin for skin, and all that a man hath he will give for his life' (Job. 2.4.) and Satan might be in the way of knowing.

Kaluapuna got well, and 'went bush' for two months till his hair had grown again, because, as he told me afterwards, he was ashamed of the mark of his sin.

Due to the enormous distances to be covered and the sparseness of the population in most of these regions, the span of a priest's life is not long enough to allow him to attend to the religious instruction of each individual person. When I say enormous distances, I do not mean thousands of miles, but, rather, distances which take an unusually long time to cover on account of the complete lack of roads or even crude bridle paths which would take a horse.

To illustrate that point I may mention that when I left Rabaul by plane on holidays, we flew directly over my parish. I timed the plane from my mission station at Malmal to Ti village in the gap of Nakanai mountains, and it was fourteen minutes. When I walked from my mission station to that same village of Ti, following the native tracks through the mountains and taking in all the villages, it took me sixty-one hours and twenty minutes of actual walking time.

The direct route is about forty or fifty miles, but going there from village to village, as parish work has to be done, it comes to one hundred and twenty or possibly one hundred and forty miles.

Fourteen minutes against sixty-one hours is an awful shock to the system.

My parish was divided up later, but at that time I had sixty-five villages to visit and a complete round of the parish took eighty-five days' walking. In localities like this, ninety-five per cent of our time and energy is spent in trying to get to the place. Two visits a year were the most I could ever afford for the mountains and sometimes even less, because the coastal people were already Catholics and demanded most of my time.

This, then, is the great work of the catechists. They go into the remote villages and live there with the people and instruct them in their religion. The programme is laid out and the progress marked off. This progress varies from tribe to tribe and from village to village, and also from one catechist to another.

In order to baptise them, it is not considered sufficient that the people know the tenets of their religion. The main thing is that they know and are prepared to follow the Catholic way of life, and the only way for them to find that out is to practise it for a number of years and, incidentally, in a manner more strict than that of the 'born Catholics'. If then, after a number of years, they are willing to be accepted into the Church and if the priest on his part is satisfied with their progress, he will baptise them.

The time varies from place to place and depends on how near the village is to the priest. It also varies with the tribe, for experience shows that some tribes are inclined towards religion and piety and others are not, and it would be a mistake to apply hard and fast rules. Villages have waited twenty years for Baptism and once I baptised some villagers who had been fifteen years under a catechist.

In our youthful wisdom and boundless zeal we used to take a dim view of the older missionaries who used to say: 'Beware of the itch for sprinkling Baptismal water in a hurry. You'll have the rest of your life to regret it, and the priest that takes over after you will have some nice things to say.' And: 'Any fool can fill a Baptismal Register with names but it takes more than that to fill the Church with people. Don't talk about fat Registers, let's see the Church on Sunday, and baptising in a hurry will never fill it.' We were inclined to think that these old men 'had lost their punch'; the truth was that it was they who were doing the real work and we were the glamour boys.

When a house is built it is difficult to repair or replace the foundation and a little extra work and care in the beginning save untold worry and frustration later on.

It is not fair practice to stampede a primitive man into the Catholic Church. He must take his time and fully understand its ramifications into every aspect of his life. Ephemeral enthusiasm is no substitute for sound religious instruction and acquired good customs and habits. Nor indeed would Mother Church be very complimented with thousands of 'baptised pagans' who never darken her doors after Baptism.

I have had requests for Baptism from several villages, possibly two thousand people in all, but as they were not ready they will have to be satisfied with Baptism-in-danger-of-death for a while yet.

All the religious instruction and all the schooling in these villages are done by the catechists. When the time comes for Baptism, the priest examines each candidate individually to assure himself that he is fully instructed, knows and performs his obligations regularly and is freely undertaking the Catholic way of life.

It is not difficult to get the children to school here. It might even be said that they are very keen on school. Attendance is not compulsory, not even in the new Registered Schools, and yet I find the average attendance never below ninety per cent. I find too that it is not unusual for a group to badger the teacher into giving them night-school.

I have always encouraged them to miss no chance of advancing their education and yet, deep down, I felt that I was in some way a hypocrite, for if I were a little copper-skinned fuzzy-headed pot-bellied Mengen brat I would never go to school at all. But when the sun rose high I'd take my little dug-out canoe and trout-spear and paddle along the warm green waters of the lagoons. You'd see my empty canoe wheeling slowly on the surface and you'd know that I was down among the fairy-castle coral reefs with their caves and pillars of blue, green-gold and red. The brightly coloured fish are down there, slowly weaving in and out of their trellised homes. Some are busy grubbing down on the sand where the water is cold and some are drifting above me like a toy balloon-barrage. I can see the white of the sand beneath and the dull glitter of the sun on the water's surface above me. Around me is a sphere of clear vision fading into dark and darker blue at the edges.

When I'd speared a fat and lazy little fish I'd climb to the surface and run a length of liana through his gill and out his mouth, and hang him round my neck and feel the satisfied thrill of his flapping on my chest while I dived for another. For that is the way my father told me to wear him to keep him alive and fresh, and to protect him from the other little boys and from the crabs and the birds of prey on the sand. And when my necklace of fish was complete, I'd beach my canoe and roast all my fish on hot embers and suck them back one by one and rub my little pot-belly and crow: 'Iau ka ponu: I am full.' And then I'd roll over in the shade on the warm sand and sleep, as Nau my mother taught me, with my bottom up.

Or I might spend the day laying traps for the wild pigs in the bush, or for the wingless bird the cassowary, or for the possum or the wallaby. Or I might ramble along the beach looking for the place where Kurasina, the green turtle, had laid her eggs, and when tired of that I'd search for the eggs, bigger than goose-eggs, of the tiny little bush fowl the Ngiok, or of the heron, the Gao which lays her pale blue eggs in her nest on the mangroves. And then I'd start all over again with my little canoe.

But go to school with its ink and chalk and dusters? Where

the cat is always on the mat and two and two always make the same old four? O sorrow!

Papa would shout at me of course, and threaten me with the cane on the ankles, or to cut off my food-supply or even to report me to the Father . . . but when the time came I am smart enough to know that he would be too blubber-hearted to do anything at all.

O sorrow, Father, if I were a little Mengen brat you'd never get me inside the door of your old school. No-no-no! Noken turu!

The Jungle . . .

THE PARISH which was so large at first appeared to shrink with time. The fact was that I was becoming accustomed to it. I had also made some mental adjustments. If I had to go to a village thirty miles away I began to realise that there was no need to put up a speed record, nor to return the same day, nor the same week for that matter. It was all part of the parish and each village was entitled to as much of my time as the next.

I began to tinker with the Golden Rule: never put off till tomorrow what you can do today, and I came up with a version that seemed more suited to local conditions: never do today what can be done as well tomorrow . . . and I still hoped to get to heaven.

Sometimes I did parish visitation by motor launch and sometimes on foot. There were great advantages attached to the launch. I could leave before dawn, do my day's work and be back home that night. A thermos of tea would see me through the day and hence there was no need to move the kitchen and bedroom. The disadvantage was that if I was moving according to a fixed schedule among people who had never heard of clock or calendar I came away with the feeling that I had skimped my work, for it was only when I was ready to leave the village that they came to ask me about this and that. But the sea would be rising and I hoped to be home before dark so I would say: 'Well, see me about it the next time, I've got to go now.' And I had to go because I arranged things that way. By and large, it was a stupid arrangement.

Sometimes I went on foot, the main reason being that I could then stay as long as I liked and was needed in any village without worrying whether the boat might drag its anchor during the night and finish up on a reef; but I also had another reason, tucked away in the back of my head and so little mentioned even to myself that I pretended not to know it was there. I wanted to know just how I would stand up to walking in tropical conditions.

Most of the coastal villages are near one another and a day's walk might vary from one to three hours on tolerably good track with few climbs of any consequence. I did the one hour's walk in a masterly fashion but the three-hour walk knocked some of the nonsense out of me. However, I improved as I went. Later I increased my distance and my pace and succeeded in shedding many unnecessary pounds and hardened up considerably. The first time I did twenty-two miles in seven hours I felt very cocky. Then I wanted to find my limit, which I did very effectively. I walked thirty-six miles in fourteen hours and nearly died of cramps that night. However, I knew that I could now do twenty or twenty-five miles day-in and day-out and that was consoling news.

All the time I had my eye on the mountains. They rose up, range behind range, from the whole coastline. They harboured three native groups: the Mamusis on the west, the Bush-Mengens in the centre and the Kols and Suis to the east.

We knew little about these people. Father Culhane had once visited three Mamusi villages back in the 'thirties, one Kol village and all the Bush-Mengens.

The Mamusis lived on the southern side of the island and the Kols and Suis straddled it from coast to coast. I made up my mind that I would get over those mountains and visit all those people, hence all the fancy foot-work along the beach. I was

still very ignorant and did not know that walking along a
coastal track bears the same relation to 'jungle-whacking' as
crossing the Atlantic by ship does to swimming it. All that
wisdom would come later and after much hardship.

The moment a person decides to stay out overnight here, he
is faced with problems unknown in the land of the Christians.
The jungle has no roads, no towns, no hotels, no store where
one can buy things, no food, no means of transport, nothing
but an abundance of sharp-faced mountains, turbulent un-
bridged rivers, rocks, trees, foul undergrowth, fetid swamps
. . . and human beings.

I suppose I have covered a few thousand miles of that kind of
country. From those of my diaries which I have not lost I can
count nearly eight hundred hours on the track. I have made
some mistakes, but few repeats among them, for they sear the
brain like a hot iron and one is not likely to forget.

Distance is never referred to in miles but in hours . . . one
hour's walk, five hard hours' walk, two days' walk and so on.
Mileage is deceptive. A mile along the beach may be only
twenty minutes and a mile in the trackless mountains may be
two hours, and as fatiguing as ten along the beach; but when a
person has the distance in hours he knows that, far or near,
he will get there in a certain time.

The usual routine is to go from village to village, staying
at least one day in each. According as the villages are placed,
a day's walk may be anything from one hour to eight.

When one decides to take on a twenty day journey, he must
prepare accordingly. Knowing all the unforeseen delays that
can occur, he adds fifty per cent to his supplies and makes pro-
vision for thirty . . . a box of food may get lost in crossing a
flooded stream, he may be marooned for two or three days, or
he may find it necessary to take in a few extra villages.

The three most important items in his boxes are Food, Food
and Food. The rest he may be able to improvise or do without.
There is no known substitute for food. Without it, he is more
helpless than a car without fuel . . . at least that can roll with
the fall. To assess what he needs for thirty days' walk he must

first know what his normal daily consumption is. He will allow twice as much for each day's walking. Thus two months' food on the home station will last only a month on the trail.

The tidiest bed to carry is a long canvas sheet about seven feet by four with loops or sleeves on the long sides. For carrying purposes the bedlinen can be rolled inside this. Six straight saplings and some jungle rope are all that is now necessary to make a comfortable bunk. Two saplings are run through the loops in the canvas and left protruding a foot or two at the ends. With the other four saplings one makes two X's tying the intersection with jungle-rope. The two X's are placed facing each other and separated by the length of the canvas. The saplings bearing the canvas are placed on the lower half of each X and pushed down on the outside as far as they will go. The spreading legs of the X draw the canvas taut. The saplings of the canvas are lashed in position with more jungle rope. A mosquito net is draped from the top four points of the two X's. Lonra and Kenpale would get this bed together in less than ten minutes with a lot of laughing and fooling thrown in.

A chair is also useful unless one relishes sitting on a box for weeks. The easiest one is the canvas collapsible. By undoing a few strings it can be rolled up like an umbrella.

Everybody has his own weakness, and mine is bread. I am in bad humour and a most disagreeable and unpleasant person if I haven't any. To avoid this bad humour I take along a tin of flour and some yeast. Any container of a few gallons capacity will serve as an oven, provided it has a lid. The lightest and tinniest material will do. I usually used the one that served as packing case for the tea-pot, cups and such like. Kenpale or Lonra made the bread and we usually took a day off once a week or so for that purpose. The yeast was prepared overnight in a bottle which was stoppered. In the morning it was ready to blow its top. Then it was mixed with the flour and took about five hours to rise. In the mountains, Madame, you must be more careful because the shack is open and the winds are blowing and the yeast can easily catch cold and fail to rise;

hence you cover it well and keep it near the fire. In the meanwhile Kenpale dug a deep hole outside, away from the breeze, and filled it with dry firewood. When that was burning at its best he put a layer of round stones on top of it and then consecutive layers of firewood and stones, about four layers each. The whole thing blazed like blazes and after half an hour all the stones were in the bottom with the hot ashes and so hot that they would keep the heat for hours.

The dough was now ready and any empty food can served as a bread form. They come in all shapes, oval, round and square, and add variety to the bread. All these small tins of dough were placed inside the big tin or oven, which was then embedded in the hot stones with some more hot stones placed on top. A fire was lit on top of the lot. The oven was placed in such a manner that the lid could be removed for inspection without disturbing the fire.

The oven had no thermometer nor automatic alarm, and Kenpale and Lonra had no watch. But when the work was done they would saunter off down the village and seemingly forget about everything. They had, however, an acute sense of time and just when I was ready to throw an apoplectic fit, because I was not as handy at removing the bread as they, they would be on their way back.

What else is necessary? . . . a lamp and some kerosene, a few books, a box of clothes, towels, soap, etc., two boxes of medicine for the bush people, a box with all the necessary items for Mass, a box or two of canned foods, cooking utensils, a quantity of newspaper and twist-tobacco for paying the daily carriers, a dish, a bucket, an axe, a bushknife, and perhaps a spare pair of spiked boots if the journey is going to be a long one. A pair of boots will last about 600 miles on the beach and only 250 or so in the mountains. Since I might have to wade streams fifty times a day or more, I cut two holes in each boot in front of the heel and at each side. The water would now run in and out as it pleased and it was not necessary to drain the shoes after crossing each stream . . . a boot full of water can be more painful to walk in than one full of gravel. A shotgun for pigeons and a service rifle for wild pigs just about complete the list.

Ten or twelve tidy boxes were always ample. These were all numbered. Kenpale knew, for he did the packing, that Box No. 4 was always the Mass-box; No. 6 was my own, and if he wanted the salt he knew it should be in the right near corner of No. 2, and that the bully beef would be found near the lard and the matches in No. 3.

The maximum weight of a box permitted by the Government for a carrier is 40 lbs. Mine would usually (starting out) weigh about twenty or twenty-five, as each box would have a blanket or some such light bulky article to keep the tin cans from creating too much of a din. There was no scarcity of carriers.

The people of each village took the boxes along to the next, for which service I paid them in tobacco or some such commodity. The cost per day usually totalled about fifteen shillings. When villages were near each other it was a present; mostly, however, it was well earned and if the journey extended into the afternoon the carriers got 'overtime'.

In daily life most if not all the carrying is done by the women. They put the most astounding weights on their heads. A particularly large one attracted my attention on one occasion. It weighed 110 lbs. The woman had a baby on her hip at the same time. A twenty-five pound box would scarcely flatten their crinkly hair. I had little pads to be put under the boxes to make them lie more comfortably, but at first the women would have no part in them: 'Ai-oo! does the Father think we are sissies?' they said. After a while they accepted them and the men said I was teaching their women bad habits.

In the beginning I found it difficult to accept the fact that the women carried my baggage; but after a time I became accustomed to many strange practices. It is useful to recall that the code of etiquette varies from people to people. If I had insisted that the men carry, in some villages I might have had to shoulder the lot myself. It is a dangerous business to flout the accepted custom, the more so when one is the exception and the novelty.

In New Guinea the code is Men first! If a woman had the bad manners to sit while a man had to stand she would be considered rude and boorish, just as we would consider the man who buries his face in the newspaper on a bus while a woman laden with parcels strap-hangs beside him.

If, in some villages, for the custom varies slightly, I insisted that the men carry while the women lazed around, I would, Madame, be greeted in the same way as would one of their people if he insisted that you should stand in the rain while your husband kept the umbrella all to himself.

Politeness is only doing what one's host expects, and one is more bound by it in the jungle than anywhere else.

As a result of carrying loads on their heads the women are erect, strong, slim and extremely graceful in their movements and carriage.

Back in civilisation I once suggested to the women of Our Lady's Sodality that they lift their pastor over a slushy road so that his shoes should not be soiled. They brazenly refused, and their men-folk backed them up! We the people will never understand the fashion of the white man.

✻

Down at the western end of the parish lies the Tolo River. About twelve miles east is the Ba, with Bairaman village at the mouth. The land between these two rivers was never one hundred per cent Mengen. In fact it seems that the 'true' Mengens are not found west of Bairaman or east of Motong.

The neighbouring tribe on the west is the Lote (pronounced Low-tay), those of whom explorer Dampier wrote in 1700: '. . . carrying with me all such Trifles and Iron-work as I thought most proper to induce them to a Commerce with us; but I found them very shy and roguish'. (Damp. Voy. II, p. 538.) It would seem that the Lote tribe does not come further east than Atu village. Between Atu and Bairaman is a sort of buffer state supporting a mixed breed of Lotes, Mengens and

Mamusis, the predominant blood being Mamusi with a tincture of Lote in the west and of Mengen in the east.

The Mamusi is an inland or bush-tribe that has in a halfhearted manner overflowed here on the shore. They do not take kindly to the sea and the canoe is little used amongst them. Any time I visited this western end of the parish, half the people were absent in the bush.

Ma'una village is a more recent foundation and entirely Mamusi, taking its origin from the inland village of Serunguna. It is a valuable asset to the mountain people. It is their sea-side cottage.

The bush people always have difficulty in obtaining salt and so it is a most prized commodity. The coastal people who cannot obtain salt from a trader supply the need by cooking their food in sea water. The Mamusis, being inland, and far away from traders and the sea, have to make their own salt, and that is one of the great advantages of their sea-side village at Ma'una. A band of men comes down from the mountains and spends a few weeks there evaporating salt-water in a petrol drum. The residue is brownish and mainly salt in flavour. This is carried back to the mountains and bartered in the villages.

I always took a supply of salt tablets with me to the mountains and the children, who are less self-conscious than the parents, would stick out their grubby little hands for some and go off sucking them as other children suck lollipops.

At Ma'una I fell into conversation with the Mamusi potboilers. They squatted round the drum in the traditional pose. They were dark-skinned, sturdy, chesty fellows, shorter than the Mengen but yet of fair dimensions.

The scene has been depicted in cartoons since we first heard of cannibals.

'You have no food in your pot,' I said. 'Ah! You must be men-of-the-eating-of-men! Now you are going to put me in and boil me.'

They paid me the courtesy of rollicking laughter. 'We do not eat men,' they said. 'Anyhow four of us could not consume the Father, there is too much of him there.'

I returned their courtesy by laughing loudly at their sally.

'You must be waiting then till you catch me in your village where there are plenty people to help you, and the babies will be given my toes and the small boys will get a finger each.'

This brought another burst of laughter and they said: 'We are lost in the mountains. No priest ever visited our villages. Could the Father come and see us?'

'You are inviting me and I shall go. Tell your people that when the sun moves to the South they will see me, and that I should like to see them all too.'

It must have been a month or two later that one day I found a small spearhead wrapped in momolo leaves on my table. I asked the house-boy about it but he didn't know a thing ... cross my heart and may I die in sin ... but that he heard some one say that it was from the Mamusi.

The momolo is a sacred shrub and a leaf is always attached by the people to all important messages in the same manner as Kings or Governments attach their seal to important documents. If the house-boy's version were true then I could translate the spearhead and momolo leaf in the following officialese (Native fashion):

'That whereas We have been made aware that you have expressed the intention of trespassing on our Lands and Whereas We do not wish to grant you permission to commit the said trespass

Now therefore, be it known to you by These Presents, that by the powers of the Mamusis and all other powers Us enabling, that should you devilishly, maliciously and feloniously disobey

Our Most Excellent Wish herein expressed, We shall avenge with a Spear this insult to Our Exalted Person.

Given under the Momolo in the Mamusi the day after they nearly caught the big fish at Salumpuna.

As Nutu is Safe, O may the Luluai be Safe.'

Perhaps someone was going to push a spear into my ribs and in a most gallant fashion was giving me due warning. I dismissed the incident and it did not recur to my mind for a month or two.

On my way home from Bairaman I was walking through Drina Plantation and as I approached the labourers' quarters natives ran in all directions, all except one elderly fellow who stood with his back to the door laughing his head off.

'What's going on?' I asked him.

'Have a look inside,' he said. 'There are four of them up on the rafters.'

I peeped inside and four scared men gazed down on me from the rafters. 'What's it all about?' I asked.

'Oh! They're just from the bush,' he said, 'and when I told them that you were the Father they all ran off. I can't explain their lunacy.'

'Where do you come from?'

'I'm from the Mamusi too. They are all my boys.'

'And why didn't you run away?'

'Run away for what?'

'Oh! Nothing! By the way, how long more will you be working here?'

'We are all finishing at the end of the month,' he said.

'What village do you come from in the Mamusi?'

'I'm from Paka . . . way up at the back, near Nakanai.'

'Very well. Now when you pass through the other villages on your way home will you tell the people that I'll be along before the following moon dies?'

'Sure, Father,' he said, 'I'll tell them that . . . and they'll be glad.'

I asked myself was it these four boys on the rafters and their brothers who had sent me the spearhead, and foolishly thinking that I might recognise them, had now run off? I had no answer.

So far the episode had had little effect on me except to cause me to add a sort of ignorant bravado to a decision I had already made: these fellows might be trying to scare me (I had met similar stuff before) but now I (the great I) was going to show them it was not so easy to scare me (the great me). Very natural and very stupid.

Later, a catechist who had been stationed in a near Mamusi village came along to me with a tale of sorrow. He had run away from the village at night because the people had threatened to kill him . . . 'and they will do the same to you,' he said, 'if you ever go up that way.'

Was somebody spreading silly prattle amongst the Mamusis or did they simply want to be left alone? A third explanation, very obvious in hindsight, did not present itself just then.

At any rate I was going to see for myself what the situation was like. I wished to find out if there had been some prattle spread among them and, also, I had no intention whatever of leaving them alone unless I heard that wish coming from their own lips.

And beside any religious motive or pioneering instinct there was the ordinary physical fascination that high blue mountains exercise on any healthy soul with the slightest love of the open spaces. I just cannot sit there under miles of mountains and know that up there are people . . . and maybe valleys, rivers and waterfalls. A blue sky, blue mountains and a white cloud? I just cannot resist. I say: 'some day I'll go, I must see what's in there.' It acts on me like an unopened letter.

When I had packed my boxes I turned to my array of guns: which would I take? There were Springfield rifles, .22 rifles, a shotgun, a .38 revolver and so on. I used to have a Bren-gun that I picked up in an army dump but as that looked too dangerous I had dropped it in the sea. Anyhow I do not think the Government would have issued me with a permit.

I always carried a shotgun or a .22 because pigeons and bush-fowl were in abundance everywhere and are a great delicacy in the bush.

This time, however, I regretfully took no gun, but instead took down my Butu from the wall. This I had received from Kawarea of the Kols. It is a strong and solid walking stick. It is made of hardwood about three feet long and shaped like an attenuated dumb-bell. It protrudes beyond the handgrip for about six inches, usually fashioned into a spear point or an axehead. It is a humane weapon and the Kols use it for caressing each other's skulls or for delivering local anaesthetics when the neighbour becomes fretful or difficult, or unwilling to do what one knows is best for him. It was not quite virgin to the trade and had one notch on the handle. Kawarea told me it would never let me down, for at his insistence the sorcerer had enshrined a dancing devil in it.

Even to grip the thing sent a thrill up the arm. The sleek hard surface, the beautifully balanced feel! Hold the knob loosely between the thumb and forefinger and it began to swing like a pendulum, slowly at first, and with ever increasing magnetism towards the nearest human skull. Psychologically it was a far more dangerous weapon than a gun. I'm sure that in the heat of battle the thing would shout and cheer and drag me along with it.

Finn McCool and the Boys used it widely. . . .

Armed with my Butu I turned to Gogoreakapangamologa and said: 'Procedamus in pace,' and he answered: 'In nomine Christi, Amen.'

I was tempted to slip a revolver into my pocket but it was a foolish temptation and I recognised it as such, for contrary to popular belief a gun is a useless weapon in the jungle. No idiot of a bushman is going to stand in front of me to collect an ounce of lead. If he is after my hide he will either fall over me with kindness and then poke me in the ribs or else sneak up on me at night when I am twenty or thirty miles inside the tribal bounds.

If a person travels with an armed battalion, then he is pretty safe in the crowd but it is most unlikely that he will see anyone on the whole journey, and of what use is that? In any case, training guns on the parishioners would be a rather startling innovation. I must go in peace or stay at home.

To be sure of a reliable line of carriers I went to the local village, but nobody would budge . . . is it to be killed by the mountain people? On reflection I found that this was a silly procedure on my part because if the future parishioners from the bush failed to show up then it would be futile for me to go on a prolonged picnic through the jungle. And also, if I supplied foreign carriers the first time I'd probably have to do it always and this would be a great burden on everyone.

One local was necessary: Qiaukaina, son of Kena, who was then my cook. But Qiaukaina would not hear of going, and the same day we parted. But I did find one: Patrick Gogoreakapangamologa, he-who-deceives-them-by-his-speech, a lad of mighty words. He used to mess about in my kitchen and should do in a pinch. He was only fifteen and I felt I was acting meaner than a Sanauga.

✵

Let me pause to say Ko Lolago (Go Well) to Qiaukaina. He was a full-grown burly lily-livered loud-mouth who in a scrap one day with a schoolboy got so hopelessly clobbered that he ran to me squealing for help. As a spouse he was herculean. One day he burned a square foot of skin off his wife by sizzling her with a live fire-brand. Another time he removed the hair and a square inch of her scalp with his teeth. He did a stretch in gaol for that and the poor wife cried her eyes out, not because he was gaoled but because she would not be allowed to go to gaol with him. Conjugal love, you know, and all that. Powerful stuff.

✵

My last contact was Kaluapuna, the catechist. He should be very useful in establishing contact with the Mamusis because he knew a few of them already. The ancient tribal Mengen incisions on his face would give him prestige with the Mamusis and their older men would say: 'Here is an elder, here is a man we can speak to and understand.'

I had told him of the spearhead and momolo and also of the other catechist's story. Kaluapuna was now to work quietly and find out all he could.

Samo . . . Interlude

ON MY way to the Mamusi I spent the first night at Bairaman village at the mouth of the river Ba. The river was flooded but abating.

Samo, as I have said earlier, was the Luluai or Burgomeister of Bairaman. He was a great actor, an innocent liar of the most magnificent proportions and hence very good entertainment. This evening he told me how he alone (iau kaskena) had won the war in the Pacific, but that his guiding genius had never been recognised by the Allies.

He was in form for story-telling and insisted on repeating some he had told me before and which I had also heard from many of the older Mengens. In previous tellings I had often asked him to explain those parts which, to me, seemed contradictory, but he would hastily brush me aside with: 'What contradiction? There is none!' or he would say: 'These are only stories for the children'; a realm where it is recognised among all peoples that logic and reality can claim no rights.

Samo was sitting on the veranda of the village resthouse with his feet dangling on the ladder and his mouth full of the red juice of betel nut and lime. His sluiced lower lip wriggled dexterously to collect a run of juice that was only too often trying to escape. Sometimes he could not quite manage it and two red

147

streams would flow down from the corners of his mouth, hop off his chest and splash his laplap with red blobs.

'Did I ever tell the Father the story about Nutu and the canoe?' he asked.

'You scandalise me, Samo,' I said. 'I have never heard a Mengen bandy Nutu's name about like that before.'

'Ah, don't be always so serious,' said Samo. 'This is only a story. The things we tell our children. I am not laughing at Nutu. This is only a story. This is different.'

'Very well, Samo, go ahead with it so.'

'Wait a while,' said Samo. 'I must clean my mouth first. It stinks . . .' and with a few fleeeeeps and prrrrts he got rid of his betel nut and washed his mouth with handfuls of water from the sea. Then he sat down and took a small home-made cigar butt from above his ear, looked deprecatingly at it and replaced it saying: 'Maski, it doesn't matter.' Accepting the broad hint, I gave him the makings.

'Nutu,' said Samo, 'lived a little way in from the beach on the Kelamalagi River . . . you know the spot . . . up from the broken footbridge at the back of the Father's house.'

I was glad to know that I had a block of land on the slopes of Olympus but I said to Samo: 'Samo, you're as bad as the old Irish ballad-writers. They never told anyone where anything was exactly but only in the general area: Patrick Sheehan was born "not far from Galtymore" and something else of equal importance happened "not far from old Kinvara" and . . .'

'I don't know what the Father is talking about,' said Samo.

'Maski,' I said, 'it doesn't matter. Go ahead with your yarn.'

'Right,' said Samo. 'Very good. O.K. Now then . . . but this is only a story . . . it isn't true . . . it is what we tell our children. All right. There were two Nutus, Nutu e Volau and Nutu e Sina, Nutu the Great and Nutu the Less. They were brothers. They had a wife each. No one knows where the women came from. They were there, that's all. They lived at a spot called Marana along the old track from Tatongpal to where the Mission now stands at Makaen. The ruins of the two houses are still to be seen.

'Nutu the Great made everything but he was somewhat awkward and he didn't do a tasty job. Nutu the Less was a very handy fellow.

'Nutu the Great built a house ... oh I'm on the wrong track ... I was going to tell you about the canoe? Maski, I'll continue now and tell about the canoe later.

'Nutu the Great built a house. He built it of mud, red mud and more red mud. He put no timber in it. Just mud. Pure mud. Only mud. Nutu the Less stood by and looked. Just looked. He didn't speak. He stood there just looking. Nutu the Great put no thatch on the house. Just mud.

'All right. Nutu the Great now spoke to Nutu the Less saying: "Brother mine, the day after tomorrow (navongalua ... navongalua ... Nutu the Great invented that word for the day-after-tomorrow) you and your wife must come and have a little feast with me. But first you must perform a sorcery which will bring down heavy rain and stir up great winds to test my house." And, navongalua, Nutu the Less did as he was asked.

'And when all four were eating in the house a great wind arose and heavy rains fell and the wind and the rain washed the house away. It just flowed away in a red stream down the Kelamalagi river and out to sea.

' "O Big Brother," said Nutu the Less, "and you try to show me how to build a house!" And Nutu the Less laughed at his brother.

'Nutu the Less said that he would build a house and "Brother Mine," he said, "I shall return the feast you made for me."

'So he called his wife and said to her: "Wife, we go to fetch some cane and pandanus leaves," and going they fetched them, and built a house with them, a big house, a good house, a house with many things inside it.

'And Nutu the Less said to his brother: "Brother Mine, navongalua you and your wife must come and feast with us."

'And they came. And they all sat in the house and they ate taro and pork and they beat their drums and their joy was full.

'And the winds and rains came but they could not harm the house.

'And the sun shone and the house still stood and Nutu the Less said to his brother: "Brother Mine, oh, how you deceived me with the thing you called a house!"

'And Nutu the Great hung his head for he was ashamed and he spoke no speech but departed, he and his wife.

'. . . And the Mengens till this day build their houses of cane and pandanus as Nutu the Less showed them . . .'

Ringringana, Samo's eldest daughter brought along a baked taro for Samo but he put it aside with the remark: 'My mouth is ashamed to eat before the eye of the Father.

'I don't know the story about the canoe too well, but I shall tell it as best I can. Nutu the Great cut a manang, that is, a canoe with an outrigger, and he said to his little brother: "Navongalua I shall see you."

'Now, that is the custom with us the people to this very day; when someone cuts a canoe he goes around to all his friends and each one gives him something, a pig, taro, fruit and so on. Then he makes a feast to launch his canoe and invites all those people and so the gifts are returned.

'So, Nutu the Less came, bringing a pig, some taro, shell-money, dog's teeth, kakal and so forth. And he also brought his wife.

'And Nutu the Great met them and escorted them to the house and they all went inside and they ate and they sang. And they danced.

'And Nutu the Less said: "Brother mine, that thing you made is only a manang. I'll show you how to make something really good, a mono (a canoe without an outrigger)."

'Nutu the Less went back to his house and he took his kiila with him and also his wife. And they cut planks and collected "molos" and he glued the planks together with the "molos" and he completed his mono and he came to Nutu the Great and speaking to him he spoke: "Navongalua I shall visit you."

'And Nutu the Great told his wife and they prepared a feast.

'Nutu the Less and his wife adorned themselves and they

put all their goods into the new mono and they came to the house of Nutu the Great. And they feasted and made merry. And when it was all over they collected all the food they could find and took it along to the mono with them. And they piled it in and the mono did not sink. Nutu the Less went in first and his wife followed him and there was still room so he said to Nutu the Great: "Let your wife come into my mono too." And she did. And Nutu the Less said to her: "You sit up forward. I steer." And she did. And the three of them came down the Kelamalagi River in the mono, Nutu the Great following along the bank.

'And when they came to the mouth of the river the mono shot straight out for the Three Islands and Nutu the Great could not follow but he went along the beach towards Palmalmal and when he got there he saw the mono shoot the passage to the open sea. And he shouted to his wife to come back but she did not hear him. Then he ran along the beach as far as Malmalkaen and he saw the mono turning towards the rising sun and heading for the land of the Sulka, and then he ran as far as Kalaipuna and when he got there the mono was disappearing over the horizon.

'Nutu the Great came back alone to his house walking slowly and he cried, cried, cried.

'He never saw his wife again, nor Nutu the Less again. And Nutu the Great came back to his house. And the name of his house is Mekael.

'. . . And that is why we the people use a canoe with an outrigger . . . Nutu the Great left it with us. But the Sulka people have a mono which they got from Nutu the Less.

'That too is why we Mengens have only one wife, after the fashion of Nutu the Great and the Sulkas take a second wife after the fashion of Nutu the Less.'

So ends the Burgomeister's tale.

Next morning I was glad to see that the Ba was running only a slight flood. I would push on to Ma'una about three hours down the coast. From there I would go inland.

In Bairaman there was the usual run of village duties: Confessions, Mass, a marriage and two Baptisms. At eight o'clock all was packed and we were on our way. Samo put his canoe at my disposal to ferry the boxes and ourselves across the river. It was an average sized canoe, capable of holding about eight persons. I smoked a cigarette while the baggage and the carriers were going across.

The river was about one hundred and fifty yards wide but narrowed suddenly as it raced out to sea through a channel over submerged rocks and niggerheads. In order to allow for the pull of the current the paddlers had to tack up-stream at a sixty-degree angle and then paddle furiously for the last forty yards. For every foot they advanced, the current swept them down another foot.

I set off in the last trip of the canoe and about halfway across everything happened at once. The outrigger came clear from the hull which immediately turned turtle. My first recollection was that I was under the water and held there by my boots which were jammed firmly in the narrow opening of the hull. I looked up through the yellowish water and could see the form of the upturned hull above me gradually sinking lower and going with the current, carrying me with it. I doubled up to gain the surface and get free of the hull. I do not recall doing so but I must have kicked violently, because I got my feet free at the expense of a few strips of skin. I came to the surface gasping and spluttering. Luckily, we were as yet only on the edge of the main current.

A few men were holding up two bush-women who could not swim and a few more dived for the hull which they eventually found and resurfaced. They rocked it to and fro to splash out the main body of water and then quickly inverted it. The air thus locked inside the upturned hull made it buoyant.

As it was the only sizeable canoe then at Bairaman several people swam out to help us. I was ordered to straddle the upturned canoe amidships. One of the women who could not swim was placed in front of me and the other one behind. A squad of people gathered round in a group and with great yelling and hullaballoo swam the guided missile across the river.

Total loss: one box of matches, fifteen cigarettes, one wrist watch. Total gain: experience. If you must wiggle your boots to force them into the hull of a canoe, don't.

❧

The next morning I left Ma'una for the Mamus and I was all keyed up because this was my first trip inland. I knew the day's walk was a matter of six hours for the carriers and that there were a lot of climbs and descents before we reached Serunguna village which is at about two thousand feet elevation. 'Leave at eight,' I thought, 'and we are there at two.'

I had no appetite that morning and took only a slice of bread for breakfast, and we were on the track at eight o'clock. Three hours non-stop those carriers went and at the deuce of a clip.

Behind Ma'una lie several miles of level ground before the foot of the mountains is reached. It is not swampy but it is always wet and so one walks in strong sticky mud up to the ankles. The track is not discernible through the jungle so that one must trust blindly in the person in front if he can be kept in sight. There are many deep stagnant creeks to be crossed. This is done wherever a tree has obliged by falling across.

These creeks are a nightmare to the rookie ... a fifteen foot span of blue-black water perhaps twelve feet deep. 'The lilies revived and the dragon-fly came back to dream by the river' ... so they did, they are all here now, in this poet's dream. To sit by shaded streams all day might excite my soul to elegant verse, but when I'm hungry and weary and have to wade them a few dozen times they produce an oddly different effect.

Let us contemplate this one in front of us. It is twenty feet wide and ten feet deep in the centre. There is a ledge at each side a few feet above the water. The muddy river-bed slopes in abruptly. The water is shallow and transparent at the edges and I can see the mud, soft and loosely knit. If this river flowed at even a mile a day all that mud would have been washed away. I throw a pebble in where the water is a foot deep. A column of mud rises to the surface and slowly subsides. There is no trace of the pebble. It is being slowly sucked down through the loose and watery mud.

There is a crooked fresh log nine inches in diameter lying across the water. The bark has been stripped off in patches and the exposed timber is oily-looking. At midstream the log dips a foot under the water and rises sharply towards the other bank. There is a broken branch, just off-centre, half way up the rise.

I pause to let the carriers go first and learn how these things are done. Perhaps what I'm really hoping for is that the line of carriers will be so long that my turn will not come at all. Four are now on the log, at this side of midstream and it is bouncing and swaying. The leading lady puts her toe in the water and turns to speak to the one behind her. What does she say? Nothing, only that she saw a crocodile there yesterday . . . but it's all right, he was fifty yards up-stream. Doesn't the idiot know that a crocodile is not a milestone?

They have all walked casually across now without even breaking their chatter on the job. The off-half of the log is dripping water from their wet feet.

It is my turn and I think: 'This is not fair. This is not part of the work of the Lord's anointed. Was it for crossing slippery logs that I had to study Aquinas? And sweat through exams?'

Kaluapuna is standing beside me having quietly cut two long saplings. I will use these to balance myself on the log. He takes my Butu now. That crocodile should not worry me unless I fall in and if I do fall in I'll probably be choked in mud anyhow. That's a happier thought, things are brightening up, and knowing that a crocodile usually grabs only the last person across I address him affectionately: 'O crocodile, please believe me when I say that there are a thousand people coming along behind me.'

Armed with the two poles I inch my way along the log. Out in the deep they are a great support. I push them down a foot and advance two feet, push them down again and advance further. Then I boldly push them down for another few feet but find no bottom and they go in six feet and I nearly follow. The forward thrust of my body buries them hard in the mud and for all I know they are still there. God's universe vanishes at the same instant leaving nothing but a nine inch log and me and the yawning jaws of a crocodile that is not there. Nothing for it but to tear ahead madly and when I do that the job is so easy that I can play the fiddle all the way . . . but I learn only as I go along.

The carriers had gone well ahead and so there was ground to be made up. I did so only with great difficulty and after half an hour, by which time I was soaked in sweat and mud. (I was doing all this to keep up the prestige of my race, so I know you are on my side. Ireland über Alles, Long live the Ould Sod, I sang as I sloshed in the mud.)

After three hours we halted for the first time, by a little stream at the foot of the first climb.

The carriers sat around on stones and stumps and ate their taros. There was little sign of perspiration on them. I had enough for the lot anyhow. It dripped off my nose and chin, trickled into my eyes and my clothes could be no worse if they had come straight from the wash-tub. I was mighty thirsty and drank mugs of water and everybody stared at me and I didn't know why. I had prepared no lunch and was still too stiff and proper to beg a taro from a circumcised Mamusi.

There was no water between here and the village so I filled up a billy-can to be prepared.

We rested for half an hour but at the end of it I was still in a dangerous mood. I felt like a boxer who thinks he is going to have the little fellow squashed in the first round and finds that he himself is glad to have the ropes to lean on.

'Wait,' I thought, 'till I get these little pint-size runts on the climb. That will separate the men from the boys! They'll realise that bone and muscle are not to be despised. After all hadn't I done thirty-six miles on the beach in one day? . . .' but it was when they got me on the mountains that they played havoc with me.

The rain came down in bucketfuls and they grabbed the

boxes and went off with a wild and primitive yell: Oh-ho-ho-ha!

We were on to the first ascent, up a thousand feet at an angle steeper than that of the roof of any house, up over rocks, fallen trees and tangled undergrowth. I could feel my heart beginning to pound in my ears and beat against my ribs. My face grew redder and hotter. Muscles began to complain and to weary. Footwork became less sure and kicking my ankles a habit. As I had to use my hands to pull myself over the rocks, the muscles of my back and chest began to scream. My hands were scratched from grabbing thorny shrubs and sharp rock-edges, and my fingers were fat and swollen and stuck out like bananas. I was becoming weaker all the time and losing ground rapidly on the carriers who sprang ahead from rock to rock like mountain goats, only that now it was the nannies who were leading the flock . . . and these were the poor lassies I had pity for down at the beach! My God, what an ass!

The separation of the men from the boys was now complete.

Eventually I gained the top of the mountain and looked around for the reassuring sign of a village. O sorrow! The track now descended eight hundred feet, one similar to that we had just climbed, and going down was just as bad as going up. When I arrived at the bottom I was confronted with another climb and this see-saw was to go on and on just to cover four or five horizontal miles.

The rain had added speed to the carriers and I was already half an hour behind. When I got to the top of the next climb I could not see them at all, but could hear them on the climb ahead singing: Oh-ho-ho-ha. There was now no question of catching up, in fact at my best I was barely crawling, and began to consider what I should do if I could not make the village at all.

I sat down where I was, piggishly in a puddle, and really glad that there was a dirty puddle to sit in. That's the humour I was in, like a child in a tantrum. I was frustrated and angry, the only thing left to a man when he's licked, angry with the rain, with the slippery tree-roots that sent me sprawling, angry with the liana vines that tripped me up, with the mountains for being mountains, and especially with myself for being a softy. Just four hours in the bush and I was bushed and bewildered. I had learned, too, that four hours in the bush can be worse than forty on the beach.

Kaluapuna stood nearby and encouragingly remarked that the village was not far off as we had already passed some gardens. I tried to cover up by saying: 'Oh, I'm only waiting here to give Gogorea a chance to have a cup of tea ready. I'm already soaked in mud and sitting here is as good as any other.'

And that was really true, and the cold water helped to cool me off. I passed the time plucking bloated squirmy blood-leeches off my legs. My blood was then as nourishing as red ink.

We crawled to the top of the ridge and then I saw the smoke of Serunguna about half a mile away and over a small rise of ground. The track here was open and rough but had no hills. That was welcome. I had to rest three times in that short span, not because I was tired but because I had reached the end of my tether. I was physically exhausted and it was my first taste of that terrible condition. I could not move my feet and if I had seen a tree fall on me I would gladly have said: 'Thanks be to God. It's all over.' It was little consolation to me to know that we had chipped forty minutes off standard time for the journey.

I ask pardon of my race, of every member of it. I let you down badly before the eye of them the people. I also lost my chance. Future generations will never gaze on the painting of the proud and commanding 'O'Neill Entering Serunguna' . . . just a washed-out character, bedraggled, dishevelled and mud-covered slithering along, too tired and too disinterested to look left or right, and hoping he would not collapse before he reached the rest-house.

I had, however, rid myself of a bagful of delusions on many things and felt the better for it.

❋

Serunguna village lacks tourist facilities. A rest-house stood on posts outside the village, four latticed walls and a woolly roof of grass, with a floor of round saplings so far apart that if a person didn't spread his feet on two of them he would fall in between them. The creek was five hundred yards away and the villagers brought their water-supply inside bamboo poles about six feet long and holding a few gallons.

Gogorea had hot water ready and I had a shower by dipping a mug in a bucket of water and using the sapling floor as a duck-board. Washed and dressed I tucked away a substantial meal. The empty tins said six and a half pounds, twice the consumption of a normal day at the mission-station.

I tried to find out how I had failed. Though I had neither intended nor expected to make a record yet I was convinced that the day's performance was poor and would have to be improved upon. My full list of do's and don'ts took many days to be completed, and the main points of it, should it be helpful, are: eat to capacity before starting out, the army marches on its stomach and so will you; for anything more than a three-hour hike, take a prepared lunch and prepare it before breakfast when you're hungry, otherwise you may underestimate your needs; shorts are preferable to long pants and puttees, a smearing of insect repellent will keep both mosquitoes and blood-suckers at bay; boots should have good sharp spikes and should fit snugly; never, never drink water no matter how thirsty, you'll lose your strength as sure as you drink; never try to keep a conversation going; this is almost as bad as drinking water. Develop the habit of deep, even breathing. Find your cruising speed and stick to it; your cruising speed is the one you keep when you have forgotten that you are walking and still intent on getting along. You can't invent it but when you forget all about it, it sneaks out. At that speed your body will act effortlessly, automatically and almost tirelessly. And, I nearly forgot, get in a lot of practice, a few hundred miles will do for a start.

By keeping to those few rules I found I could walk all day in the mountains on tracks many times worse than the one from Ma'una to Serunguna, which I came to recognise for what it was: a fair day's mountain hike, inclined to the easy side.

※

Serunguna village (the old one now deserted) is situated in the round end of a horseshoe mountain range, stuck like a swallow's nest at the top of a 1,500-foot wall of mountain. Lakalona village is an hour away to the west on the banks of the river Lea, surrounded and hidden by sharp high spurs, cones and ricks reaching a few thousand feet and all clustered together. With the aid of binoculars one can see an old garden about two hours beyond Lakalona and near the top of Kilingsi peak. It is discernible against the black-green of the jungle by its yellowish colour. The track to Viosapuna goes through that old garden and on over the mountain to the village and then down a thousand feet in forty minutes to Nunopu and then up the river Loi and a few thousand feet to Paka. Bili, Salumpuna, Elalona and Mao are on the left and all in a general westerly direction.

'Hang your lamp out here on a pole,' said Kansopa, 'the night is clear and the men of the Mamus will be able to see it. They have been watching for it of late!'

Within an hour the message would be rapped out on the garamut from village to village: A lamp in Serunguna . . . a lamp in Serunguna . . . They'd expect me within a week.

I stayed an extra day in Serunguna because I wished to make a map of the hinterland villages for my own use. This map would be inaccurate, yet precise enough to give me a good idea of the position of the villages. I began from two coastal villages twelve miles apart and got the people there to point a stick at Serunguna. I took a compass bearing on the average. In that way I made the first triangle. At Serunguna I took back-bearings as a check. I estimated I had Serunguna's position within half a mile. I continued in like manner with the other villages. Sometimes I could see them and then the bearing would be dead accurate, more often I had to be satisfied with a possible error of five degrees, which I could reduce later by cross-references. In each village I took a long list of bearings on other villages, on peaks, and waterfalls. Later on, at my mission station, I was able to correlate them and bring out a tolerably good bushman's map.

*

The next day I left Lakalona village for Viosapuna, or Mamus as it was also called. We followed a creek down a gorge, crossed a junction of several creeks, and then followed the western one up another gorge, criss-crossing it waist-high every few hundred yards according as our progress was hindered by bluffs, cliffs or boulders. A few miles up-stream we left the gorge and the creek and struck out in a westerly direction over a steep mountain side. The climb was very stiff and the carriers paused every five minutes. As I watched the carefree expression of their faces I wondered more and more how much they knew about the spearhead and momolo-leaf. I argued with myself for the next two hours up the mountain. One thing I knew for certain: when it was all over, no matter what the result, there would be an abundance of veterans who would say: 'Well, the outcome should have been obvious to anyone.' If the threat were carried out they would say: 'Only a fool would have done as he did. After all, he got a fair warning. He should have realised that these were primitive people;' and if it were not carried out, the same folk would say: 'What was he worried about anyway? If he had the slightest knowledge of Natives he would have paid no attention to it.' It is so easy to solve other people's problems when you are miles away and not involved. But now I was involved and that made all the difference.

I remembered that less than a year before, and not a hundred miles from here, a European had trekked into the jungle. He was on the perfectly peaceful errand of recruiting Native labour. He knew many of the tribe and felt quite at home with them and they with him. Yet he never got back. In an inland village he was speared and hacked to pieces.

'But you are a priest,' I told myself. True! But then, do jungle folk know the difference?

I studied the faces of the carriers again. I could not believe that they were up to mischief. Their faces belied them; they could not possibly all be such good actors . . . but then . . . perhaps they knew nothing about it? Perhaps it was a well-guarded plot of a few? A few? What few? Who knew me in here or who could have any interest in keeping me out? Nobody knew me except the Catechist a few villages back. Rule him out! On second thoughts: No! Nobody can be ruled out of this.

I called Kaluapuna, the Catechist who was accompanying me. 'Do you remember Qiaukaina who used to cook for me?' I asked him.

'Yes, Father,' he said.

'Do you know, by any chance, whether he is a relative of the Catechist back there in the village?'

'Yes, Father, they are "brothers".'

'Oh! What sort of "brothers"?'

'Their grandmothers were brothers; the same father and mother.'

'I see! By the way, what sort of fellow is he? You should know him better than I do?'

'He's . . . we-e-ll . . . I don't know. I was talking to a few of the older men back there, and well, they didn't say much. When he comes to the Father's place for big Church Holydays he doesn't mix much with us, the other Catechists.'

'I see! On the way back do you think I should make some discreet enquiries from the older men of the village?'

'That would be a good idea, Father. I think it might be necessary.'

'You think it might be necessary? Look! Just tell me what you know.'

'I don't know anything, Father, but there's a lot of gossip. You can't always go on gossip, but on your way back, make enquiries and draw your own conclusions.'

'Thanks, Kaluapuna, I'll do that.'

I had already drawn one, about the spearhead and momolo-leaf, and it relieved my mind of a heavy burden.

Lalompita, the big man of Viosapuna, had all his people lined up to welcome me and escort me to the rest-house. This was piled high with all sorts of food: tomatoes, Chinese cabbages, shallots, corn, bananas and various other vegetables and fruits.

After a wash and a meal I was sitting on the open veranda easing my bones. Four men gathered in the middle of the village. They conversed for a while and looked occasionally in my direction. Lalompita freed himself from the group and moved over towards me. It was the only time I felt suspicious and thought I heard the Butu singing its war-cry beside me. Lalompita stood a few paces in front of me and asked me without ceremony if I had a gun.

'Oh, a gun?' I said. 'Come in here a minute.'

I was very relieved when he walked in casually.

'Yes.' I said. 'I have a gun. In fact I have six of them, but I have left them all at home.'

'That's a pity,' he said. 'We thought you might have a gun with you and would shoot the wild-boar that's raiding our gardens at night. But didn't the Father bring any gun at all?'

I pointed to my Butu and he laughed.

'The white man never goes without his gun,' he said.

'Quite right, and this is the first time I ever moved out without one too and I'll tell you why . . .' and I told him the story of the spearhead and momolo, and that I did not bring a gun in case the people were hostile and might interpret it as a provocation, even though it were only for pigs.

Lalompita was quite angry and said: 'That was the meanest trick I've heard of. After all you are only a newcomer. Whoever sent it to you, you may rest assured that it was not a Mamusi.'

I believed him. It was not a Mamusi. It was a Mengen; and I entertained some very unkind thoughts about my Catechist.

And I thought too, how easy it sometimes is amongst strange people to make a mountain out of a mole-hill, to build up imaginary fears and see an enemy or the devil in every crooked creeper or snake, especially if one is scared or hysterically inclined. I am glad that I am neither; yet this can be rather a disadvantage, because by being too sober and unimaginative one can miss the stirring poetry and romance of events.

I spent a few weeks now going from village to village in the Mamusi, treating the sick, meeting the people and carrying on with my survey. Then I headed back home and spent a week-end at the village from which the catechist had run away. I sent Kaluapuna off with some tobacco. He was to get talking with the elders and find out all he could about the catechist. He came back later accompanied by three men. We sat and smoked and talked on various things for a while and then introduced the question of the run-away.

'He was a good man,' said old Novola. 'He did a lot for our children. He taught them in school and used to give good talks on Sunday. But, O sorrow, he was like that!'

No clarification was necessary because we all knew what 'like that' meant.

'He was like that, then?' I asked.

'Yes, Father, he was like that.'

'And then?'

'We just think he found things becoming too hot for him in the village so he ran away. We did not know he was going. He left by night.'

Then I was going to say: 'And he sent me a spearhead as coming from you so that I would not come in here and learn about him,' but instead I asked: 'And now?'

'We would like the Father to send us another in his place, if you are agreeable to it.'

'Are you sure,' I asked, 'that it is not too hot on the heels of the other one? I am sorry for what he did and disapprove of it as much as you do.'

There was one old man there with a weary face and two soft brown eyes. He had not added anything to the conversation beyond an occasional nod. He sat on his haunches and doodled on the ground with his finger. He now turned to me and said: 'I should not worry, Father. He is a man. That is the way with all men. To fall. That is our nature.'

I thought I had never heard a more beautiful reply. Any

further remark would have been out of place. I could only silently admire the way the words came from him with that easy and generous tolerance which comes to us only with age and a deep human sympathy. And I remembered that the same answer had been given two thousand years ago by Somebody he never knew. And He, too, was doodling on the sand.

❊

The Mamusi country is rough, but not in the ordinary sense of the word. It is, in many ways, difficult to describe and almost impossible for any person unacquainted with similar country to visualise it. To say there are mountains there is as inadequate as to say there is water in the sea. It consists of mountains only; peaks, razorbacked ridges and gorges packed side by side and going apparently in all directions.

There are no valleys properly so called. Sometimes I had the illusion that there were when I saw what appeared to be an open stretch of country between mountain ranges, but when I came to these apparent valleys I found they were, in reality, a series of lower peaks and ridges just as rugged as the bigger ones and often more difficult to traverse.

Fast-flowing, tormented little mountain-streams babbled along on rocky beds at the base of the mountains, combining and splitting as they rush on to form a larger stream.

There were waterfalls too. I have seen them drop clean a few hundred feet into the Melkoi River, one more glorious than the next, with scarcely half a mile between them. Some like Kiwa, on the steep sides of Nakanai, are not waterfalls. They just lack those few extra degrees of inclination to give them a clean drop. Instead, they rush down a thousand feet, one white, mad, swirling streak on the mountainside, pitching, kicking and tossing with the sun making rainbows in the spray, a river gone crazy with all the fire and the fury of a hell behind it.

There are many waterfalls that only a few eyes have seen and many that none have seen. They are hidden in the deep and inaccessible clefts in the mountains, but I could hear their solemn thundering and watch their white veil of spray rise up above the tree-tops.

And I would say: some day when I am not too tired I will go and see those falls that no man has ever seen. I'll watch that mighty black and white sinuous column of water pour into dark cavernous pools and see the giant ferns, the blood-red flowers and the mosses dripping foam. But there is a loneliness about them all, a wearying feeling of dereliction and solitude, the sadness of a joy incomplete that galls and pains till you say: Here is the glory of God.

The mountains are mainly limestone rocks with a thin covering of soil in most places, though I have often walked for miles with nothing under my boots but bare, jagged rock and tree-roots. Towering trees grow straight up from the rock-bed without a thimbleful of soil about them. They live on rain and sun. They send out high surface roots sometimes fifty yards from the trunk. Hundreds of trees in a small area can form the most intricate rootpatterns. They crawl over and fasten on to one another, forming narrow deep holes full of dark brown water and rotting leaves. The hard slippery bark of the roots makes progress a difficult and dangerous business, for that is the road, the track, the path or whatever one wishes to call it, and it has to be done on foot, for neither horse nor mechanical invention is of any use in here. Sometimes that track even defies footwork and one goes down on all fours; if all the patches I covered on all fours were totted up they would come to many a mile.

It is not always the height to which one must ascend that is the hard element in climbing, but rather the steepness of the gradient and the nature of the ground underfoot. In other parts of the parish I have sometimes gone up a thousand feet in a day's march, and so gradual was the gradient that I scarcely knew at any moment whether I was going up or down. Also I have often found the going easier at five thousand feet than at one thousand.

It is possible that some engineering genius will build a road through the Mamusi but he will not take the track we follow, because the villagers, living as they do among the mountains and climbing daily to their gardens, have little interest in finding the easiest path; they just hit out for their destination and take the country as it comes. Detours are only for sissies and the Mamusis breed no such animal.

There are no flats. One is always going either up or down on gradients that vary from one in ten to three in one, climb one foot to advance ten feet on the horizontal or climb three to advance one.

Two villages, Paka and Bili are about four miles apart as the cockatoo flies. The track leading out of Paka first drops and then rises so that at the end of the first horizontal mile it is about two thousand five hundred feet above the village. The next mile is a cat-walk along a razorback. In the third mile the track drops two thousand feet to the Gaute River and in the last mile goes up another two thousand, so that in those four miles one has descended three thousand feet and climbed five thousand. The journey of four miles takes four and a half hours. It is enough for the day.

In many places the side of the mountain may be almost perpendicular and I could get along only by gripping saplings and stumps and pulling myself up with my face a few inches from the mountain. Sometimes the track follows the rib of something that seems a cross between a parapet and a flying arch. Look left, right or behind and there is a drop of perhaps a thousand feet. There is a constant danger of falling, though a person could not fall far before being stopped by a tree, for they grow right up the mountain-side in the most precarious positions and at the most daring angles.

If a portion of the track is unusually steep and bare one must keep about thirty feet between each person. This is done so that, should anyone fall, he will not start a human avalanche but have a fair chance of cracking his neck in solitary comfort.

Niowa . . . Comforter
of the Afflicted

VIOSAPUNA (ALSO known as Mamus) is a tiny village of only fifty people, and the smallest of the whole Mamusi. Yet it enjoys a local reputation far beyond its size. Two hundred yards away and on the road to Miresi is a hill known as Mamus. This hill has given its name to the village and by extension to the whole hinterland of some five hundred square miles, the tribal grounds of some three thousand people. In the olden days it must have enjoyed some notoriety because travellers from the coast were always presumed to be going to Mamus, hence the extension of the name.

I sent the first available catechist to Viosapuna, Gerard To Minus, a Tolai native, and his wife Ia Girada. They spent three years there and did excellent work. The little bush-church at the upper end of the village served Viosapuna and three neighbouring villages. There were, of course, except in danger of death, no Baptisms.

But the people of Viosapuna had, like so many others, a little pagan temple of their own at the other end of the village and both temples carried on in perfect harmony. This temple was known as the Niowa. I had never shown any interest in this Niowa; it was just a thing a person pretended not to see.

It was my custom in a village to walk around with the

headman and have a look at the houses, miserable shabby little structures of grass, saplings and bark, and to suggest a few small improvements within the scope of the people. We passed that Niowa several times and I should have loved to have gone inside, except that such a procedure would have been very impolite and possibly quite embarrassing to both of us.

It could also bring on an unwelcome crisis. What would happen if worse than pagan rites were going on inside there? Lalompita would ask me if such were all right, and if I said, 'No,' he might say: 'Well, we like them and if it comes to a choice between them and your religion, we'll stick to our own.' I find it better to let these things alone for a long time, until the people themselves understand Christianity, and usually then I do not have to condemn them because the people themselves will quietly have got rid of them. I never considered it my duty to challenge idols to single combat with my Butu. Sound Christian doctrine and the Grace of God do a better job than a legion of fiery Butus.

The people will of course still cling to a few superstitions, but why worry unduly about that? Should we exclude them from the Kingdom of Heaven because they believe that a stone placed in a certain position will have a good effect on their gardens? If so, what should be done with those of the Kingdom who believe that No. 13 brings bad luck? Have a peep, in your spare time, inside the planes of international airlines and see if you will find No. 13 on any seat. In the few I took particular notice of I found only 12, 12a, 14 or just 12, 14. It seems that many children of the Kingdom will not sit on No. 13, no doubt in case they'd arrive in the Kingdom too soon, which, if we are to judge by all the nice things they say about it, seems to portray a rather contradictory state of religious conviction.

During my second last visit to Viosapuna, Lalompita led me round the village according to custom. In front of the Niowa he said: 'That's the Niowa there. That's the Sacred House of our ancestors.'

'Is that what it is?'

'Yes. Hasn't the Father seen it yet?'

He knew well I had not seen it. He knew everything I had and had not seen, or had or had not done in that village, because everything connected with me is the subject of conversation for months after each visit. It is told and retold, each one adding a fresh detail which he has observed.

I knew that his question was only his manner of telling me that I was now being invited to enter the Niowa if I wished to go.

The Niowa is a very small hut, fifteen feet by nine by eight feet high. The hut itself is not easily seen from the outside because it is surrounded by momolo shrubs. These are planted all around it in three rows about eighteen inches apart and they reach higher than the hut.

The momolo is a shrub that grows long, red-and-yellow, fleshy, sword-like leaves directly from its stem. These are the sacred shrubs and their history is longer than Lalompita could relate or than I could follow. It seems they had many previous habitats but a long-long-long time ago they were brought to Viosapuna and found a final resting place there.

Now, the Mamusi people, like so many others, are divided into two main clans or sects according to the two chief totems, usually known as the Big Totem and the Little Totem. Each village must have representatives of each Totem.

The building of the Niowa, so Lalompita told me, must be a joint work of the members of the two totems, each one having its traditionally defined work to do. Under no circumstances may one totem do the work of the other. Building the Niowa, or Sacred House, is the only work in which everyone co-operates unhesitatingly, because on it depends the prosperity of the village.

The whole ceremony of building, blessing and opening the Niowa was related to me by Lalompita and I give it here as I took it down from him, with a few remarks to help clarify it.

The Niowa is built by driving piles into the ground. These serve as a support for the roof, and the walls will be made by laying tree-bark between the piles. When the frame is erected and the last rafter in position all the workers assemble at one spot and go through a ceremonial washing of the hands 'lest the juices of the timbers affect their stomachs'. This washing is followed by a small ceremonial meal.

The women collect the leaves to make the thatch for the roof which must consist of the leaves of the Lau or pandanus tree. At the same time the men collect jungle-rope and bind the rafters once more before putting the thatch on. When the thatching is finished, another ceremonial meal follows.

The side-walls and gables are now closed with bark and two doors are placed opposite each other in the end-walls.

Inside the house two lines of posts about four feet high are placed three feet from the sidewalls, each totem placing its own line. A shelf of Tumulata (rattan) is then woven between these posts and the sidewalls.

A long length of Oal (a very straight tree) is fixed in the middle of the house and a section of the bark is cut away. The exposed timber is smoothed off with the rough leaves of the Tramani tree. A kalipo (lizard) is drawn on the smooth new surface and when that is done, each one may add any private symbols suggested to him by his own genius. Then follows a third ceremonial meal.

The Niowa is next blessed by fire, one fire being lighted at each door and allowed to burn itself out. The fourth ceremonial meal follows.

The Niowa is now complete but for the planting of the Momolo shrubs and though this action takes no more than two minutes it has to be preceded by a most elaborate set of preparations featuring mainly a feast and a dance.

The dancing dress or Urasen takes about four months to be prepared. There are usually twelve Urasen, each one prepared by a group of men. The rudimentary form of each Urasen is constructed in the Niowa and later taken secretly and at night (so that the women may not see it) to a special hut concealed from the women in the jungle. This jungle hut is never left unoccupied and if a woman accidentally approaches it the guardians will sing and shout so that she will know there are men about and go off.

The dancing dress of Urasen is made in two parts, the head-dress which rests on the collar-bone, and the body-dress which hangs from the neck and shoulders. No part of the wearer's body may be visible through the Urasen.

A collar, round and loose and made of Tumulata, in such a manner that it can be slipped on over the head and which rests on the shoulders, is the main support of the body-dress, which is a loose affair, and consists of pandanus leaves cut in thin strips and in sufficient quantity that no movement of the dancer can reveal any part of his body, not even his feet. This body-dress can be assembled in a few days. Most of the time is spent on the head-dress. This is designed like a tiara-cum-mask and tapers to a point at the top. It is crowned with the yellow crest of the white cockatoo. The foundation of this head-dress is a light wicker-work frame covered with very thin bark which has previously been well dried. This bark is painted in grotesque and gargantuan caricature of the human face, in the three main colours—black, white and red. These colours are home-made, extracted from the sap of different trees. They are applied in the most lawless manner.

A body-dress may weigh thirty pounds but a head-dress seldom exceeds one or two, though it is of very ample dimensions.

No man has a right to fix the day for the feast and dance, at least in theory. All he can do is to say: On such a day the Urasen will come. The Urasen is supposed to be beyond human control since it embodies the spirits of the dead. Hence the time of their arrival is their own business and all the mortals can do is to hand on the news.

The inauguration of the Niowa is a tremendously important event for all the people. For a few weeks previously some of the men are busy making traps for wild pigs, wallabies, cassowaries, possums and birds, while others make fish-traps and dam the rivers. Towards the appointed day, these traps are visited and the catch collected. All domestic pigs of any worthy size are rounded up and killed. The women are busy bringing load after load of food from the gardens: taros, sweet potatoes, yams, tapioca, bananas, pineapples and other foodstuffs. The neighbours are called in and then all is ready to begin the ceremony.

The dancers are dressed in the hut in the jungle. They have clothed themselves in the Urasen and have now lost their mortality and identity. They are no longer men from the village but spirits from the other world. They are not in the Urasen; they are the Urasen.

The sun is straight on top, and friends and relatives are chatting happily all over the village. A few dozen women holding momolo leaves form two lines in the village square and facing each other they bob and shuffle backwards and forwards, conducted by an elderly woman. There is a beating of drums in the jungle, the women disperse to their huts and the square is emptied.

One lone dancer appears dressed in Urasen but carrying a spear. His duty is to clear the village square of all females. He is free to kill any woman he sees (and occasionally does so) and he cannot be brought to order because he has no identity, he is not a man but a returned spirit. There is a hush as he enters, a whirling mass of greenery and colour. He jogs and weaves his way around the village a few times, making passes with his spear at a few points. He peers behind a stack of food or behind a big log and jabs with his spear. His step is short, high and jerky and all the rattlers on his legs and arms jingle and clack. He lunges forward, pirouettes, hops backwards and weaves crabwise; and as his dress is symmetrical nobody knows after a while which way he is facing. At last, when he is satisfied that everything is in order for the arrival of the Urasen he jerks and bobs his way out of the village to take his place among the other dancers. The women may now appear in public again.

Excited boys come running out of the jungle, pushing, falling and scrambling ahead with the news: 'The Urasen is coming! It is nearby already. It is almost right here! Listen, you can hear the drummers.'

Heads peer out of huts and around corners and all turn their faces to the noise of the drums. The dogs begin to howl, but an older one that has seen this before takes the opportunity to sneak over to a leg of pork on a banana leaf. He is booted and pelted from all sides and goes off whimpering.

A dozen drummers appear through the trees, singing and beating their hour-glass drums with open palms. A few long feathers ornament their hair and their faces are splashed with last minute daubs of red and white. There has been no intention of concealing their identity. They are now entering the village and the Urasen is just breaking through the jungle about forty yards behind, flanked by the important men of the village bearing ceremonial spears. The Urasen advances in a slow colourful mass, bobbing and bowing from side to side.

A posse of men armed with spears jumps, shouts and kicks up a fuss in the village square and charges about at full speed in a mock attack on the Urasen. The men of the posse halt abruptly a spear's throw from the advancing Urasen and dig their heels in the soft ground, hurrahing and brandishing their spears before the oncoming Urasen. The Urasen ignores the warriors and advances on them. These now retreat, confer hurriedly for a moment and charge again in the same manner. The Urasen keeps on inexorably. Again the warriors retreat, this time right into the village, hold an excited council and make one last desperate charge on the Urasen and brandish their spears right up to their faces, but the Urasen ignores them completely and advances on the village with the warriors now retreating before them. Then the posse breaks ranks and flees in disorder. . . . They have done their duty; they have shown to all that the Urasen is not afraid of the fiercest attack of humans. Why should they be? Are they not the spirits of the dead?

The Urasen now occupies the village square. The dancers circle round it three times in formation and then break up, each member of the Urasen performing a solo on his own to the rhythm of the drums and the music and song of his fans.

You may see a young woman break from the crowds and trail a dancer. Her dancing step is a variation on the theme of slipping feet on greasy slope. She has a raw taro in her hand.

She bites it and spits the pieces at a dancer's feet. 'Why, O Maiden?' 'I recognise by his gait,' she says, 'that he is the spirit of my dead lover.'

An old woman shrieks and screams and her voice trails away in lonely sobs: 'Oo-ee-oo-eeee-o!' You ask: 'What is the matter, O Woman?' She says: 'The last time we had a feast my man was here. Now he is dead. Oo-ee-oo-eeee-o! Today he has come back to me. I see him among the dancers' . . . and the tears flow down her face.

The Urasen dances on, maybe for an hour, and then goes back the way it came, in formation and bowing its appreciation to the mortals.

The rest of the day is now given over to feasting and dancing. Young men in modified Urasen perform solos for the benefit of the guests. It may be a new step or perhaps a dance which imitates a fish on a hook, a cassowary or a pig in a trap or any other event which could amuse or edify.

That night, the dancers' Urasen is brought in great secrecy to the Niowa. The men of the Big Totem place their masks on the shelf prepared for them and the men of the Little Totem follow suit.

The planting of the sacred momolo shrubs now follows. They must be planted by the members of the two totems, secretly, quietly, silently, quickly and simultaneously. Any person who fails in his duty here will die within a month and there is no sorcery that can cure him.

When the shrubs are planted (the women are told next day that the spirits planted them) all the men congregate inside the hut and the Sacred Stones, the Mao-pako, are placed at the foot of the Oal post with the lizard's image.

The Mao-pako are bigger than goose-eggs and much the same shape. They bear several marks and some are sculptured in an excellent resemblance of a man's head and features. The stones are next placed on the shelves beside the dancing masks, and in such a manner that they are always exposed, for should they become covered or concealed the gardens will yield a poor return.

The main reason for all this ceremony, Lalompita assured me, was to placate the spirits and so ensure the prosperity of the village. Unlike some of their neighbours, the hunters, fishermen and gardeners of Viosapuna are always successful.

Now, if the crops should fail on a rare occasion, another and minor ceremony is needed, not to influence the gardens directly but to remind the spirits politely that while the villagers have done their duty it might seem that the spirits have been unusually slow.

A woman collects a basket of small taros, wraps them in taro-leaves and bakes them, or more correctly, to use Lalompita's phrase: she does not really bake them, she only fools them with the fire.

The keeper of the Niowa then strings them like a necklace around the Niowa. He retains a small one and this he offers to each man present, who must refuse it with the words: I am full. This scapegoat taro is then placed by itself in a basket and hung in the Niowa till it rots. All food has to be kept well away from it.

Women are debarred from the Niowa. Men and boys have free access. Women beyond child-bearing age may come as far as the door and look inside. Somebody must always be present in the Niowa, otherwise the wild pigs and the parrots will ruin the gardens.

A small wrinkled old man named Kivolo was the Keeper of the Niowa . . . a sort of Sacristan. He brought the Taro-stones (Mao-pako) out in the open for me to photograph them. He handled them and spoke to them as to old friends, and laid them gently on the ground, dusting and patting them as he communed with them in murmurs. He gave me each one's name and traced its history.

'Now this one,' he said, 'popping his eyes wide open, comes from a-l-o-n-g time ago.'

But as he does not understand numbers and I am no expert at interpreting eye-popping, I did not know whether the stone was a hundred or a thousand years old.

As we left Kivolo, Lalompita said: 'Old Kivolo is worried. He is afraid that the Niowa will die with him.'

A later visit to Viosapuna was made on the heels of an epidemic. Pneumonic influenza flowed along the beach, infecting three villages a day, and spread into the mountains. Most of the Mengens on the coast were affected too, but with no damage because we had the necessary drugs. The Mamusi lost about eight per cent of its population. Like all others, they attributed the disaster to the evil spirits, who had possessed the people and their villages. The only solution was to leave the villages and settle down elsewhere.

Serunguna was deserted, the little huts keeled over and grass grew on the village square. Lakalona had crumbled, Viosapuna was derelict, as was Nunopu and many others. The people were on the move, men, women, babies and the sick, all refugees from the anger of the hidden spirits. The unseen hand had struck the hive and the terrified occupants were dispersed, seeking a place in the vast jungle where they might hide from the evil spirits. And no sooner have they built a new village than the hand strikes again. This is the saddest and most pathetic sight you can ever see.

. . . And then some happy humorist drops his evening paper and lazily sips a snorter and says: 'Rather a waste of time going out there, isn't it? After all, aren't those people perfectly happy the way they are?'

Should I tell him . . . and would he believe me if I did tell him . . . that the South Sea Islanders live in no paradise? Should I tell him that they are perpetually mentally befogged, spiritually bedevilled, and without any reason are confused, frightened, suspicious, frustrated and lonely? Should I tell him that they live not in Paradise but in Purgatory? I should not, because he would not believe it. He'd just think: that chap has been too long in the sun. He might even vex me to such an extent that I'd imagine I heard my Butu dancing and chanting its war-cry on the wall.

Viosapuna was deserted. All that remained were a few heaps of ashes that marked the places where the houses stood. The Niowa had fallen in, and there was no sign that a Niowa was being built in the new village. Kivolo, the old Keeper, had died in the epidemic.

'I don't think there will be any Niowa here,' said Lalompita, 'the people have no interest in it any more.'

Here was a great change in their way of life, a change I can in no way explain. I was sorry to see the old custom die out. Most probably no one will ever know why they abandoned so easily such an important and central function of their lives. It was as if a whole community of solid church-goers suddenly gave up the practice without a word and carried on unconcernedly.

Was it because they were accustomed to see the white man prosperous without recourse to the Niowa? Was it that the catechist had changed their view in a few years? Would that Niowa still be going strong if I had openly opposed and condemned it? I just don't know.

I have often wondered what way this tribe will finish up. Will they seek to improve their life by adopting the better things from the European, will they continue as they are, almost immune to all outside influence, or will they drift into European settlements in dribs and drabs, lose their identity and vanish as a coherent tribe?

The present indications are that they will drift from the tribal grounds and dissolve. Their life is extremely hard, and unfortunately little can be done at the present moment to relieve it. If they did not know of the outside world they would, of course, continue as before. But now the attraction of that world may appear too strong to be overcome by homesickness for a gruelling and spartan existence in the mountains.

It might seem ironical that a race which has existed from time immemorial at the heart-breaking stone-age level should vanish now when the tools of comparative ease are put in their hands, and yet on such ironies is the history of mankind built.

'Now in Ancient Times' . . .
Lifting the Veil

AFTER THE Mamusi hike I decided to go and see Father Tony Gendusa down at Uvol; we had quite a few interests in common as our parishes bounded each other from the beach to the Nakanai mountains.

I left one night by boat and got to Uvol at five-thirty in the morning just as Father Tony was going to say Mass, for he worked early and late. There was the line of sick to be attended to, a new canoe a-building in the shed, some butterflies to be sent overseas, rosaries made from bush-berries for an American film star (male), a footbridge to be put across the chasm above Ruakana village where Explorer-pirate Dampier on St. Patrick's Day A.D. 1700 'filled two Hogsheads of Water and all the Barrecoes', schools going up and a thousand other items. It was on this occasion that we dug the sand in search of Father Culhane's body, but we never did find it.

'Something for you to read till I come back,' he said, tossing an Aero-Digest my way. 'I've got to go to Maso on a sick call. These fellows never seem to get sick except when a visitor arrives.' (Father Tony was a pilot too, but at present all his flying was done on foot.)

'Take the boat, Tony.'

'What use is that to me? That has to go around the point

The parish—from sea to jungle

178

and will take an hour. I can cut across the neck of land in that much time myself.'

There was no use pointing out that it would spare energy to go by boat. His difficulty seemed to be to find ways of using it up.

He was back in a few hours and in the meantime I tried to memorise the difference between an aileron and a flap. 'Ha-ha!' he greeted me from fifty yards, 'Ha-ha! 'Tis great, great! I found him!'

'Found whom?'

'A Kanaka (south-sea islander) from Missouri!'

'A what?'

'A Kanaka from Missouri, right out from the wild and woolly!' (Kansas speaking.)

Father Tony was American and often used phrases I did not understand. 'I was just coming out of Maso,' he said, 'and I saw these two guys on the track. I guessed I hadn't seen their faces before. I spoke to them in Tokboi. No go. I shot a bar of Lote at them. No reply. Heck, says I, what have I got here? Then a few chaps from Maso came along and found the two lads were from away back in the bush. They were on their way to Rano looking for work and had gone astray. They should have come out up at Meingi.'

'And where are they from?'

'They didn't want to tell at first but I guess they were a little scared in a strange place. They're from a place no one ever heard of ... Ulutu ... way up beyond Matewan. Ho-ho, 'tis great! That should be an interesting place.'

Father Tony was attracted by places in direct proportion to their distance and the difficulty of getting there.

'How about your coming back with me by boat,' I said, 'and then the two of us can strike off together, you see my bush and I see yours, and then we'll find this place Ulutu.'

'Sure. When do we leave? I'm ready.'

... He was always ready to go anywhere or do anything for anybody.

We packed some gear and left for my station where we

Where God grew weary.

packed some more and next day we were on our way to the mountains.

'We'll take it easy,' he said, 'and do it in style this time.'

For Father Tony, taking it easy meant doing not more than twelve hours' walk a day and doing it in style meant that he would allow us to have such luxuries as bed sheets. In a momentary mood of sheer recklessness we packed a gramophone and half a dozen records. This was to be our venture into Anthropology: 'A Study and a Report on the Effect of Different Harmonious Noises on Primitive Man.'

We varied the records: Grand Opera ... bored Primitive Man. Light Opera ... faintly interested P.M. Male Voice Choir ... much appreciated by P.M. Soprano ... shocked P.M., who wondered why white man allowed a woman to make so much noise. Bagpipes ... enthralled P.M. and produced a state of near ecstasy, Primitive Man and Primitive Woman scramble out of primitive house dragging Primitive Child. Clerical resolution passed that a request be made to Church Authorities for permission to use Bagpipes instead of Church Bells on Sundays. Tenor sings 'The Rose of Tralee' which has a sequel.

The last line runs: 'That made me love Mary the Rose of Tralee.' It was sung by John McCormack and he puts great emphasis on the word Mary. Now it so happens that Mary, spelt meri, is the Tokboi word for woman. The emphasis caught the ear of one P.M.

'Oloboi, he's cross with his meri again. What did she do?'

'She stole his liver,' we said.

'Steal, steal! That's all the women ever do. My meri stole my smokes in the garden today. I belted her for it. 'Twas she did it. Nobody else. What did you say that one stole?'

'His liver.'

'Sure a man can't live without that or can he? And what did she do with it?'

'He says she broke it.'

'O sorrow! Indeed he's telling the truth. I believe him. She deserved a whacking. Indeed she did! Can that plate cry twice?'

'I think we can manage it.'
'All right. Wheel-wheel that plate again.'

Aside from our religion, Father Tony and myself differed on most things, as may be expected of Latin and Celt. On one thing, however, we did agree, that the jungle was a hard but fascinating place. It exerted a sort of hidden magnetism on you. It threw down a challenge, you considered, got annoyed and took it up. Sometimes you won, sometimes you lost, but always you learned something new about it or about yourself, and your one rule was 'Never give in', because you would often be sorely tried. When you lost you were annoyed, when you won you were happy, because there were always unexpected difficulties. Each day's walk was in the nature of a fight with something wild, impassive, stupid and unyielding. It never fought back, it just sat foursquare on your track, an obstacle in capitals. Each victory brought the consoling hope that one day you would know how to get along, each defeat was good for your humility. You never beat the jungle unless you abolish it. As long as it exists you have won if you can live in peace with it.

It reminds me of the Catholic Church in that it is a hard place to live in, but a wonderful place to die in; for who wants to look out for the last time over a stiff white sheet and see through a misty eye a mummy-looking nurse in white draw a screen of white and softly pad away on a noiseless floor? Here is the lush green-blue-green of the jungle and the magnified rumble of violent streams billowing up through the mouths of gorges. The thousand-foot faces and escarpments of Nakanai dip down towards the western horizon with rainbows in the hair of its waterfalls. There is a deep and heavy loneliness of soul and body, a loneliness in which it is easy to remember God.

Father Tony and I conversed on many things but hardly a day passed that we did not put such questions as: I wonder is there a track from this village to that one; or, that's forbidding looking territory. I wonder is there anybody living in there?

We were dissatisfied with a mere two or three week tramp over ground we already knew, the jungle was luring us on and at heart we were glad.

The trek we had planned to last three weeks eventually lasted two months and would have lasted three or maybe four if we could have arranged a food-supply. But now, through the loss of a box of food in crossing a stream we were already on short rations to complete our three week trip.

Father Tony decided that when we got further into the No. 2 Mamusi he would leave me on my own for a few days while he returned to his Mission station for more supplies. He would meet me at Matewan on his return and from there we would set out to find Ulutu, which we believed to lie further up the Melkoi river. At Ulutu we could decide on the rest of the journey. Accordingly at five o'clock one wet morning he poked me in the sleepy ribs and said: 'See you later. I'm off. Wait for me at Matewan. As MacArthur said: We shall return'; and he vanished in the fog and the rain and the jungle.

I came first to Matewan village overlooking the turbulent Melkoi river, and I was waiting for Father Tony. It was only the seventeenth day of the walk but the food was finished on account of our recent mishap crossing a river. But I was not hungry; I was full of sweet potato and bananas and never again did I want to see them raw or roasted.

I lay on my bunk to help me contemplate heaven, a very solid and earthy affair consisting mainly of sizzling steak, beans, chips, tomatoes, eggs and a glass of beer as bitter as vinegar and so cold that it stuck to my hands.

'Father Tony is now approaching Aulo,' I thought, 'or maybe Olpopo. I can recognise his bright orange T-shirt. He has a ball-chain round his neck and dangling from it are a medal of Our Lady, one small and two large safety-pins and a pocket knife. "When you've got those, you've got everything you need," he says. They are swinging across his chest like windshield wipers as he strides along, his black beard parted by the wind and his hair matted down on his forehead with perspiration. The carriers are strewn out for hours behind him and one is saying: "O Brother mine, this our Father is likened unto what? He walks not as a man. No. He bounds along like the bush-wallaby. He sits for a flicker and Pst! he has gone! O sorrow!"'

A villager brought me some bananas (Ugh!) which reminded me that I was still at Matewan and that Father Tony, for all I knew, might be still at Uvol.

At about five o'clock two chestnut-skinned men came pounding up the track. Their skins were glistening and wet. They had had a long walk. 'The Father is here,' they said. 'He is already at Kuru ...' about a mile away.

In that case either he had not gone to Uvol at all but sent someone to collect the food or else he had packed seven long days' walk into four.

I met him half a mile down the track. He had a baseball cap on his head and he had said that he would collect that at Uvol.

"Hiyah," he shouted at fifty yards, 'find everything O.K.?'

To encourage him, I sat on a tree-stump.

'Let's go,' he said. 'What are we waiting for?'

'Hold it! Gently now! Is there cargo? There's nothing at Matewan but a kettle of water.'

'It's coming right along,' he said.

He pulled off his T-shirt and mopped himself with it ... 'Where's that kid? He has my towel, I'll bet ...'

A young lad of sixteen came waddling along in a hurry like the last tired duckling in a line, with the towel. He looked at me and then at Father Tony who was busy towelling himself, and he shook his head and smiled. Father Tony's feats of walking were a by-word.

'You lost no time, Tony,' I said.

'You remember when I left you?' he said. 'O.K. I kept right on till seven that night. (Fourteen hours' walk, I noted.) Next morning I left again at five. Heck, says I, I'll make Uvol. I got in there at one next morning. (Twenty hours' walking out of twenty-four!) You should have seen how surprised everyone was when I woke them up. But we lost the track a little at night ... we kept on finding and losing it ... it's difficult to find your way in the bush with a lamp . . . but there was a moon and I knew that if I kept south by the moon I should hit the beach somewhere. We didn't do too badly after all, but we missed the ford at the back of Uvol and where we struck the river it was wide and deep and running a little, so we floated my few boxes across with the lamp atop and swam behind. There was a current at the other side but we managed to grasp some jungle-rope on the bank and haul ourselves out. No loss. The boxes stood up well and didn't let in a drop. When we got across, I recognized the place. Ha-haaa! about a hundred yards above the crocodile pool. Oh! I'll bet that croc won't stop kicking his behind when he heard it! The ass was probably down the rivermouth that night and got nothing! Serves him right. A few of the boys worked all night packing the stuff but I went to bed. I left next morning at eight, that's yesterday morning and here we are now. Only two days to come back.'

Out of eighty-four consecutive hours, he had been scrambling through the mountains and rivers for fifty-four, and he was now rearing to be off to find Ulutu!

Back at Matewan, he said, 'Ulutu is around here somewhere and we've got to find it.' Looking at a map, he said, 'We've covered all that section there to the east, also the northeast and the south. I know everything west of here to Gasmata already so the place must be up in that block between northeast and northwest . . . but the beggars here won't help much for it will mean a day's carrying for them. Look, that is as far north as anyone has gone on the Melkoi and I've always noticed that if you want to find the people you must find the rivers. Follow them right up to their sources and you'll find that the people have done the same thing ahead of you.'

This was a sound observation and I used it later in a different area to unearth a few other obscure places.

'Coming in to Matewan the other day, Tony, I think I saw what looked to be a clearing up the river. I'm not sure, of course . . .'

'How far up?'

'Maybe three miles, maybe five. I just don't know.'

'That's Ulutu,' said Tony, 'and if it isn't it's some other equally attractive place. There is nobody known in this locality that could have gardens there. Wait . . . I'll be back in a minute . . .' and he was.

'Ha-ha! 'Tis great, great! That's Ulutu alright. I went down to the village and told those beggars I knew all about it. They fell for it. Four have now gone off with bush-knives to open a track. They say it is a hard road and boy, if the Mamusis say 'tis hard you can be prepared for anything.'

The following note is from my diary: May 4th. 1951. 18th day. Ulutu. Population seen: 55. Elevation 2,500. Time from Matewan 6 hours. Estimated distance: not four miles. Average estimated speed 1,000 yards an hour.

It may be a stretch on the credulity to consider covering a little over half a mile an hour as hard work, yet this was without question one of the most gruelling days we ever had.

The Matewan boys had cut less than half a mile of track. It led down a sharp mountain side to the river. The track was a green tunnel less than five feet high. We had to stoop forward and try to keep our balance at the same time. We didn't.

The track finished and we were faced with a long steep drop through close-packed scrub and jungle-creeper. We pushed the scrub aside with our hands only to find as we advanced that the surface which had appeared solid was a growth of creeper over holes. Our legs became so entangled when we fell into a hole that we could extricate each other only by hacking away the creepers and dragging ourselves out. We were cut and bruised before we got to the Melkoi River, but our difficulties had only begun.

The Melkoi river ran deep and fast and about thirty yards wide. It spilled over rounded boulders and rushed out through narrow channels, a black oily-looking living thing, and then rumbled along through white foamy eddies. It was the bottom of a gorge, with the mountains rising sheer on each side. A margin of loose boulders and shingle sometimes lay between the river and the mountains. In flood time this would be covered too: today, however, it was the road.

At times these boulders were piled as high as a house and we had to pull and squeeze ourselves up over them. More often they were strewn out loosely and precariously balanced on an edge or a point. They made a most maddening form of torture. When you stand on one it wobbles and tosses you among the others where you knock your head or elbow or where your foot plunges down between two and comes back without the skin on the ankle.

We kicked off our boots and tried the track with rubber-soled canvas shoes, but a recent shower had made the round, bald rocks so slippery that it was near suicide to move. Then we tried going barefoot but the stones were too hot for our feet. Nothing for it but to make the best progress possible with our boots.

High rocks jutting out over the river forced us to cross it several times. The river bed was boulder-covered and the water rushing fast. We were lucky to have got through without having our brains bashed out.

Ulutu consisted of a dozen huts on a ledge about three hundred feet above the river. There was one hut larger than the others and this was given to us for the night. It was quite comfortable and roomy but was infested with rats and all sorts of lice and vermin. As no one could speak Tokboi the Matewan boys had to interpret.

The village site was extremely fouled. There were all sorts of sores on the people, yaws and tropical ulcers by the hundred. 'Tomorrow,' said Tony, 'is going to be a hard day on the two quacks.'

That afternoon we strolled around the village trying to estimate the number we would have for treatment next day. They were a pitiable group, and we had wrongly put the population at about thirty.

Tony saw the implications. 'How can we go on up the river tomorrow?' he asked. 'There isn't a man here fit to hoist a box. We'd better hold on to those lads from Matewan, they can take us back to Tauve and the Tauve people can take us to Sona.'

Lots of things went wrong next day. After we had said Mass at dawn, the Matewan boys wanted to move off with as much gear as possible because when they got to Tauve they still had to go back to Matewan for the night. Consequently we split up our boxes and retained only those we needed for medicine and two more to act as a table. The carriers had left by seven.

At nine o'clock we had sterilized our equipment and lined up an assortment of stuff for treating sores and infections. Only a few people had arrived so we went off to round them all up. Instead of the estimated twenty we found we had fifty-five all in dire need of care.

A tropical ulcer is a vicious thing. It starts from a wound in the skin. Infection follows and bores in towards the bone. Later, a patch about the size of a wrist-watch swells around the infection and in due course falls out leaving a round open wound. This now spreads and grows from the edges and in a short time may be the size of a saucer or a dinner plate. The worst cases we saw were a woman who had an ulcer which stretched from her hip-bone to her knee and a man who had one which almost covered his back. Many of these bigger ones caused us considerable discomfort even at twenty feet.

Yaws are no less unpleasant. They usually manifest themselves first around the mouth and other orifices where they erupt in the form of a large scabby-looking running sore. Later they break out all over the body, tiny little volcanoes that erupt and grow. A large one on the head could at first lead you to believe that the skull had been broken and the brain was protruding.

When we had collected all the sick, we knew that we had not a hope of getting through with the work in time to leave for Sona. We would have to stay overnight ... and all our supplies had gone ahead! The carriers had had too much of a start to think of calling them back.

The two extra boxes we had retained as a table contained mainly cooking utensils, soap, carriers' tobacco, two oilskins, some linen to be washed, a small tin of bully-beef, tea, a tin of condensed milk and a lot of inedible stuff. Had they been properly packed there would have been no food at all in them. Thank God people can make mistakes.

We worked all day without a meal because we had no meal to eat. Towards sundown we had finished the job. The place was littered with empty medicine jars, sterile-water phials, plaster spools for the children to play with, swabs, bandage wrappers, cotton-wool and forty-eight penicillin bottles.

The villagers gave us some vegetables and we made tea but spared our bully beef for next morning to give us a kick for the road.

We slept in our clothes, each of us lying on two boxes fifteen inches wide in order to keep clear of all the things that crawled along the floor. But we had no protection against the rats. We managed to protect our feet but we had no shoes for our ears.

Next morning we left Ulutu at five minutes to seven and got in to Sona at twenty minutes past six that evening with barely enough strength and light of day to climb the last hill up from the Kiwa River, which we had crossed only by the help of our boys who hauled us over on a jungle-rope.

We ate a full meal at seven and another full meal at ten that night.

Of the fifty-five people we treated at Ulutu, fifty-two were healed within a week and three died. Unfortunately there was little we could have done for those three as gangrene had already set in when we found them.

How do people manage to survive under conditions such as Ulutu had? We found them, I think, in the last silent and heroic struggle. The woman whom I have mentioned earlier was a case in point. In any other place she would have been long in hospital. We saw her coming from her garden aided by a stick. She had worked all day in the garden and was now coming home with a load of food on her head. She carried a small hungry child on her hip. He too, was covered with yaws. We had seen her fall once and she rested for a few minutes in that position to gain strength and then slowly rose and crawled along. Her life depended on the work she could do; her baby's life depended on what nourishment only she could give him. The day she could work no more, she died, for there was no one to help her; she was only one of many, and when she died the baby followed soon after.

'You see now,' said Tony, 'what a native means when he says: There used to be a village there long ago: I heard my father speak about it.'

We yarned far into the night building fairy-castles with a few thousand pounds we did not have, cleaning out all disease and sickness from the neighbourhood and making thousands of people happy. We wondered why we had not got the money and decided it was because our own civilized tribesmen had to pay out millions to make bombs and bombers to inflict suffering, disease and death on other civilized tribes. In a bitter moment we wished them all the best of luck. Never before did we realise that Christianity and civilization could be so different, much less so hostile to each other.

If all civilized tribes, we thought, could only love their neighbours for just six months, and turn their genius into helpful channels, how happy could they make the whole world.

We made a few exceptions, one of them Sir Alexander Fleming who discovered penicillin. We owed a lot to him and so did the people here. Yesterday we saw fifty corpses shuffling in agonising pain. In two or three days from now there will not be a sore upon them. We will be thanked for the happy change, but the miracle is his. And a miracle it surely is, more noticeable among primitive people than among others. We treated some people so covered with yaws that we had difficulty in finding enough healthy skin on their arms or buttocks to take a hypodermic needle, yet not one in a hundred will need a second injection in a few days' time. The disease vanishes right before your eyes. Apart from the wonderful help from the drug these people must have the most extraordinary natural healing powers, powers which unfortunately decrease according as they adopt European habits or avail themselves of his medicine.

We had a personal interest in a place like Ulutu, and not

particularly from a desire to be the first to get there. In that respect the people had beaten us by a few thousand years and by a road that was harder, though now unknown and even beyond conjecture. At any rate, it is easy to be the first white man to go some place in New Guinea; all he need do is climb a high coconut-palm in Moresby or Rabaul. But we wished particularly to be able to compare a completely uncontacted village with those under our care. The comparison gave us hope and courage, and confidence in the progressive ability of the native.

It also gave us the final word against the romantic-minded, those people who still believe in the Happy Life of the Noble Savage, an idea that is shared by brown and white alike. Down on the beach there are even a few native smart-alecs who imitate the European in every possible manner but who, at the same time, spread the insidious nonsense to the younger set that the European has destroyed their happy golden home of the good old days, and that they should try to re-establish it before it is too late. What their motives are I cannot imagine; possibly they too are pressed by the too-common desire of always glamorising the past and the unknown.

If a man from Ulutu should read these lines in a few hundred years from now, when Ulutu may have skyscrapers, or even superhighways that give the tourist the best possible view of its tumbling waterfalls and its awesome mountain scenery, he may feel that I have done his people less than justice. Neither Tony nor I will be around to argue with him, but if his vanity is piqued he can remember that his origins were no more lowly than those of the rest of civilisation. If he says that we exploited the ignorance of his people I will call his ancestors from the grave and line them up as they lined up in the village to see us go away that morning. They need not speak, because they did not speak to us then; but I will show him one of the most beautiful sights in the world: 'Thank you' written in the eyes of men.

If he wishes to be contrary or sophisticated and says that his ancestors exploited our credulity I'll say: 'Where there is gratitude there is no exploitation. The same expression of gratitude should be written in our eyes because we are priests of the Catholic Church that has been stumbling into Ulutus for 2,000 years. We were grateful that your ancestors gave us the opportunity to carry on the great traditions of our own.'

And when I have relieved myself of those lofty sentiments for the gallery I will quietly take him aside and say: 'Thanks, chum. Thanks, especially to the old folk, for the proud and sinful satisfaction they gave me when I laid an early hand on them. You are descended from a line of heroes, from the Great Men of Yore.'

The Diary

IF HE picks the dry season for travel in the jungle a man will rarely be trapped by flooded rivers, and if such a thing should happen it will not last for more than a day or two. Heavy rains high up in the mountains can cause a torrent lower down, even though the place is basking in sunshine, but as the rivers run fast they usually empty themselves in a day or two unless fresh rains fall.

I was going down to Mao village from Bili through Salumpuna, travelling, against my better judgment, alongside the Loi river because it was running a fair flood and we had to wade it several times. There was little risk to life but a grave risk to my baggage.

There are certain places where a river can be crossed. The people know them and it is a good thing to follow their advice. Half a mile from Mao we crossed the Loi for the last time through a wide and deep pool with a sandy river-bottom. The extra width had reduced the current. Nearly half way across, the water was already up to the carriers' armpits. Then they placed the boxes on their heads and faced the deeper centre. Here the water rose to their heads. Then they held the boxes over the water with their hands while they walked along completely submerged. As they neared the other bank they rose out of the water.

Below the pool the river ran only a few feet deep over a sloping bed of large gravel, a death-trap to the newcomer. No sooner does he step on those round loose stones than they sink beneath his weight and bring an avalanche of stones on top of his feet from above, or else roll away from under him and he finds himself racing down the river with the speed of a boy on a bannister.

Bili village is built on the side of a mountain range which falls away sharply to the south to reach the Megigi river flowing east, and to the west where it meets the Loi river flowing south. The Loi and Megigi join at Mao just two thousand feet beneath Bili and three and a half hours' distant. The Mao village is on a few acres of sandy plateau about ten feet above the Megigi which is the larger of the two rivers. Sometimes it floods the village and the people get away by crossing the Loi, or if that is in flood too, by scaling the mountains.

At the dry period the Megigi is about a hundred and fifty feet wide and only knee high. In flood it can swell to three hundred feet wide and fifteen feet deep, filling old pools with gravel and scouring out new ones and rolling heavy boulders along with it. At the point of a little spit of sand a few hundred yards east of the village it is joined by the Loi and the new river, now called the Tolo, heads south between high green cliffs of mountains and sweeps along in black and white fury sixteen hundred feet beneath the village of Kaitoto. There is enough wild and majestic scenery along that river to satisfy anyone for the rest of his life.

Both rivers rose during the night I was at Mao, and although they did not threaten the village they left only one path open, the one for the hills and Bili, and as I had already been there I decided to stay where I was till the floods went down. Mao had as yet no catechist, so my day's work was light. About ten o'clock I retired to the rest house and found it leaking. Someone cut large banana leaves and placed them on the roof to stop the leaks.

The rain was heavy and continuous. Everybody was indoors. A few inches of water eddied and flowed through the village carrying along all sorts of flotsam. The village pigs took shelter under the houses. The dogs climbed up the cumbersome ladders and continued to scratch their mangy heads with each leg in turn. I had nothing else to do but to watch them, and I settled down for a day that was not on my schedule, a day marooned in a native village. This could be a day of boredom so I lay back on my bunk and dozed.

The limbung floor vibrated under a footstep and I woke up. There was a man standing at the door. I took my diary and thought: I'll write everything that happens today, even the things that go through my mind, it will relieve the tedium; and I wrote, taking my first visitor as a beginning:

'I should like to converse with the Father,' he said, 'about my insignificant affairs. Yesterday I helped to bring your boxes from Bili and I got no tobacco.'

'Go down and get two pineapples from your wife,' I said. When he brought them along I gave him a stick of tobacco.

'And paper?'

I gave him a few sheets of *The Kerryman*.

'And matches?' he asked.

'Do you think I'm Woolworths? Isn't there a fire in the house?'

'How about it, don't I get anything for the pineapples?'

'Beat it, chum!' I said and waved him away.

He did. He hadn't brought any box of mine yesterday; all the carriers were from Bili and Salumpuna. He just wanted a smoke and couldn't think of any other way of getting it. Poor devil. I didn't want those pineapples. Kenpale and Lonra might like them, but I had to ask for something for the 'smoke' or the whole village would be on top of me.

Now did he tell me a lie? Was it a *locutio contra mentem ad fallendum prolata*? Did deception follow? Was it necessary that it should have followed to be a lie? I wonder what Aquinas would think of it.

It is hard to remember the white man's world right now. Let

me see. Cars, trains ... trains? Haven't seen one for years ... people rushing to telephones and away from them, to hospitals, to get the evening paper, to races, from races, to get into cinemas, to get out, oh dear, what's it all for anyhow? It is a wonderful civilisation and the farther you get from it the better it is ... but not too far, because it has its advantages. A couple of thousand miles with a monthly service is about right. I find it hard enough to understand that civilisation and I was born in it, so what hope has the chap here? Take the case that happened yesterday.

When the carriers had deposited all my boxes in the rest house I counted out the necessary number of sticks of tobacco and paper, and gave them to the leader of the group to divide them out. The men, of course, lined up first in accordance with polite custom, to receive their share. The leader placed the tobacco in each man's hand. Then the women came. The giver of good things stood before the first woman and dropped the tobacco on the ground. When she stooped to pick it up he kicked it beyond her reach and messed it up in doing so. She went after it and picked it up, tapping it on her hand to knock the sand out of it.

That woman is the leader's sister-in-law and by tribal law he may never touch her nor touch anything which she is touching. He dropped the tobacco on the ground so that she could take it, but he dropped it too near and fearing she might touch him when she stooped to pick it, he kicked it well away 'lest the people think evil things of her', thereby paying her the highest courtesy he knew: a tribute to her virtue.

Savages? I don't know. Savage seems to be a word that has a strong appeal to the arrogant and ignorant mind ... it might even have been coined by one. Unlike poets, savages are made, not born. Anyone can turn one out as a hobby if he mixes a little pride, conceit, complacency and self-righteousness with a small dash of superiority and a flavour (un soupçon, the French discerningly call it, a suspicion) of learning or civilisation. Believe me there are far more savages outside the jungle than inside it. 'But don't they bash in each other's skulls?' I hear you ask. 'Sure! Proper fashion too! How else keep law and order?' 'But surely a cannibal is a savage?' Cannibal, Madame, as Shaw might say, is a word we should approach with circumspection. It is purely a matter of taste, not a very elegant one, but we are in glass houses. Wasn't it Jonathan Swift who made up a list of the different manners of cooking babies, affecting that he had received it from an American lady-friend of great wit and gentle breeding, and offered it to the landlords with the caustic remark that since they had already devoured the parents they seemed to have the strongest right to the children? There are more ways of devouring a person than with salt.

Cannibals are decent folk. What is more commendable than to hear Slup-slup say: 'Let us not kill Tobulbul, there would be too much left over. Rather let us take a smaller child and then there will be no waste of good human meat and our hunger will be satisfied.'

For headhunters and skull-crashers I have no time at all. They just kill and leave the body there to rot. Some do it with a Butu and others with a bomb. The result is the same. Skull-crashers, both kinds, might be cured if they were forced to eat the dead bodies. There is a lot to be said for cannibalism.

Oh! Would some power the giftie gie us to see ourselves as others see us . . . so spake Bobbie Burns. Pity he is not now here. I should like to ask him to make me a handsome couplet enshrining rather: Would some power the giftie gie us to see others as they see themselves. Then I'd be on his side.

A wise Providence has denied us Bobbie's wish, and apparently for a good reason, because if we could see in ourselves the mean and snivelling little cheats that others see in us, only those of us completely destitute of honour could refuse the hemlock. But it would be an important advantage to us all to be able to see others as they see themselves. It would be especially advantageous to me now if I could see the villagers as they see themselves. I would give my right eye for the loan of the head of one of the villagers just for one hour.

Pangarea has reminded me of all this and of much more. British Law requires that not only should justice be done but also that it should be seen to be done. When a primitive man runs foul of the Law and has sentence passed upon him, few will ever know whether the sentence appears just or otherwise to his primitive eyes.

The Australian Government treats the crimes of primitives with admirable circumspection and tries to strike a very delicate balance. Any institution which attempts such a generous ideal is, however, bound to be criticised.

Pangarea killed a man. He did it after due deliberation. He admitted to doing it. There was no question of self-defence. No provocation. The victim had never caused him a personal injury, yet Pangarea split his head with an axe. Pangarea is a sane, reasonable and good-natured sort of fellow. He believes he did a worthy deed. He was sentenced to one year's imprisonment.

He is now back again in the village, a respected citizen, twenty-five pounds heavier and able to speak a second language, Tokboi.

Was Justice done and did it appear to be done? Was the sentence too light, too severe or just right?

The case may be argued interminably.

There was an immemorial feud between Pangarea's tribe and that of his victim. There had been other killings on both sides. Were those killings murder or the justified taking of the life of a murderer? Was Pangarea a murderer or a State hangman?

These are all very difficult questions to answer.

The Law takes into account some other factors, such as: How long has Pangarea been associated with the White man through a Christian Mission, a White employer or the Government? How far can he be expected to have realised that he should not have dealt with such matters in his own manner?

Then there is the consideration of Commutative Responsibility versus Personal Responsibility, in that each member of a clan shares the honour and the blame for the deeds of any other member of the same clan ... a kind of Mystical Body. If a person cannot take revenge on the actual culprit he can always adjust matters by dealing with any of his 'brothers' since they are all as guilty as he is. That was the principle on which Pangarea decided on his deed.

How far is this idea of Commutative Responsibility a peculiarity of primitive people? How far is it accepted by civilised people? How far can it be said to spring from the very nature of man himself?

It would seem, then, that the idea is not a trait peculiar to primitive man, nor is it a refinement of the cultured man but seems to be a thing that grows automatically on human nature regardless of creed, breed or culture. St Paul was enunciating more than theology when he said that we are members one of the other.

Even Adam becomes implicated in all this. We are commutatively responsible for his sin. We are punished for his crime. Is this solely by Divine Decree or is it an automatic result based on the oneness of the human nature in which we all share?

When God freely became Man, he became a member of our tribe and in that way He took on the responsibility for all the crimes of the tribe, that by His Sacrifice He could atone for the tribe. Wasn't it Isaias who said of Him: He was wounded for our iniquities; He was bruised for our sins; For the wickedness of my people have I struck him.

For the wickedness of his brother, Pangarea, too, struck his victim, the same commutative responsibility, the same vicarious punishment, the same vicarious atonement.

The system works both ways: by His bruises we are healed. We become initiated members of His spiritual tribe through Baptism and share in the profits of His good deeds.

There are those of us who consider this as either too profound or too far-fetched or totally incomprehensible except to the gifted intellect, yet here in the jungle it is the traditional conviction of the people and they take it for granted without batting an eyelid.

When Messrs Pangarea and Co. later receive instruction on

the Doctrine of Atonement they will find it terribly common-place.

From whence did these jungle-folk receive these ideas? They have had no revelation and have never engaged in discursive reasoning, yet they seem to have hit unerringly by a sort of direct intellectual vision, on things whose discovery we attribute to the sages of our civilisation.

There is scarcely a belief or a custom known to civilised people which is not to be found here either in identical or in parallel form.

Here comes Weita from Bili; he has travelled in the rain. He has come all the way to fulfil a promise. Weita is by nature talkative, effusive and good-natured. He offers me a sharp stone nine inches by two and a half. It is a stone axe-head or kiila.

'I knew the Father would be delayed by the floods,' he said, 'so I brought the kiila I promised.'

He also brought a crude axe-handle and showed me how the head was affixed to it.

This stone axe was the acme of progress of Weita's forbears. The stone was fished from the river and the handle obtained in the jungle by selecting a hooked hardwood branch of correct thickness. The axe-head was fastened to the hook of the handle by means of four splints bound with jungle-rope. It was not purely an axe; by rotating the head it became an adze.

Weita remembers when it was widely used. If a person had no axe and wished to make a garden he had to fire the base of every tree. Dead leafless trees were no obstacle to his garden. Only rarely was the kiila used to fell a tree; its purpose was to ringbark them.

Weita told me how one day he accompanied his father who was bent on felling a tree with his kiila. From memory he estimated the tree to be eighteen inches in diameter. The idea was revolutionary and the people were amazed that he felled the tree in a week.

A kiila was a powerful social boost to the owner. It could be lent out under great compliment. It also gave the owner a name. 'There were not many kiilas in Bili,' said Weita, 'but my father had three. Everybody wanted to borrow them. That pleased my father because then the people who borrowed them had to give a few days' work in our garden and that was why my father had the biggest garden of the lot. The people agreed to do anything my father wished because they were afraid he would not lend them the kiilas.'

'So the man who wields the axe makes the law, Weita?'

'That's it, that's it,' he replied.

'It's much the same in all tribes, Weita.'

'I think so,' he said, but he didn't get my meaning.

And with this axe which was never a battle-axe they won the greatest battle of all, the battle for survival.

Weita and I were, in a way, old friends. He had helped me on many occasions. One I like to recall happened at Bili. I had hoped to meet a priest from the north coast doing his rounds in the hinterland; instead the people told me he had been very sick in bed for weeks. The account may have been exaggerated but I knew he must have been in some way indisposed when he did not meet me as arranged. And when you hear of a sick confrere in the bush you don't need to be told what to do.

To get to his mission station by the known route would mean eight days. If my map were reliable and if I struck out through no-mans-land on a compass course, I reckoned I could do the trip in two days. A difficulty in going through a no-mans-land was that I would have to cut my rations to the limit as there were so few carriers available for such a journey. The rest would have to remain at Bili or be taken back to my mission station at Makaen, a journey of some fifty or sixty miles, at any rate twenty-two hours' walking time by the shortest route.

I had explained the position to Weita.

'I have three men that are willing to go with you,' he said, 'and that makes four with me. Only three can carry. The fourth one is to relieve them in turns. Put what you don't need into the other boxes and leave the rest to me. I'll fix all that.'

There was no lock on any box and one contained about 15

pounds of tobacco for paying carriers, enough to set a Mamusi up as King for the rest of his days. Yet, when I got back to Makaen some weeks later, all those boxes were stacked on my veranda and not a match missing, which further reminds me that in all my time I never turned a key in a door, even though I went off for a month or more at a time.

Weita's team and I went off on our errand of mercy and covered the distance in two days, and the poor man at the other end was right glad to see us.

Three hours out of Bili we had already climbed two thousand five hundred feet which put us now more than five thousand feet above sea level. The rest of the climb was gradual or non-existent because we followed the top of the range. The undergrowth had thinned out and given way to moss. There was no more jungle but high open forest.

After three and a half hours we rested. We were now miles beyond the gardens most distant from Bili.

'We the people seldom come as far as this,' said Weita, 'except to lay traps for wild dogs and wallabies. The people are afraid of the wild men that live about the jungle here.'

Weita said the wild dogs they trapped were bigger than the domestic type. We saw or heard none that day but I did see some tracks and they were large. I do not think there are wild men in that stretch between Bili and Ti, but we the people have no doubts on it. As we went ahead after our rest the men kept close together against possible attack. Weita kept up a constant jabber about wild men and wild dogs till I got bored. I imagined it was because he was scared.

'Weita,' I said, 'look down there. A wild man!'

'Where, where?' said Weita.

'Down by that big tree.'

'I don't see a thing.'

'He has moved. He is now behind that clump of scrub. I'm afraid he has gone.'

'It wasn't a wild man,' said Weita. 'It must have been someone from the village.'

'No, no!' I said. 'I know a wild man when I see one.'

'How can you recognise a wild man?' asked Weita.

'That's easy. He had a wild dog with him.'

Weita was not as obtuse as one might imagine. He threw me a quizzical eye and let out a wild yell of laughter, slapping his thighs and rubbing his hands. And that finished all reference to wild dogs and wild men.

❋

Weita went off with a few sticks of tobacco. I put the kiila carefully in a box and said: 'I will take this treasure back to the land of my ancestors and show it to my tribesmen.'

A dark form appeared at the doorway. It was Palak. Years ago he had given me his little son Mumu to take along to my mission station and send him to school there, so that later he could come back and teach the others.

Palak came to enquire about his boy. He also knew that if I was in any sort of mood at all he would get a few sticks of tobacco; Palak is a gentleman but not a scholar.

The Malmal people were very kind on these occasions. At one period I had ten lads from the jungle parked out on them and there was a waiting-list of foster-fathers. It was a happy change from the day they refused to go with me to the Mamusi for fear they would be killed. A couple of years and a little acquaintance and they were calling each other 'Brother'. Why is it that they never fear the white man and are very scared of each other? They possibly have some good reason . . . 'old forgotten far-off things and battles long ago' . . .

Mumu was quite an intelligent boy. To help him make up for lost time I used to give him home-work. One day when I went to correct his home-work, Mumu shifted uneasily. He riffled through one exercise book after the other and looked at them and at me in surprise. 'It must be somewhere,' he said, 'I know I did it' . . . indeed he didn't, for I had used that same excuse in those same words years ago in school and thought too that I was fooling the teacher. But when Mumu fresh from the jungle said it, I wondered what is inside us that makes us all the same and so true to type.

May I have the honour of borrowing George Washington's words to his lady-love: 'Mistake not my intention, misinterpret not my meaning'? They are very useful words of advice here.

I do not mean that the primitive is all virtue. He is just flesh and blood like the rest . . . but he is flesh and blood, and if you study his conduct you will know when you can trust him and when you can't and that will offset many disappointments on both sides. If his behaviour seems irrational or savage, be prepared to grant him a good reason for what he's doing; search for it and you will find it because it is always there. Allow that there are more view points than your own . . . and forget the word savage; it will only harden your prejudices, keep you from ever learning and lead you into untold mischief.

It is easy for them to mistake our intention and for us to mistake theirs. I am reminded of two cases by a woman who has just passed along here now. Her entire dress consists of two or three strategically placed leaves. Is she immodest? Is she loose? Many people I know would say: definitely immodest. Are they drawing from their own experience or from their upbringing? Let it pass. I have no reason to think she is one or the other.

There is, I suppose, a certain connection between modesty and dress. They are not, however, the same thing. Clothes may help modesty but they do not constitute it. I do not mean that piling on clothes makes one more modest. It may or it may not. Sometimes it is an aid to modesty to take off clothes, sometimes to put them on. Modesty is a quality of the soul and the lass with the leaves has got it. Everybody knows of people who use clothes to look immodest and succeed. Whether a dress is modest or not is best decided by the right judgment of the people concerned. What's right in one country may be wrong in another.

A coastal trading ship called into my mission station one day. Among the few passengers was a young European woman. She was dressed conveniently for the conditions of travel and for the climate. She had on a pair of slacks and a blouse. That evening a venerable papé from the village came to me:

'Did the Father see the missus on the ship?'

'Yes, I did.'

'How about it, was she a good missus?'

'I'm sure she was.'

'We the people are talking plenty in the village. We think she is lewd.' (This from a man whose own grown daughter wears a few leaves and flowers.)

'Well, well! And why should anyone think that?'

'But isn't she wearing a man's clothes? Amongst us the people, if anyone wore the clothes of the other sex, that person would be speared to death.'

'Ah well! Don't worry on that account. The white man has different customs.'

'True. Some of the men in the village said that too. They said she was all right. That 'twas the custom of the white man. He's different. I just wanted to ask the Father.'

'The white man sees nothing wrong in it,' I said.

'That's all right,' he said. 'That's good. We know some of the white man's customs differ from ours. That's his affair. But there was a lot of talk in the village and I came to enquire.'

I wondered if a primitive woman wearing her own garb of leaves in civilized society would be treated with as much sympathy and understanding? The more tolerant would probably put her in gaol to protect her from civilisation; the more virtuous might like to tie her to a stake and burn off what little clothes she had.

It is so very easy to misinterpret the intention.

❀

Three school-girls from the top class came to me one day and asked if they could go to the convent-school at the central mission station. Their school records were good and their parents consented, so off they went on the next boat.

For obvious reasons the girls could not wear their purpurs of leaves in the convent-school. What are those obvious reasons? Well, any well-dressed girl needs twelve croton leaves a day. For the school that would mean 2,400 leaves a day or

16,800 a week (and 20,000 if you allow the usual 20% for damage). Since Vunapope is a built-up area the hedges could not withstand such a denuding, so the nuns did the only wise thing, they made frocks for them all.

Three years later the girls came back to Malmal and you should see the eyes of us the people! Two-tone frocks with frills and piping and the rest.

I lay low for a few days waiting for the reaction. Then one evening going to night-prayer I heard: 'Harumf, harumf!'

'Oh, good evening, Paulus.'

'God bless you, Father.'

'And Petrus, and Joannes . . . and is that you old Matemage?'

'It is only I,' he said with true humility.

'So?'

'We should like to approach the Father in conversation about our insignificant affairs.'

Then followed the usual sitdown and a smoke, and various discussions before the deputation got round to the point.

'Has the Father seen the convent-girls?'

'Yes. I just saw them come off the boat.'

'What does the Father think of them?'

'Well, I haven't spoken to them yet.'

'But what does the Father think of their appearance?'

'They looked fine and fat, didn't they? And you fellows said they would be thin.'

'Ah! We don't mean that. Certainly they are well-fed.'

'Then what do you mean?'

At last we had arrived at the point and all drew closer.

'We were thinking of their clothes.'

'Oh!'

'Does the Father want them to wear dresses?'

'You know well the Father doesn't care a *kavivi* what they wear. I have already told you that your dress is a matter for yourselves.'

'That's true. Now we would like them to dress like the other girls.'

'That's fine. Please yourselves.'

'But they won't obey us,' said toothless old Matemage petulantly.

'Today I told Catharina to take off her dress and she wouldn't!'

'And what did you expect?' asked Paulus who never missed a chance of poking fun at poor innocent Matemage.

'Oh sorrow!' the old man replied, 'you can't talk like that before the eye of the Father. Father, Paulus is laughing at me and he's talking no-good too.'

'I'm sorry, Matemage,' I said. 'I'm deaf on that side.'

'Then that's the side I'll go to Confession to in future,' laughed Paulus.

'Sorrow! He's mocking again now,' said Matemage. 'This man Paulus, what kind is he?'

Eventually the deputation left and I beckoned Robertus. He was old and steady, though young of heart.

'Tell me Robertus, between you and me, why do the people object to dresses?'

'It is like this,' he said. 'We the people have a custom for clothing our men and women. That's our fashion. It is good to our eye. What we see like that we see with innocence. But when we see things dressed up and covered like the convent-girls are, our livers become agitated.'

Agitation of the liver is not found in any medical book, but if you look up the catechism, you should find it under one of the Ten Commandments.

Next day 36 extra croton leaves were plucked from my hedge. The Recording Angel laid down his quill, smiled, and softly flew away.

It was four o'clock. The rain had ceased and the sun shone from a washed blue sky. Steam rose from the village square and from the thatched roofs of the huts. It rose from the pathways, from the gardens and from the dripping trees and floor of the jungle, swelling up in white, loose, billowy clouds from the valleys and padding each mountain range with a layer of white cotton-wool. In half an hour no trace was left of the downpour.

I strolled down the village accompanied by a few young men. In a short time we formed quite a gathering. This was the idle hour of the day for the men, the hour before the big meal. The women were busy cooking in the huts, and every pig had converged on the doorways, grunting, squealing and savaging one another. Occasionally a handful of offal came flying through a doorway, and the squealing ceased while the pigs bore down on it en masse. In a few seconds it had vanished and there was a new scramble for an advantageous place in the queue.

We visited the first Giung (men's common house). The walls were lined with tobacco leaves, fishing nets, spears and the skulls of some twenty wild pigs and bush-wallabies. Old dancing masks were tucked away among the rafters. I imitated the dance of the Urasen amid such cheering and shouting that a large crowd soon gathered outside . . . The strange white man was on display, like the elephant of the circus. One villager offered me a bunch of native tobacco in exchange for razor-blades. After we had agreed on the exchange, he said he could not sell because the tobacco was not his. All part of the game! They only wanted to observe me and size me up, for they knew that I was doing just that with them too.

We moved on to a second Giung. Outside the door lay a 'garamut', a drum-shaped, hollowed-out log a few feet long, which was used for tapping out messages to neighbouring villages. To satisfy everybody's curiosity I had to do some tapping on the garamut. In this Giung the senior members were gathered, smoking and yarning. It also had its quota of pigs' skulls and dancing masks. The old men asked me to repeat my version of the dance of the Urasen for them. I did not think it was quite so funny but they seemed to derive extraordinary pleasure from it, slapping their thighs and rocking to and fro with delight. They proudly showed me the pigs' skulls and other trophies of the chase. I pretended to believe they were human skulls, and holding an unusually long one said: 'Now, isn't that just like the skull of an Arowe Native?' I thought the cheering would never stop. My popularity was unbounded because I had disparaged a neighbouring tribe.

This was all quite silly, but what other common topic could we find for a few passing moments of conversation?

The evening meal was ready and so I drifted back alone to my rest-house, hoping to get in my Rosary on the way. Poor hope! Some of the children followed me but when I turned to look at them, they ran off, glancing back over their shoulders; and as soon as I went on, they followed me again. Without the use of any words, this became a little game between us.

Back at the rest-house my meal was ready: baked Kaukau, sliced bully-beef, tomatoes, shallots, and a pot of tea with sweetened condensed milk.

A large yellow moon rose over the mountains shining dimly through the scattered trees of the clearing, and spilling silver on the fronds of the solitary palm-tree. The air was still and the smoke of the village drifted slowly down, with shafts of smoky light between the village and the mountains. The houses lay like black humps, and as the moon rose higher the few trees in the clearing reflected more silver from their trunks. I strolled up and down listening to the soft subdued murmur of voices from the village, and watching the deep-red flickering firelight from my boys' rest-house where a few locals were also gathered to hear them crooning a Kyrie Eleison. Cicadas maintained a constant chirping and the frogs were croaking, barking and laughing on all sides.

Down near the rest-house was a lime-tree, studded with fire-flies. There were thousands of them on it, all flashing their green lights together, like fairy-lights going on and off. I counted their flashes; like the heart-beats of the tree they were seventy to the minute; later it may be eighty but, no matter, they would always beat and flash in unison.

I went inside and wrote up the day's log, almost as you have read it now. I turned the stud on the pressure-lamp and the light went out with a hiss and a smell of kerosene, taking with it the solitary evidence of the white man's intrusion into this lovely and lonely jungle village. The night now differed none from any night for a thousand years: the mountains, the moonlight and the river; the frogs and the cicadas; a baby's whimper and the hushing murmurs of its mother crooning it back to sleep; the dying fires and the steady flash, green flash of the fireflies through the lattice.

The Gentle Art of Converting
a Primitive

THERE WAS more than enough work for any one priest in Malmal. I had inherited fifteen hundred Catholics and the number was increasing by about a hundred and twenty-five a year, more than a third of whom were adults. In a short time it would top two thousand. To cater for the spiritual needs and often for the temporal ones of these people left very little time free.

There was the routine visit to each village with its Baptisms, Confessions, Marriages and so on. The schools had to be visited and the Wailing Wall set up, where some came with 'their insignificant affairs'.

Besides that, most of the able-bodied came to the Mission station at Malmal for the greater Church Feasts, and Mengens are not satisfied with going to Mass on these occasions, they also go to Confession and Holy Communion, and hearing a thousand confessions will take thirty hours at least, and tropical confession boxes with all possible ventilation and on the coolest day are still little better than a Turkish bath. To get through them I usually spent two or three days before each feast-day going from village to village just hearing Confessions.

In spite of the continuous pre-occupation with the Catholics on the coast I was anxious to find time to visit those bush-people who were in my area and who, so far, had received no attention.

My aim was to make and to keep contact with them. I could not hope to give them all the care they needed on account of their numbers and the great distances involved, but they were part of the parish and I had to do my best for them and that best was very, very small.

Ultimately, I hoped that when I had visited them all I would be able to plead with His Lordship the Bishop and obtain priests for them. The parish needed at least three more priests.

Much later, I was glad to learn that two could be assigned, and so two new parishes were sliced out of Malmal; a priest was placed at Motong for the Kols and one at Ulamona for the Bush-Mengens and Sui. But that was still to come. I had yet to make first contact with the Kols and the Sui.

By juggling time, I had been able to make a trip to the Mamusis the first year. If I could contact the Kols and the Sui the next year I would be happy because I would also have to visit the Mamusis again.

Now, to make hare-soup one must first catch the hare, and to make fillet of salmon one must first catch the salmon. To convert a Kol or Sui one must first catch him and that is a more difficult job than catching hares or salmon.

Imaginative writers have depicted for us the ideal missionary. He has a well-trimmed beard (that first *sine qua non*); he is dressed in a newly pressed soutane and has a biretta with a silky pom-pom. He is accompanied by cherubic altar-boys carrying candles, incense and bells. He is holding a Crucifix aloft. In the background is the savage, the Kol, dragging a man by the hair towards a ring of dancing brothers. A pot on a fire completes the picture.

At the sound of the holy bells and at the whiff of the incense wafted by a favourable breeze to his distended and bone pierced nostrils the Kol sniffs, paws the ground, sniffs again and recognising the sanctity of the sweet smell drops his victim and prostrates himself before the missionary and craves Baptism.

He then joins a monastery and spends the rest of his days chanting and transcribing the Psalms.

O sorrow!

Here, we fall short of the ideal. No conversions are sought or accepted on the first trip, nor on the second either. The sole object is to see the people and be seen by them and return home in one piece and with no damage done. Anyone who achieves that may be considered reasonably successful.

No damage done! It is so easy to do the wrong thing even when you mean the best. It is so easy to mistake their intention or for them to misinterpret your meaning.

This might be a case: you come to a village for the first time; you see a little child and wishing to show, like a presidential candidate, that you do not eat children, but in fact are fond of them, and also meaning to compliment the people, you pat the child on the head and say: 'Atta boy, Tootsie-Wootsie, Fuzzy-Wuzzy Pikinini' and move along swollen up with good-will towards all.

It will never be forgotten that at such a village on such a day you patted little Melemveda on the head. A few days later little Melemveda got a fever and died. It is now known from one end of the tribe to the other that you cast an evil spell on him. Didn't everyone see you do it? Wasn't the child all right till you did it? Surely you meant something by doing it and hasn't everyone seen the result? Your next visit will not be a glorious success.

Or maybe you are walking through an old garden and you are thirsty from the hike and you pick a paw-paw from a dere-lict paw-paw tree. What harm is it? Are there not plenty over-ripe ones rotting on the ground? ... But someone has seen you and the fame precedes you to the village that you are a robber of gardens. Maybe you did not do it, just one of your boys did it. The result is the same.

So, on your first trip, you hand-pick your boys and instruct them carefully on their behaviour. Amongst a new tribe you try no fancy tricks or cleverness, but stick strictly to the rules. And in all cases you know that your assurance of your own good-will doesn't mean a thing. You must learn to keep looking at yourself through the eyes of a Kol. Since you know nothing about a Kol you must draw on your experience of other tribes, because they are all much alike.

It is prudent to avoid trying to make a good impression. One must be satisfied with and very grateful for not making a bad one. Should some person wish to be very friendly with you at first sight, it is usually better to dismiss him after a polite interval ... you don't know what reputation he enjoys among his own and the Kols, like everyone else, say: Show me your company ... Most often, your first acquaintances are not the best. The Kols produce the best wine last. An impression of aloofness may be preferable to one of exaggerated affability. Primitive people are not easily fooled, in fact they're not fooled at all.

You might let it be known discreetly that on occasions you are prepared to attend to the sick, that is, if anyone should like to come at his own risk. If one or two approach out of the tribe, it is sufficient. When you have left, your handiwork will be well and truly examined and if you have effected a cure, there will be no scarcity of patients the next time.

You make no mention of religion to them, for you have no means of explaining the whole lot to them in an hour. At the moment you are not even interested. Your object is to see and be seen.

If your first trip has been successful within its narrow confines, you will make a second. A change is noticeable. More people approach you. There is a marked feeling of guarded friendliness. An ever-increasing number want medical attention. You might even find a small present of food in your camp.

They have noticed you said Mass the last time and now ask you about it. You cannot explain it fully yet but you say a few things about it and ask them to come along and attend. They do, and their eyes won't leave you for a second.

They recognise your boys from the previous round and become friendly with them and may even invite them to their houses, if they have houses. The main topic will be you; you and your religion, but mainly you. Your boys, perhaps without knowing it, will be preparing the ground for future evangelisation.

After a few more trips and much tribal politicking in between they have got a very hazy idea of what this is all about.

Then one day, you are sitting in your rest-house. You are lying back in a canvas chair with your bare feet on the veranda railing. They are fat and hot from the day's walk and you are wiggling your toes and enjoying the cool breeze on them. You have washed and changed. There is a heap of clothes ready for the boys to wash: sweat-soaked khaki trousers, a singlet dangling from a sliver on a rafter, a pair of socks all covered with mud and burrs, a pair of muddy boots and your old canvas hat that's dripping wet because you have used it all day to wipe the perspiration off your face and neck. A few tribesmen come along to you and say:

'We, the people, were thinking. How about it? Could the Father send us a catechist as we would like to become Catholics?'

This is the moment you have been waiting and praying for and unless you are cool and careful you'll lose your tribe and your Catholics. All the previous perspiration is forgotten, all the hunger, the weariness and disappointment. You say a fond *Ave* and the world is rosy. And if you say a few more *Aves* you'll remember to look at yourself and your religion through the tribesman's eyes.

You might remember the Great Healer of Souls. He was walking along one day and He saw Peter and his brother Andrew fishing. And He said: 'Follow Me and I will make you fishers of men.'

Fishers are patient people. Often they fish for days and catch nothing. They just cast, pay out line and reel in. Then one day there is a nibble. The angler is tense but he does not strike. He pays out more line, and even when he is sure he has hooked the biggest yet, he still does not strike hard because his fish may be too strong for his frail tackle. Instead, he patiently plays his catch up and down the stream. He has plenty of line and time is on his side. He silently prays the fisherman's old prayer : 'O God, grant that this one may be so big that in boasting about it later at the pub I need not lie.' His patience and prayers are rewarded and at last he grasses his troutie.

Fishers of men have to be patient too. When the tribesmen say they want a catechist, even though you have one waiting for the job, you must first do a little angling.

You look again through the eyes of the tribesman. He has seen you visit his village and cure his sick. If there is a catechist here you will come oftener and the villagers will never again be sick, and they'll increase in numbers and make a powerful village and then, May the Lord have Mercy on the neighbours. There are old scores to be settled.

You know there is always jealousy between neighbouring villages (for people are the same the world over) so you say to the honest man : 'Well, it is going to be difficult to find a catechist for you, because I intended to place the only one available at Pikaso village. They have asked me and they promised to look after him well.'

At that painful jab your fish will now swallow hook line and sinker. He'll say : 'That village is only rubbish. We've got a decent village here and anything they can do we can do better.'

You ponder. You see him already on toast. Then you say : 'Can you build him a house?'

'Sure we can.'

'And give him a place to make his garden?'

'There's plenty ground and he can live off my garden till his own is ready.'

'But then ... there is this matter of school and Church ... you don't have to attend you know, but if you didn't it would be useless putting a catechist here, he might just as well be sent to Pikaso village.'

'Just leave that to us,' they say.

'Well, then, you had better come along with me to my station and bring the catechist back with you.'

'We'll do that, and make a little feast too.'

'But I'm sorry to be disappointing the Pikaso people.'

'Oh, they'll be all right. They can have the next one.'

And they will too, because they'll want to be as good as their neighbours.

The reason for all this angling and hedging is that the newcomers must learn that the compliment is on your side. If you just plonk a catechist in their midst they will more than probably demand payment to allow their children to go to school, and also for every time they enter the Church to say a prayer.

❉

The conversion of a primitive man is a slow and difficult work and weighed down with plans that go awry, and no one is capable of doing it alone because life is too short. Conversion is best illustrated in Our Lord's parable where He compares the Kingdom of Heaven to yeast. The working is not obvious to the eye and is by nature slow. Conversion too is slow, it takes a life-time for the individual and generations for a people. Tradition cannot be hurried.

No single person can say that a conversion was his work. It is rather the accumulated effort of thousands of nameless and forgotten people working steadily and imperceptibly over generations. Each one receives a partly finished job, works on it to his ability and moves on.

Tribes do not rush out now, nor did they at any time, to ask the first missionary they see for a Baptism they never heard of. When the day comes that they do ask for Baptism and are worthy of it, a tremendous amount of hidden hard work has already been done, work that is more difficult than pouring water on the head and saying: I baptise thee in the Name of the Father and of the Son and of the Holy Ghost. Most of us reap where we have not sown, which is a very encouraging thing as long as we remember it.

Tribes differ too. Some are religiously inclined and some are not. Some are ready in five years, others with the same amount of work may require twenty. Some are tenaciously good Catholics, others are a loose lot. The difference in the external success of the apostolate depends largely on the luck of the draw, the natural inclinations and characteristics of the people. The nature of the people is more important than that of the preacher. Apart from the grace of God, national apostles owe their success to the people they had to deal with, and not the other way round. The people can make or break him.

Even when you have established contact with primitive people and all is ready to begin the work, there are still problems that will frustrate and delay conversions for years. I have had some little practice at trying to get Catholic life organised amongst these first contacts and here are some of the situations.

Village A was marked off for a Catechist. I sent him along. He was a good fellow but could not help being young and handsome. You can now guess the rest. A mountain lass fastened her eye on him and said: 'Ha! He's mine!' She jilted her own boy-friend. The villagers, rightly so, would not hear of the new liaison and trouble was brewing. The only solution was to remove the catechist.

I replaced him with a married one. That should fix things. A few weeks later I got a letter from the catechist's wife. What happened? She looked the place over once, sat down and cried '. . . you-can't-do-this-to-me . . . I wanna go home . . .' Home she went with her catechist husband trailing behind.

A year passed and I sent another catechist to replace him. Now he was an excellent fellow and his wife and children said they never had been in a more agreeable village before. Within six months I had to remove him on account of a cancer of the jawbone. When I visited him in hospital he was scarcely able to speak. But he did manage to get this out: 'Christ suffered for me. I want to suffer for the Mamusis that God may hasten their conversion.' He certainly did suffer before he died . . . Martin Vili, I bow to you.

Nearly two years had now elapsed with village A and they were still almost where they began, and if there are twenty-five villages to be catered for the difficulties will be proportionately increased.

In the meantime I was badgering the locals to let me have a

few of their young boys to take them along to my school. If suitable they would come back later as teachers. After two years they offered me Lumaluma, who is hard of hearing and has a stutter; he is no use to the village so let's give him to the Church. I am expected to teach a half-deaf boy, and he is expected to teach them.

I agreed to take him if I got four more of my own choice with him. We bargained for two. Later on Lumaluma got homesick and had to go back. That's my story and I'm sticking to it.

The villagers now wanted to know if those two young lads will eventually come back to their own village when trained. These villagers were as cute as pet-foxes.

This is a procedure I preferred to avoid, because a young catechist in his own village hasn't got a word to say and the village boss who doesn't know a thing about religion puts himself in charge of it with the catechist as the figurehead.

On the other hand, a stranger catechist must be careful in laying down the law or he will find himself the victim of a local pressure-group. A catechist must be, above all, a diplomat.

No pagan village is willing to supply boys to be trained as catechists if those boys are later to be posted to another village: Why should we supply boys to help advance those people while we ourselves lag behind?

I tried to get out of that by pairing off the villages. Thus I said to the people of Vavakena village: 'When your boys are trained I will post them to Kurumea village and the boys from Kurumea village will come here.'

'Just one moment,' they said. 'Let us have a good look at that again. The people of Kurumea village are always casting evil spells on our people and can we allow our boys to go and live there?'

'But you will have the Kurumea boys here so their people will be afraid to try any tricks on your boys. Anyhow, the Kurumea people say you are always casting spells on them!'

'Oh! No! Father, we don't do that. Those fellows are only a mob of liars at best. And if their boy happened to die . . . just died you know . . . they'd say we had bewitched him and we'd

---

A Mengen solo-dancer's individual dress. The umbrella-like head-dress may be rotated on any plane. It is decorated throughout with the feathers of cockatoos, parrots and parakeets and has all the colours of the spectrum.

have to pay compensation even though we didn't do a thing.'

'And if your boy died ... just died you know ... in Kuru-mea, wouldn't they have to pay?'

'Ah, but that's different! You see, no one just-dies-you-know in Kurumea. They are all bewitched.'

'But they say the same of your village!'

'But don't you believe them, Father, they are all liars!'

'And they say you are liars. Anyhow isn't it true that some of your villagers bewitch one another?'

'Yes, it is.'

'So even if your boy is catechist here, he can still be be-witched?'

'Yes. But we can undo those spells.'

'All of them?'

'Some of them.'

'... So it is merely a question of whether it is sweeter to be killed by your friends or by your enemies?'

I post a catechist only after long deliberation, and no matter where I send him, I always realise later on that it was the wrong place.

Mengens' traditional dancing-dress and drums.

The Kols

THE KOLS lived inland towards the eastern end of the parish. I knew little or nothing about them. Back in the thirties Father Culhane had gone as far as Nutuwe village, the first big village in from the coast.

Government patrols had been through the area and the general impression I received was that the people were no better and no worse than might be expected. Perhaps a little too quick on the draw but, on the whole, nothing unusual.

Their lands lie along the basins of three fairsized streams, fast, deep and treacherous: the Bergberg, the Iso and the Sibul. The tribe is spread out towards Nakanai Mountain range from the south, but over across the range on the north it has another section called the Kol-Sui or Sui, which occupies the land from the mountains almost to the north coast of the island.

This was known as Uncontrolled Territory. The Government sticks that label to those places which are still little known and are considered, therefore, dangerous for the white man. Such places are out of bounds. As I was leaving on my first visit to the Kols I learned that the label had quite recently been removed from the Sui. No extra patrolling had been done in the area but the ban had been lifted.

The reason given, though I cannot vouch for this even though I believed it, was a question raised in the United Nations Assembly. New Guinea is under UNO and entrusted to Australia for administration. Russia being a member of UNO has an interest in how the place is run. It seems that the Russian delegate was worried about all the Uncontrolled Territory in New Guinea and felt that Australia was not doing all it could to advance the civilisation of the people and bring them peace, prosperity and Christianity. Others said he wanted to have a dig at Australia and didn't care a rouble about us the people. Maski, it doesn't matter. All that interested me was that the ban was lifted and there were no more out-of-bounds.

But I hope it will gladden the heart of that good Russian to know that these people are now being catered for by two priests in sympathy with the Vatican. I baptised a little dying child in there and named him Vladimir Patrick ... Vladimir for the Russian Delegate because I did not know his name and Vladimir sounded right good Russian to me. The little lad is now in Heaven and I know he is praying for Papa Vladimir, who in a crooked political sort of manner is the Apostle of the Sui. Thanks, Vlad!

Travelling in the Kol country was very easy after the Mamusi. It is not extensive and I had done it in eight days.

A faithful old luluai, Kawarea by name, accompanied me as guide and adviser. He knew all the tribal land and also the land for miles beyond it. He had traversed it times out of number during the war, when he acted as guide to some Australians operating an intelligence service there. A heavy silver chain hung from his neck and attached to it was a medal about the size of a silver dollar. This was a Loyal Service Medal which he had received at the end of the war.

Kawarea was small and of darker skin than is usually found among Melanesians. He was exceedingly fit and moved with a tireless, springy resilience, up-hill, down-hill, the same steady hop-hop-hop.

He planned my journey like a Travel Agent, but went one better because he accompanied me on it, just a few hops ahead,

slashing down a projecting branch here, warning me of a
hidden stump or pot-hole there, lending a hand on greasy
patches and testing the different 'bridges' before I crossed a
stream. And if our day brought us, as it sometimes did, to an
old deserted village, Kawarea would hustle his troops and in an
hour have a tolerable shelter built for me for the night.

These shelters were made of brushwood and leaves; they
were weatherproof for a night or two and large enough to hold
my bunk and my boxes. In fact Kawarea did for me everything
that Hiawatha did for Minnehaha :

> 'Cleared the tangled pathway for her,
> Bent aside the swaying branches,
> Made at night a lodge of branches,
> And a bed with boughs of hemlock,
> And a fire before the doorway
> With the dry cones of the pine-tree.'

From this trip I remember only a few incidents that might
be of interest to anybody but myself.

The Iso River cut the track between two villages. It ran fast
and deep in a gorge between two high banks of smooth rock.
A narrow path of gravel lay between the river and the rock on
our side. For some reason best known to the Kols the track led
down the rock-face and then followed the river for a few hundred yards to a 'bridge'.

The face of the rock was smooth and made a sheer drop. But
the Kols had more ways than one for overcoming it. I was
treated to the privileged way.

A wicker basket capable of holding a crouched-up man was
fastened to an inch-thick cane about fifty feet long. This cane
was strung round the butt of a tree near the edge of the rock.
A Kol went first to give me confidence and to show how it
worked. Then I was motioned towards the basket and asked to
make myself at home. It was hanging over the edge and held to
the tree by the cane-rope. I was given two sticks to help keep
the basket clear of the rock-face. Five men now paid out rope

and as it slipped around the tree I descended in the basket with befitting elegance.

I recall this incident from time to time in the hope that if I should ever meet St. Paul we may be able to talk a little shop about getting out of awkward places in a basket.

The basket was used again only for my baggage and for some women that were following along with babies. The menfolk scaled down the face of the rock with as little apparent concern as if they were on the level. When I examined their toe-holds, which I had not seen at first, I found they would only accommodate my thumb. I asked Kawarea why someone did not cut the holds a little larger and he said he often told them to do so but nobody bothered. I asked him if anybody ever fell down. 'Oh, yes,' he said, 'a man fell down there once but he was a stupid fellow . . .' indicating that he did not really think it necessary to have them enlarged either, though I believe the job has been done since.

Further on we came to the 'bridge'. I call it a bridge because that was its purpose, but do not imagine a work of art in stone or steel with graceful arches and sculptured balustrades and statues of nymphs and poets thrown in for good measure.

It was a primitive, yet ingenious structure of about one hundred and fifty feet single-span. It was anchored to a tree on the near bank and to another tree which clung grimly to a large rock near the off bank. At the points where it was anchored to the trees it must have been about thirty feet above the water, but since the people had no means of pulling it taut, it curved down gracefully towards the centre, where it cleared the river by only a few feet. It was not a footbridge but a sort of ladder on its side. It was fashioned of two cane-ropes about an inch thick and a few feet apart in the middle of the stream, but splaying out wider towards the ends. These two canes were held together by flimsy rungs. One cane was to be used as a footrest and the other as a handrail, and a person had to crawl crabwise along the footrest. No single cane could be found to take the entire span so that each one was crudely spliced midway across the stream.

A few Kols went ahead, one at a time. Meanwhile I was making up my mind what I should do in case the bridge broke under me. Hold on to one cane was the solution, and then I would be washed over to one side. I looked down the stream. It rushed straight on between two tree-clad rocky banks for seventy yards and disappeared around a bend. I heard the local radio saying next week: 'The body of a European has been found at the mouth of the Iso River in a decomposed condition . . . a patrol has set out to investigate . . . the only person reported missing from the area . . .' I was in hilarious mood.

Nearing the middle of the bridge, I began to worry. I was much heavier than a Kol and had almost pushed the footrest down to the water already. What would happen when I got to the halfway mark? I was trying to calculate if the handrail would also be submerged.

I pushed ahead gently. The water lapped my boots, rose to my ankles and my shins. I could now feel the pressure of the stream which was sweeping the footrest with it in jerks, and inclining me to fall out over the handrail, and the more I leant on it the more I was inclined to fall over it. The whole structure was swaying and wobbling.

I was half way across and matters should improve. Wishing to get my feet over water as soon as possible I hurried my foot forward along the footrest and in doing so, jammed it into the splice, and in extricating it forced the splice apart. The footrest was now gone and I was flat on the water holding the handrail. The situation was disturbing. 'You're all right. Don't panic.' I was talking to myself.

I crawled hand over hand until I found where the footrest was again firmly lashed to the handrail and climbed on board with much splashing and grunting. The rest of the journey on the bridge was rather dull.

As I was sitting on the rock to which the bridge was anchored I watched a Kol go out to repair the damage, as a spider goes out to repair his web when a bungling bumble-bee has floundered through it. He ignored the handrail and walked down the footrest like a tight-rope walker. A long bush-rope trailed from his mouth. He squatted with a foot outside two stays with only occasional regard to the handrail. Bobbing like a bird on a windy bough, he did his repairs in a few minutes.

Now, why wasn't I born a Kol?

※

I had told Kawarea of my intention of visiting the Sui and asked him, since he was so well acquainted with the region, to be my guide. This he agreed to do.

We discussed arrangements at some length. It appeared that if we were unencumbered with baggage and carriers we could arrive at the first outpost of the Sui in perhaps nine or ten hours' walk, but as there could be no question of my going without my supplies we decided on a two-day walk of six or seven hours each with carriers.

This meant we would have to camp on the track, with the added difficulty that our carriers would have two days' walk, hence more carriers would be necessary to bring the extra food, and besides all that, the country was waterless. We had, however, sufficient containers to cover the water-supply.

Kawarea assured me that it was best to leave the final arrangements till we reached Bagatavi because it was from there we would strike over the mountains. But when we later came to Bagatavi we found it had been long deserted and the only hut that remained was overgrown with long grass.

Kawarea put his men to the job of building me a shelter while he went off to the bush to round up some people, but without Kawarea's attention they worked very slowly, and when he arrived back a few hours later, covered with mud and perspiration, he spurred them on considerably with tones and gestures that were good sound abuse in any language.

I asked him how arrangements were going for tomorrow's trip and he looked at me in silence as if to say: It's a long story so pull up a chair. 'I'm afraid,' he said, 'we cannot go. Something has been happening across the mountains and some people have been killed. The people are saying that the Malkol-kols have raided again and this man here who has just now come back from Lea's place found only an old woman and a child in the village. This is the wrong time to go there.'

The Malkolkols have earned themselves a lot of local fame, far more than they are entitled to. In fact they are not a tribe at all but a remnant of a Baining village (so I have been told). It is difficult to assess the value of the stories attributed to them, but it would appear that they were originally a Baining village of extreme left tendencies, inclined, in fact, to the cult of the personality. They did not pull too well with the rest of the tribe, all the petty bickerings finally culminating in one grand scrap with clubs and spears. The recalcitrant village fled to the unchartered wilds of the jungle, dissociated themselves from the parent tribe and kept up continual hostilities.

Their night-raids on the villages were fast and furious. The attacking Malkolkols would sneak into the village at about three o'clock in the morning and take up positions at the doors of the houses. They would then put fire to the houses and bash the skulls of the people as they came out. In a few minutes the Malkolkols would have vanished into the jungle and the night.

Others say they are an off-shoot of the Sulka tribe; but wherever they came from, their tradition is full of unpleasantness and they keep their neighbours in constant fear. But they have fallen on evil days of late. Some were rounded up by a Government Patrol after a raid in 1947 and a later Patrol showed that there existed then only a few men, women and children, in all about twenty people.

It was possible that the Malkolkols were on the warpath again, but it was extremely improbable. Still, where people with their unsavoury reputation are concerned, the Kols may be excused for using discretion.

I accepted that there was something wrong at the other side of the mountains but I could not believe the Malkolkols had a club in it, because to get into the area where the damage was supposed to have been done they would have had to pass through a large section of the Sui tribal ground. They might have succeeded with rare cunning in getting through in a couple of nights, but even so, the greatest factor still remained unexplained: If they had made a raid was it likely that they would have left an old woman and a boy behind, or was it likely that they would remain after the raid?

Later investigations by a Government Patrol showed that the Malkolkols had nothing to do with the trouble; the Sui were just settling some private business in the traditional manner, for heads lie loosely on the shoulders of the Sui.

At Bagatavi I tried to get Kawarea around to my way of thinking but he would not hear of it. I argued with him for the greater part of an hour. Really it was not an argument at all but a monologue on my part, because when he got it into his head not to go, then it was easier to persuade a Missouri mule. I promised him valuable presents if he would get a party together. He listened attentively and politely, made no comment whatever and the only sign of life he showed was to shift his eyes from one spot to another. At last I said: 'Well, what about it? Do you think we can go?'

'No, Father, it is out of the question.'

I gave up. I had now to return to the coast and he made all arrangements for the journey. He was very pleased with the new decision and was talkative again. I asked him how he had not heard of the disturbances till now. He told me that everybody knew about them for the past week but kept it secret from me lest I would have turned back from the beach and they wanted me to visit their people.

I never discovered whether Kawarea knew all the facts of the case. I'm inclined to believe he did and just did not want to drop me into the middle of a family squabble. It might be too, that the carriers refused to obey him or perhaps he was genuinely scared of the Malkolkols, because he came to me that night with a very strange request: could he sleep in my shelter?

The Sui

EIGHTEEN MONTHS now elapsed before I could arrange a visit to the Sui, where I worked my first miracle.

Towards the middle of June I had all my boxes packed and stacked ready for the wet season to break, because the Sui tribe was on the north coast, and when we on the south coast have the rainy season they have the fine. I would leave by boat for Pomio the day the rains set in. As the seas would take a day or two to rise, the boat could be safely back at anchor.

I had a little shack at Pomio but never got a chance to sleep in it. No sooner would I be ashore than a messenger would arrive from Mr. John Young-Whitford, the local Government Officer, inviting me to spend the night with him and his family. In New Guinea it is said you make acquaintances but no friends; I shall always consider it a privilege to say the Young-Whitfords were my friends.

Next morning the tropical rain had got into its stride, and was falling at an inch an hour when I set off. There were two days' walk ahead of me over the mountains before I would come to any village. After six hours walk uphill through muck and slush and slimy fetid jungle we called a halt and built shelters for the night. They were hastily constructed in the rain from materials already soaked through, and thus were not comfortable. Rivulets of water ran all over the camp area. Some tree-branches under my boxes allowed it to flow beneath them without damaging them. It was ankle deep beside my bunk and the rain and fog enveloped the outside world. The elevation at the camp was over three thousand feet which, added to the dampness of the atmosphere, made it a most miserable night as there was no hope of getting a fire going.

Twenty-five months previously I had camped in this same place, but it was then the dry season and no water was available except what we could scoop from a slimy green disused wild-pig wallow. Strained through a handkerchief to collect the grosser material, and boiled for five minutes, it made excellent tea . . . at least it tasted good then.

There was little sleep that night. I rose at four and said Mass by the light of a pressure lamp. The carriers were anxious to move on and so was I; all we needed was the first grey light of dawn to make the track discernible. At a quarter to six sufficient light had penetrated the overhead canopy of leaves to serve our purpose. It was still raining heavily and we moved like ghosts through the fog that still clung to the mountain-tops.

An hour's walk brought us to a dried river-bed strewn with dripping green mossy boulders. Water had begun to flow in it again with the recent rain. We walked the riverbed in twenty minutes. I timed it because the last time here it took me an hour and a half's painful hobbling with a damaged knee.

Towards nine o'clock the rain eased off. The heavy clouds grew thinner and moved higher in the sky. The ground showed signs of having had less rain. After another half an hour we were walking on hard, dry ground and the sun blazed down from a blue sky. We were over Mount Meisi on the top of the mountain range. We had left the wet monsoon behind us and were into the dry season of the north coast.

The day was still young and only three or four hours' walk ahead of us so we called a halt. Little fires sprang up about the place and the people were busy re-heating some taros. Kenpale got about his work with pots and pans and I wandered off among the trees to a tiny trickle of water where I washed and shaved and changed into fresh dry clothes. It was a relief to change from heavy wet boots to a pair of crêpe-soled canvas ones.

As I sauntered back I relished the resinuous smoke of the camp fires and looked forward to a hot meal, the first since yesterday morning. I have enjoyed trips by plane or by car, but when young and healthy and not caring whether a day's walk is one hour or five, I have never enjoyed anything better than jungle trips like these.

We had now crossed the mountains some twenty miles west of Bagatavi and consequently the Sui were well to the east. Right at hand were the Bush-Mengens and I was anxious to spend a few weeks among them. The terrain was also inviting, hilly but not mountainous with good open tracks and the villages not more than a few hours from one another.

Nakanai mountain range rose straight as a wall behind us with white woolly clouds sleeping on its emerald top, all that was left of the dark heavy rain-sodden clouds that were now soaking the southern side of the island with their continuous downpour. Due north was Mount Ulewana (The Father), an eight-thousand foot extinct volcano. Northwest was Mount Bamusi (The Son), like his father only not quite so big a man, and showing signs of more recent volcanic activity. Out between them and perhaps thirty or forty miles away lay the islands of Lolobau fading into the skyline, and the blue Pacific rose sparkling and dancing away to the shimmering horizon.

These Bush-Mengens were still pagan, though they were attached in sympathy to us ever since Father Culhane visited them in the 'thirties. Since then we had done little for them on account of the intervening war-years and scarcity of staff, but today I had some catechists to leave with them.

They hold that they sprang from a few families from Galue village on the north shore of Jacquinot Bay, who had pushed inland and settled down here. They still keep very close ties with the Galue people.

Pakenopita from Galue, a Mengen Paramount Luluai, had

accompanied me on this trip, as he naturally had a special interest in the bush-Mengens. He was not a Catholic though he had been attending Church for years. Today, however, he told me he would like to be baptised. After two years' instruction I baptised him.

From the Mengens I struck out east in the general direction of the Sui through little places hardly worthy of a name: Silepo, Sitoru, Bwaliu and so on. The Sui people do not live in villages and often a 'place' was simply a large rock or a prominent tree, but it was a useful landmark where little else is known.

We had set out for Tuke, a few huts on the side of a hill with a waterfall nearby. We were not heading in the right direction however, and I learned that the carriers were not on talking terms with the Tuke people, so now we were going to visit a man called Misa. He was building a house and it was understood that it would be ready that night for me to lodge in it. From Misa's place I would go on to Siwoire which was reputed to be a large village.

We crossed the Kanu river by crawling from one slippery rock to another and on the other bank we met two of Misa's friends. One of them, Titipe, seemed better fed than usual and I asked him if he had been working on some European plantation. He said he had never worked anywhere but that he had recently come back from jail having spent six months there for killing a man. He felt that he had been wronged: six months in jail! Six months for killing an old man who was already half dead!

Leaving the aggrieved Titipe by the river, we climbed a sparsely wooded slope and followed the level track at the summit till we came at two o'clock to a small clearing where Misa, my host, was busy on his house, the framework of which he had already erected.

Misa and I conversed through an interpreter and the conversation was not over-cordial. A few sticks of tobacco, however, put him in a happier mood and he agreed to let me use the shelter for the night. He rounded up some tribesmen for medical treatment and they were in the usual distressful condition of the bush-people. Later on six braves from Tuke appeared before me, bowed in unison and smiled. This was a new approach. I returned their smiles and gave them a smoke. They bowed and went off. Not a word passed between us. It was just a contact made.

I never slept in Misa's house that night. Towards ten o'clock as I was preparing for bed the interpreter came and said there was a dying man close by and he wished to be baptised.

This, of course was ridiculous. The people here knew nothing of Baptism. It later came to light that the idea came from the interpreter himself, who though still a pagan had told the locals that the correct rubric in danger of death was to have the man baptised.

It appeared to me from what I was told, that the sick man had gone down with pneumonia and had been semi-comatose since noon. With two guides and the interpreter carrying the pressure lamp we set off about 10.30 p.m.

We the people have no measures for time or space. After a while one knows how to interpret their descriptions, the five chief ones being: really far away: anything from one day's walk upwards; small distances: about five or six hours; not too far: three or four hours; fairly near: one or two hours; and right near: less than an hour. The journey this night to the sick man was between Not-too-far and Fairly-near, or to speak precisely, it was a fair bit.

An hour out from the house and I thought: 'Is this a trick? Shall I in a few minutes get a Butu on the noggin? Back at Misa's house, Kenpale has probably already gone to his Eternal Reward, God rest his soul! Amen.' I had never got anything like a Butu on the head yet, but it is disconcerting how these thoughts crowd in under certain circumstances. Since I had no imagination to retain it, the vision passed.

Some time around one in the morning we arrived at the abode of Pusua, and he was dying. He appeared to be old for a native, having successfully defied all the laws of hygiene for close on sixty years. His hut was little bigger than himself. It was bare. A dying fire smouldered on a heap of ashes inside the door. One had to stoop doubled up to gain entrance and be quite an acrobat to avoid falling into the fire in doing so. A rather useful entrance when people do not trust their neighbours too far.

The floor was dry and brittle. There was a shallow pit following the long wall. This was always warm from the fire close-by. It had a layer of dust finer than snuff about nine inches high. Pusua lay almost buried in this warm dust which served him as pyjamas and bedclothes. The pit conformed to the shape of his body.

A few friends who had been keeping watch gathered round. I bent over him and took his wrist but could find no pulse whatever, and his hand fell back limply in the dust. He was, however, still breathing fitfully and noises rattled up and down his throat.

I administered conditional Baptism ... *si capax es* ... and commended him to the great mercy of God. As there was still life in him I also gave him an injection of penicillin. Unfortunately in the circumstances there was little else I could do.

It was after four in the morning when I arrived back at Misa's house. I said Mass and had breakfast and because there was little else to be done around here we moved off at six o'clock, just before the sun rose. I hoped to arrive early at Siwoire and make up for lost sleep. But when we reached Siwoire we found that it no longer existed and had never been much more than a temporary gathering place. All that remained was the debris of a few grass huts that had rotted in the weather.

Along the day's route I had seen the smoke of many gardens in the distance but had seen no people. It was now three in the afternoon and, so far, I had failed to find any Sui in the neighbourhood of Siwoire, even though Misa had sent out some search-parties. When the last party, headed by Misa himself came back unsuccessful, I asked him to get his men together and to carry the boxes till we met the first Sui, because it might be dangerous to be stranded in the middle of an unknown tribe, without having made contact with them. Misa refused, saying that he had bargained to bring me so far and that now he wished to be paid and get away home. I paid them off and wished him the best of luck. Misa now said that they would carry my boxes to a Sui habitation if I gave him the equivalent of a five-pound note in tobacco.

I told the interpreter to thank him graciously but to assure him I was quite happy where I was, and to suggest to Misa that he move along as fast as he could lest the evil spirits and ghosts of the dead should come upon his party in the dark along the road home.

I do not know what Misa replied. The interpreter refused to say but puckered his lips and shook his head saying:

'Misa i tok nogut nau . . .' and I made a fair guess at what his talk-no-good was.

I was not as worried as Misa might have thought I was. I could see Mount Ulewana clear over everything, though it was now slightly north of west, and I knew that nearby was Kematanme village, and that if the worst happened and that we ourselves had to carry the boxes, we could still make it in four or five days.

Scarcely had Misa and his party left when four naked men with spears on their shoulders broke from the jungle, and stood motionless about thirty yards distant. I waved a greeting to them and they approached. They seemed to be a friendly quartet.

The interpreter spoke to them. They did not know we were here; they were just on their way to visit some friends. They told us of a Sui habitation of sorts, about three hours distant. We asked if they would help to get our boxes along there. They certainly would.

My own boys became suspicious and said the four had been sent along by Misa. 'Twas just a trap. They were so insistent they almost convinced me. Naturally, every native tribe is always convinced that the next one is out to trap him. They have a reasonable basis for that belief.

However, it was stupid to talk of trying to trap us because

we were trapped already. The Suis did not have to cart our boxes a few hours to trap us. If they wanted to do us harm they just had to wait quietly till dark.

I finished the argument by saying that anyone who wished to remain could do so and I would leave him a week's rations. There were no takers except Kenpale who said he could not walk as his leg had suddenly swollen up and he feared he had been bewitched by the Suis. Everything was getting out of kilter now, and with one or two more difficulties I might be inclined to believe in sorcery myself. Kenpale could not be left behind, because he was sick and he was the only cook in the team.

I do not know what Kenpale's ailment was. His leg was swollen up like a balloon from his hip to his toes. There was no mark of a snake-bite or any other wound. I had resort to the cure-all: penicillin.

Kenpale is a plucky fellow and said he would try to walk with the aid of a stick, if I stayed with him. At last we were on our way.

Darkness was now approaching so we lighted two lamps, one for the van and one for the rear of the party, which to-night would be Kenpale and myself. As the carriers were not sufficiently numerous they lashed three boxes together for every two men and they carried them dead-pig fashion. Only Kenpale's rucksack remained and this I carried. It contained two blankets, a laplap, a bamboo comb with teeth like pencils, a small bottle of insect repellent, perfume, hairdye, a cake of soap, a tiny mirror, a small tin of lime, seven betel-nuts and two taros.

We set off at a slow pace and formed a miserable procession. There was no cut track, we just followed the broken trail of the leader. It went through long grass and scrub that hid holes and stumps, and rotting logs overgrown with creepers that harboured vicious red ants and occasionally a snake, but the vanguard usually frightened them off. I saw none, only one tree python. For variety we had to traverse loose shingle at an angle on a slope, over slippery rocks and along creekbeds.

It was a distressing business but I took courage from the fact that I had the easiest part of it.

All this for the hope of contacting a few shy jungle-dwellers! It seemed horribly out of proportion if one thought himself important. I might meet forty in the whole trip. But I knew too that the number would be greater the next time and greater still the third time. Some one has to begin somewhere and some time.

At ten o'clock we came to the resting place, a lone, deserted shack in a clearing on a protruding ledge of mountain. A broken valley stretched away to the south between low mountains. Twisting lines of fog, snow-white in the moonlight, were the tell-tale marks of the rivers. We could even hear them, for the night was calm and cloudless.

We saw no Sui here but they would be here in the morning. Few of the party were in any mood for entertaining or for being entertained. For the past forty hours I had had no sleep and had been walking for twenty hours, half of which was by night, and I was tired.

The shack was as windproof as a five-bar gate. We could see the stars through the roof. Luckily there was neither wind nor rain that night.

In spite of his own sick and tired condition Kenpale wanted to hobble along and cut saplings for my bunk. This was Kenpale at his best. I needed no bunk that night. I evened out a few knobs on the dirt floor, spread an oilskin, two folded blankets and a half-empty rucksack for a pillow and another blanket to pull over me. As a concession to the blankets and civilisation I kicked off my boots though I would have slept that night in leg-irons and a coat of mail.

I slept round the clock. I woke drenched in sweat for the sun had been on me for a few hours. Kenpale had arranged an altar at one end of the hut and a fire at the other. His swollen leg was back to normal.

I said Mass that morning on a rickety altar in a shack in the middle of nowhere and as the Church gives us a chance to do so, I said a special prayer for that benefactor of the human race, whom I had now long come to regard as a personal friend though I had never seen him—I mean Sir Alexander Flemming. At that same Mass I had an even dearer remembrance to make, because, as I was about to begin, a messenger sent by Mr. Young-Whitford from the Government Station at Pomio handed me a radio-message that my father had died.

While the boys were packing up after breakfast I went off to a pool we had crossed half a mile away yesterday and there had a swim and a shave. When I got back everything was ready for me to clean up the sores and the ailments of the Suis.

I was well aware that these same Suis who were now smiling and delighted to have their festering wounds attended to, would vanish when the time came to give me a helping hand to get to Kematanme. Consequently I had all my boxes lined beside the medical table outside the hut and whenever I treated a man who had only a trivial sore, I put him beside a box and had him understand that he would have to carry it to Kematanme. They were all quite pleased.

In the middle of the work, three men rushed into the clearing from the bush, puffing and perspiring. An excited babble of voices followed for a few minutes with many people glancing my way. Then one of the three, Baligelmo by name, came up to me and spoke in Tokboi:

'Does the Father remember the man he baptised the other night and he died?'

'Oh yes! I'm sorry to hear he died.'

'But he's not dead. He was dead. But he's not dead now. He got up. He has washed and gone to his garden. Everything was ready to bury him. In the eyes of us the people he was really dead. Truly dead. Completely dead. The Father baptised him and he's all right again. The eye of us the people is dark to the fashion of the Father.'

I tried to remind Baligelmo that the old man still had life in him when I left him; he would not listen but kept on repeating: 'He was dead. Truly dead. He was dead. He was dead.'

This was not the time to explain either the theological effects of Baptism or the biological effects of penicillin so I kept on with my job, to get done as soon as possible and away before some bright Sui should get the idea of unearthing the bones of some old ancestor for Baptism.

I am still wondering what those burial preparations were because the Suis have some original ideas in this matter. Sometimes the corpse is placed on a high tree, or in a cave or covered over in the hut; but the favourite one is not to bury it at all but to hang it up in the smoke till it has dried out. The various 'natural juices' that flow from the decaying body are collected and used as poison in food. (Should be good, too.) Every time I see a can of food 'Packed in its Natural Juices' I think of the Sui and get the shudders.

When I had fastened the last bandage I went back to the hut to collect my Butu and in those few seconds every Sui had vanished into the jungle. All I saw was the bare buttocks of one as he frogleaped a shrub in his hurry. I noticed he had a spanking white bandage above each fetlock.

Why hadn't I been more quick-witted and taken advantage of my wonder-working reputation and told them earlier that if they ran off I would change them into Malkolkols? It is always too late when I think of these things.

I went to the edge of the clearing and shouted 'Bal-i-gel-mo!' and strangely enough he came back. I pretended to be in a towering rage. I flung my hat on the ground and at the same time gave off as much as I could remember of Mark Antony's 'Friends, Romans, countrymen, lend me your ears . . .' because I have found on a few occasions that one can impress a man deeply by speaking to him in an unknown tongue.

Leaving poor Julius unburied now, I switched to Tokboi and with all the dignity and highbrow I could muster I said: 'Baligelmo, I shall be pleased to take delivery of my boxes at Kematanme at four o'clock,' wheeled around and strode off. Baligelmo shouted that it was impossible, but I ignored him, for I knew it was not.

My party pushed on ahead. After half an hour we came to a stream and waited. In a short time eleven Suis, close-packed and silent filed along with the baggage, but I did not see the one with the two bandages.

We closed in behind them and pegged along steadily for three hours, wading the junction of the Kanu and Sagi Rivers and up a long slope to an open track outside Kematanme. Paramount Chief Pakenopita was there with a few hundred Mengens. I felt as if I had been re-admitted to the human race or had come back from the dead.

Like a Mengen, I dug my heel in the soft ground. That closed the ring. In three and a half years' hiking now, I had mapped the last of the sixty-five villages of the parish and had seen the eye of us the people.

To The Reader

Iᴇ ʏᴏᴜ have had the patience to follow me to the end, you may wish to ask me: how do you feel about those strange people? I shall answer, but I must warn you that I am prejudiced: I am very fond of them.

And you may further ask: what kind of Christians do they make? That I shall answer by another question: to whom shall we compare them? To you? In your humility you protest: I am not as good a Christian as I should be. To me, then? I also must beg to be excused, lest we the people learn that their gods have feet of clay.

❧

Julius is approaching the Church when the conch-shells sound for night-prayers; he hides in the scrub till the others have gone in for prayers and then he sneaks home.

There are five men half a mile out to sea in a canoe and the Angelus rings. They lay their paddles on their knees and make the Sign of the Cross together. The canoe drifts till they have finished their prayers.

They have a grip on Christianity. They also have their breaking point. So, too, have you and I. And when it comes to imitating Christ, are not we, also, primitive, no better, no worse than they?

240

Appendix ... Tokboi

ONE OF the greatest difficulties in the path of making free contact with the various tribes in New Guinea is the numerous languages which they speak. The native population of Papua, New Guinea, is estimated at about one million and a half and the number of different languages is placed between one hundred and fifty and two hundred. Nobody knows for sure. Here and there one finds a large tribe, say twenty or fifty thousand people speaking the same dialect, but for the most part it changes with every few thousand people and there are many cases of only a few hundred people speaking the same dialect, or even, in cases like the Timoips or the Malkolkols in New Britain, one finds only a few dozen people with the same dialect.

Many dialects are akin in a close degree and many have been connected only in the remote past. One thing, however, is common to most, that is the form and manner of expression, or, as the grammarians call it, the idiom. The words follow the same order in the sentences, and phrases and many turns of speech are more or less identical throughout. This idiom is very different from that of European languages, and many words and phrases defy the grammarians' classifications. The native languages cannot be forced into our grammatical forms.

It is well for us to remember that almost the whole western

civilization trimmed its various languages to fit into the Greco-Roman grammar and those natural idioms of the old languages which did not fit in smoothly were discarded as bad grammar. Languages under less influence of Latin held on to their native forms, which accounts for the fact that in Irish, for instance, there are many unusual grammatical forms: the preposition 'after' is an abstract noun, personal numerals are nouns and the qualifying 'man' or 'woman' is an adjective.

If all languages were expressed in the same grammatical form or idiom it would be easier to learn foreign languages, for the problem would be reduced to a mere question of vocabulary and direct translation; but each language would lose thereby its own picturesqueness, its individuality and its own richness of expression.

Languages are only means of expressing ideas. Each language has its own peculiar way of doing so. The ideas are more important than the language and were there before it. Ideas and thoughts are the same in every human head but find different forms on the tongue.

Ideas can always be translated, sometimes by a word-for-word translation, and sometimes a re-shuffle of the words in the new language is necessary so that the ideas are not lost. Phrases too can be translated word-for-word on occasion but sometimes they have to be substituted by entirely new phrases in the new languages, phrases of different words but of the identical meaning.

'The cow jumped over the moon' is a good English sentence. In Irish idiom it would be 'Jumped the cow across the top of the moon' which in that form would be very unidiomatic English, because in English the noun goes before the verb and in Irish it comes after it. That is the idiom of the languages and that's all there's to it.

The difference of idiom is far greater in Melanesian languages. If you wish to translate a common sentence such as 'I am angry' you will find that you will have to say, in many cases: 'My belly is hot!' You don't say 'Pull my leg', you say 'Pierce my nose'. You don't tell the cook-boy to 'put an egg in the pan' unless he is a magician or sorcerer or both; this is very vulgar since only a hen can 'put' an egg. If a man tells you that his liver is sore, or that it is agitated, or that it is his eye, take him quite seriously, but do not think he is suffering from any bodily ailment, he is merely telling you of his mental or emotional state.

Let us not enter into the more complicated idioms because they have little interest for the general reader. Enough has been said to make the reader aware that in order to understand a Melanesian one has to get away from one's own thought-process and become adjusted to his.

A most important aspect of all these languages is that they are not written but spoken tongues. In written languages we make use of several props to aid our understanding: capitals, full-stops, commas, semi-colons, question-marks and so forth. These aids are not available in spoken languages and have to be substituted by others such as: popping of the eyes, pointing of the fingers, elevation of the eye-brows, inflexion of the voice and so on. A simple sentence 'you saw the man' has ten different meanings according as we stress one or other or all the words, say it in an assertive voice or ask it in an enquiring tone.

The million and a half natives speaking their hundreds of languages are scattered thinly over 184,000 square miles. Three ways of verbal communication are possible between them and the white stranger: (i) the white man learns their languages, (ii) they learn his, (iii) all learn a common language.

For universal purposes the first method is of little value, for when the white man has learned one native language, it is useless to him if his job takes him outside the small area where it is spoken.

The second is no better because thousands of illiterate people are not going to learn the language of a passing stranger, in whom few have any interest.

Furthermore, an illiterate primitive has tremendous difficulty in explaining even his own language. He has no conception of words, phrases, sentences, tenses and so on. If you ask him to break up a simple sentence of his own language into words, he does not know what you mean. To him it is all one sound which has a special meaning. Only on reflection does he realise that it is made up of different words. If I ask an illiterate Mengen to translate: 'Tell him to come' he will say: 'rolengekeatu'. He does not know how to break it up into words and I have then to figure out by devious questions and other examples whether it is 'role-nge-ke-atu' or 'ro-lengek-ea-tu' or what is it, and gradually match it word for word with my own language. But even that is not easy because his language will always have a few untranslatable and superfluous sounds put in 'just to make it sound nice', or left out on another occasion because 'it does not cry nice'.

These difficulties coupled with the unusual idiom, the small scope of the language beyond social affairs, the absence of literature and the brevity of man's life cause the ordinary white to keep clear of native languages.

The third method of communication is a common language and that is the one chiefly in use at present. It is called TOKBOI (the 'Talk' of the 'Boys', i.e. native men). It is also called Pidgin or Pidgin English, but these names are confusing and have led to much misunderstanding and abuse of the good name of Tokboi. They are misnomers and lead people to believe that Tokboi is corrupted English or Babytalk, that no effort is required to learn it, that any old private inspiration will pass muster as long as you add sufficient and well-placed didums and wasums, and you-savvy's. O sorrow!

Who uttered the first word? There is no record except what we find in The Book of Genesis, 2, 19-20: And the Lord having formed out of the ground all the beasts of the earth and all the fowls of the air, brought them to Adam to see what he would call them: for whatever Adam called any living creature the same is its name. And Adam called all the beasts by their names and all the fowls of the air and all the cattle of the field.

When Adam looked at the cattle of the field did he say Bull! or did he say Toro! or did he say something entirely different from both? Whatever he said, the name he uttered must have been very much pidginised down the ages. All languages are mixtures and corruptions of one another.

I opened the Pocket Oxford Dictionary at random and here is what I found: Page 138-9: Common words 19, of which 10 are English, 7 Latin, 1 Irish. Again at Page 212-3 : 50 words of which 32 are Latin, 5 French, 5 Greek, 4 English, 1 Dutch, 1 Latin-English. At Page 464-5 there are 21 words of which 4 are Greek, 4 Latin, 3 French, 3 English, 1 Italian, 1 Dutch, 1 Arabic and a few unknowns. The Oxford Dictionary, by the way, is a dictionary of King's English.

The Native of New Guinea created Tokboi and in his own image and likeness he created it. We Europeans learn Tokboi from him and it is he, not we, who is the final judge as to what is correct and what is not. The words are mainly English in origin (i.e. Greek, Latin, French, Arabic etc.) but the idiom is Melanesian. However, the English words are not faithfully reproduced and for two reasons: the average English-speaker is slovenly and careless with diction and is a victim of his home-town pronunciation; and also the native is not able to reproduce many sounds common to the English language; for instance he will say P for F, S for Sh, DS for J, and P, B, V, or W for W.

In order to get conversation going when they first met, the European pronounced some words to the native, simple every-day words which were necessary for daily work and conversation. The native picked up these words and pronounced them in his own clipped fashion and as true to the original as he could possibly do. He repeated his new vocabulary to his neighbour and so the word went round and by the time it returned to the white man it was already pidginised and established among the people. The European now adopted the native version of the word as it was more intelligible to them. A few simple examples may illustrate that point. A white man refers to his house. The native gets the idea and the word. Then he refers by gestures to cooking. The boy understands. Then the white man calls his kitchen the cook-house and the native is confused because that is not the way he ties up his words; the native asks if he means the house-cook? The white man is now getting the slant on things. And so we have house-cook, house-sick for hospital, house-drink for a pub, house-paper for a Government Office, house-lotu for a Church and so on.

As the native's vocabulary grew he formed new words and phrases by combining known words in different sequences, and if an English word was not handy he slipped in one of his own which was better known. This new means of communication was dubbed Tokboi by the natives who are as slick as the Americans for sticking an appropriate tag to a thing. It is the most widely used and commonly known language in the Territory today. Europeans of different tribes who have no common language use it, European with Chinese, European with Native, Chinese with Native, Native with Native of another tribe, *wanpela tok bolong ol, Tokboi tasol*. The influence of Tokboi has been immeasurable, for it has allowed the European to get in touch with the natives and the natives of different tribes to communicate with one another.

Even in the fifty years of its existence it has had its ups and downs. In Papua it was banned by the Government and the Missions. In New Guinea it was allowed to grow as it wished and it spread like a rash. The New Guinea Missions, who at that period were the only educators, found Tokboi a very useful medium of instruction where people of different tribes were gathered. They reduced it to a written language and used phonetic spelling, for though many words were derived from English, it was impossible for the native to understand the English manner of spelling. A further concession was made to the fact that even when the native adopted an English word he did not pronounce it as an English-speaker should, and so the written Tokboi took a form resembling as closely as possible the actual way they pronounced it. Hence, Talk became Tok, House haus, Road rot, Saltwater solwara, Throw away toromoi, Drink diring and so on. This new spelling was now united with the Melanesian idiom and Tokboi as we know it today was born. The European supplied the words and the native supplied the idiom, or European body-work on a native chassis assembled in the hausboi.

When you hear it first it sounds like English out of focus, for many of the English words are no longer used in their derived sense. One last example: Ol derived from All means They; Wantaim derived from One Time means Together; Ologeta derived from All Together means All, so to translate 'Tell them all to come together' you do not say 'Tokim ol i kam ologeta' as it is sometimes said but 'Tokim ologeta ol i kam wantaim'. A lot of misunderstanding between white and brown could be avoided if the white only realised that he is often not saying what he thinks he is, and that one cannot manufacture a language.

Many people do not like Tokboi because they feel it is granting recognition to an illegitimate baby. 'These things occur even in the best families but it is not good form to encourage the practice.' It is an unfortunate misconception. Tokboi is not English and makes no pretence to be. It is just Tokboi. I have heard people denounce it with eloquent words and smooth graceful gestures that made me quite envious, only to discover that they did not know a thing about it and could not tell their cook-boy to lay the table without having resort to baby-talk and broken English. With them the dislike was pathological. What they wanted was to strike a blow for King's English by killing the little urchin from the jungle who they erroneously thought was claiming blue blood. Nogat hia ! The little lad is quite happy in his laplap and could never be persuaded to insinuate himself into a boiled shirt. It is quite unfortunate that many of his ignorant detractors have voices in the Councils of the Mighty.

The present Official drift is away from Tokboi towards a system intended to make pure English the common language. Much can be said in its favour. For a people intended to take their place in all walks of civilised life the English language can lead them along a well-beaten track; no matter what trade or profession the future English-speaking native takes up, he will, with his knowledge of English, be able to understand it and feel at home in it. With a good knowledge of English he could become one of the world's best informed citizens.

Tokboi is not intended to, nor can ever hope to, compete with English in that sphere. It may develop on its own lines and produce something of worth, or it may not. But at present it is a most useful go-between, and to discourage Tokboi is to put back the day when the native will be brought out of the past, and consequently the day when the English language will be established.

There is work and a place for both in New Guinea today.

	Date
	PRINTED

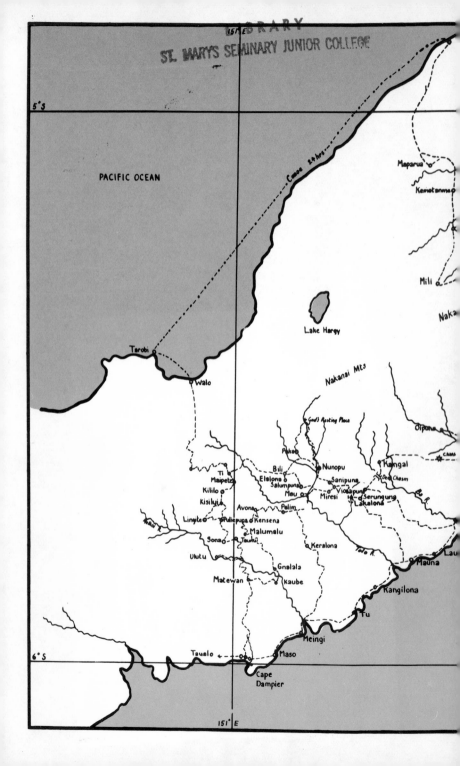